D1684212

Canon, Period, and the Poetry of Charles of Orleans

Found in Translation

A. E. B. Coldiron

Ann Arbor

THE UNIVERSITY OF MICHIGAN PRESS

For Katharine

Copyright © by the University of Michigan 2000
All rights reserved
Published in the United States of America by
The University of Michigan Press
Manufactured in the United States of America
♾ Printed on acid-free paper

2003 2002 2001 2000   4 3 2 1

No part of this publication may be reproduced, stored in a retrieval system, or transmitted in any form or by any means, electronic, mechanical, or otherwise, without the written permission of the publisher.

A CIP catalog record for this book is available from the British Library.

Library of Congress Cataloging-in-Publication Data

Coldiron, A. E. B. (Anne E. B.), 1959–
    Canon, period, and the poetry of Charles of Orleans : found in translation / A. E. B. Coldiron.
       p.   cm.
    Includes bibliographical references and index.
    ISBN 0-472-11146-9 (alk. paper)
    1. Charles, d'Orléans, 1394–1465—Translations into English—History and criticism. I. Title.
PQ1553.C5 C67   2000
841'.2—dc21   00-09134

Acknowledgments

This book was made possible by a fellowship from the National Endowment for the Humanities; thanks to the staff and readers who helped the project take shape. Many thanks to the English Department at Louisiana State University for graciously granting a leave of absence during 1998–99.

An earlier version of chapter 2, "*Translatio,* Translation, and Charles d'Orléans's *Parole*d Poetics," by A. E. B. Coldiron, was published in *Exemplaria: A Journal of Theory in Medieval and Renaissance Studies* 8, no. 1 (Spring 1996): 169–92; this material is used by permission of Pegasus Press, University of North Carolina, Asheville, NC, 28804 (copyright 1996). A version of chapter 4, "Translation, Canons, and Cultural Capital," appears in *Charles d'Orléans in England, 1415–1440,* ed. Mary-Jo Arn (Woodbridge, Suffolk: Boydell and Brewer, forthcoming).

The jacket illustration and figure 1 are taken from BL ms. Royal F 16.ii, and are used with the permission of the British Library.

Other illustrations are used with the permission of the Bibliothèque Municipale de Grenoble. Special thanks go to the learned and generous librarians and curators there, particularly Yves Jocteur-Montrozier, Marie-Françoise Bois-Delatte, Marie-Christine Hébré, Marie-Thérèse Imbert, Marguerite Pénicaut, and Monique Samé.

The Andrew W. Mellon Publications Fund of the Folger Shakespeare Library made possible the publication of color plates in this volume; special thanks and acknowledgment for this support.

Much of the work of this book was done at the Folger Shakespeare Library, whose professional, personable staff members manage to inform and encourage even the most exhausted researchers. Likewise, the staff of the University of Virginia's Alderman Library provided, for this and other projects, a decade of consistently superior assistance and resources.

Even copious lists of thanks to family, friends, colleagues, and students would not suffice; instead, epigrammatic, heartfelt gratitude for intellectual guidance, practical help, and personal kindnesses to Professors Gordon Braden, Alastair Fowler, Daniel Kinney, A. C. Spearing, Mary-Jo Arn, Anne Lake Prescott, Gilbert Ouy, Hoyt Duggan, Werner Gundersheimer, Eugene Vance, Susannah Brietz Monta, and Cynthia Horen.

Special thanks to the anonymous readers and editorial staff at the University of Michigan Press.

Contents

1. Introduction: Placing Translations in
   Literary History and Theory ... 1
2. *Translatio,* Translation, and
   Charles d'Orléans's *Parole*d Poetics ... 14
3. Self-Translation, Writerly Self-Consciousness,
   and the Early Modern Lyric "I" ... 39
4. Translation, Canons, and Cultural Capital:
   Manuscripts and Reception of Charles d'Orléans's
   English Poetry ... 76
5. Creating World Lyric: Translation, *Ordinatio,*
   and the Politics of Selection in Grenoble Ms. 873 ... 112
6. Translation and Periodization; or,
   Charles d'Orléans, Renaissance Poet? ... 145

Appendix. Bibliographic Observations on Grenoble Ms. 873 ... 191

References ... 201

General Subject Index ... 219

Plates ... 225

1
Introduction: Placing Translations in Literary History and Theory

In the autumn of 1415, in the bloody aftermath of Agincourt field, Charles, duc d'Orléans, was pulled from beneath a heap of bodies and armor into a twenty-five-year English captivity. The historical import of this fact is considerable: this prince of the house of Valois, later to become father of Louis XII and uncle of François I, would figure largely in the settlements ending the Hundred Years' Wars. However, the literary results of Charles's long imprisonment have not been much studied, given their significance and interest, and are the general subject of this book. Captive in several prominent English households, Charles composed more than thirteen thousand lines of verse in both French and English, in carefully constructed lyric sequences that are broadly (but not entirely) parallel in content.[1] The English side of the parallel oeuvre, found in BL ms. Harley 682, is in fact the first one-author love-lyric sequence in English. Not only is it the first, it is remarkable for reasons both theoretical and literary-historical. The bilingual oeuvre appears at a crucial moment, that of final separation between two nations that had been as one since 1066 and between which powerful connections and tensions persist even today.

That crucial moment, if not this remarkable oeuvre, has been the focus

---

1. In BN f. fr. 25458, the autograph manuscript. The chief modern edition is that of Pierre Champion, *Poésies,* 2 vols. (Paris: Librairie Ancienne Honoré Champion, 1923–24). Some of the French poems were written after Charles's repatriation in 1440. There is also a parallel French-Latin lyric sequence, Grenoble ms. 873, unedited since 1842, containing many of the poems that appear in French and English, introduced here in chapter 5 and described in the appendix. The English sequence in BL Harley 682 has been recently edited by Mary-Jo Arn, *Fortunes Stabilnes: Charles of Orleans's English Book of Love* (Binghamton, N.Y.: Medieval and Renaissance Text Society, 1995). Only two previous editions exist: R. Steele and M. Day, eds., *The English Poems of Charles of Orleans,* 2 vols. (London: Oxford University Press, 1941 and 1946; rpt., 1 vol., 1970); and G. Watson Taylor, ed., *Poems Written in English by Charles, Duke of Orleans during his captivity in England after the battle of Azincourt* (London: Nicol, for the Roxburghe Club, 1827).

2   *Canon, Period, and the Poetry of Charles of Orleans*

of recent critical and theoretical reevaluation. The work of such scholars as A. C. Spearing, Lee Patterson, Seth Lerer, Carol Meale, H. Marshall Leicester, and David Wallace has established the fifteenth century not as a literary dead zone or a slumber before England's great awakening into print, but as a period of tremendous, overlooked interest with resonant consequences for literary theory, for literary history, for canon and curriculum.[2] The fifteenth century's wars, diplomacy, and nationalisms, its linguistic and literary dynamism, and its social and technological shifts make it an era we can no longer consider "minor."[3] Furthermore, it is in

---

2. One line of fifteenth-century literary scholarship has sought to redeem the era's reputation as a "transitional" period between medieval and Renaissance, not as the drabber precursor to C. S. Lewis's "drab age"; this line revalues the work and looks for continuities across period boundaries (for example, A. C. Spearing's now-classic *Medieval to Renaissance in English Poetry* [Cambridge: Cambridge University Press, 1985], but also Seth Lerer's *Chaucer and His Readers: Imagining the Author in Late Medieval England* [Princeton, N.J.: Princeton University Press, 1993], which views the period's literature as consequent to Chaucer in some additional senses). Viewing the continuities at least as much as the discontinuities between the fifteenth and sixteenth centuries means giving attention to the early Tudor courts, attention granted in the work of, for example, Peter Herman, ed., *Rethinking the Henrician Era* (Urbana: University of Illinois Press, 1994); or David Carlson, "King Arthur and Court Poems for the Birth of Arthur Tudor in 1486," *Humanistica Lovaniensa* 36 (1987): 147–83, "Politicizing Tudor Court Literature: Gaguin's Embassy and Henry VII's Humanists' Response," *Studies in Philology* 85, no. 3 (1988): 279–304, and "Reputation and Duplicity: The Texts and Context of Thomas More's Epigram on Bernard André," *ELH* 58, no. 2 (1991): 261–80. Another line of recuperative thinking, working by analogy but without succumbing to "presentism," highlights the fifteenth century's several similarities to our own: a time of great technological shift, of revolutions in communication and transportation; a time of warfare, internationalism, political struggle, and the redefinition of national boundaries and even of the conception of nationhood. An excellent example is David Wallace's *Chaucerian Polity* (Stanford, Calif.: Stanford University Press, 1997). Recent work from, for example, H. Marshall Leicester Jr., *The Disenchanted Self: Representing the Subject in "The Canterbury Tales"* (Berkeley and Los Angeles: University of California Press, 1990), has stressed the importance of this era to the history of early modern authorship and "subjectivity." Likewise, the century is crucial in any scholarly consideration of textual and literary transmission, as the work of Carol Meale, "Patrons, Buyers, and Owners: Book Production and Social Status," in *Book Production and Publishing in Britain, 1375–1475*, ed. Jeremy Griffiths and Derek Pearsall (Cambridge: Cambridge University Press, 1989), 201–38; Janet Backhouse, inter alia, "Founders of the Royal Library: Edward IV and Henry VII as Collectors of Illuminated Manuscripts," in *England in the Fifteenth Century: Proceedings of the 1986 Harlaxton Symposium,* ed. Daniel Williams (Woodbridge, Suffolk: Boydell Press, 1987), 23–42; or Julia Boffey, including *Manuscripts of English Courtly Love Lyrics in the Later Middle Ages* (Bury St. Edmunds, Suffolk: D. S. Brewer, 1985) has demonstrated.

3. Gilles Deleuze and Félix Guattari's theorizing of the minor as a result of certain kinds of colonializing actions in *Kafka: Pour une littérature mineure* (Paris: Éditions de Minuit, 1975) is particularly misleading in this case since Charles, of royal blood, was higher in rank and status than any of his noble captors. His capture depended on, yet in some ways inverted, accepted linguistic and social hierarchies, placing him in a position as much to colonize as to

such complex cultural moments that our largely teleological models of literary history fail and can be fruitfully reconsidered. Some of our chief organizing categories of literary study such as authorship, influence, and period do not adequately explain this important material and generally do not much address its contexts. In such a period we can test our own methods and find illuminating examples; "placing translations" is both a geographical and a critical endeavor. This large body of lyric translation reveals a poet crossing between nations, among languages, and between literary traditions, negotiating several sorts of conflict and finally establishing a voice and poetics in English that might best be read as an illuminating tertium quid.

The Poems

So unusual has been the poetry's reception history, and so unevenly known is it, even among scholars, that a general description is a helpful prelude to its theoretical and literary-historical interest. BL Harley ms. 682 is a vellum manuscript containing Charles's English lyric sequence. The lyrics are set in three main parts, introduced and separated by rather elaborate narrative-verse sections (but not fully framed with a closing narrative section).[4] The narrative verse begins with a fairly conventional documentary appeal to Cupid, with "letters patent" and a designation of the young Charles as a servant of Cupid. The ballades that follow do not narrate the lover's story but rather offer a series of brief, expressivist snapshots of the lover's varying experiences: admiration, anxiety, despair, delight, frustration, joy, and so on. These poems often focus on the lover as a writer, and while many contain traditional love-topoi, nearly as many are experimental and playful in treating the topic. For example, the conventionally epideictic speaker promises faithful service and praises the lady's beauty, virtue, and honor. But less conventional poems also praise her wit, her clever speech, and her physicality or sensuality, and other poems celebrate intimate moments spent with her. There is also something beyond the expected degree and kind of trouble in this lover's paradise. Not only the

---

be colonized; the social politics of language in this case are more nuanced and complex than contemporary theories of "colonizing the Other," potentially anachronistic anyway, are likely to explain.

4. For a fuller discussion of the larger sequence and its narrative sections, see Arn, "Charles of Orleans and the Poems of BL MS Harley 682," *English Studies* 74 (June 1993): 222–35.

usual delays and absences, but the sniping of other people, an expressed need for more than the usual duplicity and secrecy, and a certain mistrust of each other's fidelity render this first English love-lyric sequence less idealizing than most. (Charles does not quite enter George Meredith's territory, but by the latter half of the English sequence, he is closer to troubled Wyatt than to awestruck Petrarch in this respect.) Additionally, the speaker undergoes severe mood swings and experiences something resembling a postmodern psychomachia. Various parts of himself are split, reified, and given voice in inner dialogues. This fragmented subjectivity is a feature of the English version in particular, and the English diction, much more than the level and abstract French diction, tends to swoop and dive along with the speaker's mercurial moods. The ballades are as dramatic as they are epideictic, containing a variety of imagined and real encounters in which speaking participants enact either a conflict, a news event, a lovemaking scene, a game, or a memory. There are, in other words, an unusual number of presences in a sequence about absence.

The progress of the poems, as I said, is not primarily narrative. What narrative progress there is is generally found in the narrative-verse sections that interrupt or frame the lyrics. One could say, as one could say for many lyric sequences, that in the lyrics themselves there is hardly any progress at all, that "story" is after all not the point of lyric poetry.[5] And despite the narratological potentials available to Charles in Petrarch's *Rime,* the prime model for European lyric sequences, Charles's English sequence rejects the obvious *in morte* opportunities in his chosen narrative frames. After nearly sixty ballades, we learn that the lady sickens and dies. Soon another narrative-verse section introduces a new lady, who seems uncannily to resemble the old one (at least from a distance). When the speaker encounters the new lady, only slight deliberation ("Fie, fie, schal y me make a lady new?") is required before proceeding. Instead of a transcendent Petrarchan response to the lady's death, then, the sequence records the speaker's worldly, pragmatic return to the speaking-position of lover, if not to the usual ethos of that position. The second half of the sequence treats the experience of loving this new lady, again in nearly expressivist snapshots rather than in linear narratology: there are roundel sets, chansons, and in the English sequence, over three dozen more ballades, many of which are without French analogues. The English sequence ends in a

---

5. But see chapter 5 for a treatment of the *ordinatio* in the different manuscripts, which may imply Charles's experimental understanding of lyric sequencing.

resonantly complex and polysemous poem (examined below at the end of chapter 3) of which there is no French equivalent.

The verses that frame the lyric speaker's un-Petrarchan response include a number of traditional, courtly set-pieces, but like many medieval conventions found here, these are playfully revised to suit the witty and in some respects unconventional persona. For one thing, Charles writes his speaker's detachment from love by naming the place in which he finds his heart "nonchaloir" in the French, "no-care" in the English.[6] This of course draws on the topographical method of love-allegory, invoking the traditions of the *Roman de la Rose;* yet Charles eschews the traditional *locus amoenus.* Likewise, there is a prosopopoeia of Venus, and a banquet-of-poems motif; but Venus is much racier than usual and the banquet is pun-filled. There are heart-and-eye debates, but they are highly varied and taken to nearly self-satirizing extremes. The lover ages and complains about it, but he is no *senex,* and aging does not seem to impede the witty, sensual, and experimental record of his courtship(s).

The Present Book

For a number of reasons, in short, this is a sequence unlike the chief European analogues or predecessors it might reasonably have claimed: no *Vita Nuova,* this, no *Voir-Dit,* and certainly no *Rime sparse.* The French poems do bear a fair resemblance to European lyric poetry of their day, particularly the ballades of Alain Chartier and Christine de Pisan, but the English sequence is quite unlike the French, and is also in a number of important ways unlike the work of the fifteenth-century English poets in whose milieu Charles found himself for so many years.

His translations, then, are not about "influence" as traditionally construed: it is not a matter of a translator bringing a French literary tradition into English. Charles does bring words and phrases, does bring the new presentational mode of the single-author lyric book, and does bring a new sort of *sprezzatura* into English. But the present book is not an influence study: something more exciting and complex is at work in Charles's poetry, for it seems that linguistic and political contexts shape a lyric poetics uncannily like that of English lyric writers working in the 1590s and

---

6. *Nonchaloir* is a word Alain Chartier, for example, uses, but not as a topographical trope. Chartier, Rondeau XII, l. 5, and *Le Débat des deux fortunés d'amours,* ll. 103, 295, in *The Poetical Works of Alain Chartier,* ed. J. C. Laidlaw (London: Cambridge University Press, 1974), 380, 161, and 167.

after—a distinct poetics (distinct, I mean, from the French, but also distinct from the post-Chaucerian literary system in which it appears). To put it bluntly, the poet is a different poet, the subjectivity a different subjectivity, in French and English, even when the content is essentially the same. Belgian author Luc Santé, writing in the *New York Times Magazine* about his own trilingualism, remarks,

> My three languages revolve around and inform one another. I live in an English-speaking world, of course, and for months on end I may speak nothing else. . . . I cannot snap back and forth between languages with ease, but need to be surrounded by French [his first language] before I can properly recover its rhythm, and so recover my idiomatic vocabulary—a way of thinking rather than just a set of words—and not merely translate English idioms. . . . [D]ifferent aspects of my self are contained in different rooms of language, and a complicated apparatus of air locks prevents the doors from being flung open all at once. Still, there are subterranean correspondences between the linguistic domains that keep them from stagnating. The classical order of French, the Latin-Germanic dialect of English, and the onomatopoeic-peasant lucidity of Walloon work on one another critically. . . . I like to think this system helps fortify me in areas beyond the merely linguistic. I am not rootless but multiply rooted. This makes it impossible for me to fence off a plot of the world and decide that everyone dwelling outside those boundaries is "other." I am grateful to the accidents of my upbringing, which taught me several kinds of irony. Ethnically, I am about as homogeneous as it is possible to be. . . . Having been transplanted from my native soil, though, and having had to construct an identity in response to a double set of demands. . . . I have become permanently "other." The choice I am faced with is simple: either I am at home everywhere or I am nowhere at all. . . . Mere tolerance is idle and useless—if I can't recognize myself in others, . . . I might as well declare war upon myself.[7]

Naturally, bilingualism in the fifteenth century could not have meant what it means today.[8] And we do not know if the historical Charles, deracinated

---

7. "Living in Tongues," rpt. in *Best American Essays,* ed. Ian Frazier (Boston: Houghton-Mifflin, 1997), 130–31.

8. For fascinating speculation on this point, see Leonard Forster, *The Poet's Tongues: Multilingualism in Literature* (Cambridge: Cambridge University Press, 1970), especially chapters 1 and 2 on medieval and Renaissance poetry; or John R. Edwards, *Multilingualism* (London: Routledge, 1994); or Uriel Weinreich, *Languages in Contact* (The Hague: Mouton, 1974).

and multilingual, at the center of wars in which boundaries of otherness (boundaries both political and linguistic) were being clearly and permanently drawn, found this sort of value in becoming "permanently other." We cannot know if his continuing friendship with, for example, the duke of Suffolk indicates his transnational humane sympathies, nor if he were grateful to the accidents of history that led him to construct multiple authorial identities. But his work clearly reveals those multiple identities, as well as a capacity for irony and for "a way of thinking rather than just a set of words, not merely [translating]" between English and French.

Such contextual and linguistic shaping of writerly identity is a phenomenon with implications for even the most monocultural literary studies, of course, but is also a phenomenon that monocultural literary studies are ill-equipped to appreciate. Placing these translations, then, means not fixing them in a single framework, which would clearly not be the best way to read a trilingual, bicultural, period-liminal body of work. Rather, it means considering the unusual literary-historical and theoretical problems such figures pose, and seeking new approaches to them—a contextualist criticism, if you will, that includes comparatist and historicist methods. As David Wallace has recently pointed out,

> Rather than developing a comparative historicism, critics have often settled for national and monolingual frames of reference, even while calling for multicultural approaches. Renaissance critics, with some exceptions, have expanded their horizons westward (hence reinforcing rather than critiquing myths of Anglocentric teleology) while ignoring continental Europe.[9]

Wallace calls for a literary-historiographic criticism that "make[s] visible ... relations and developments that would otherwise remain obscured or unconnected" (xvii), and for a cross-period, cross-cultural approach to early modern literature. The cross-cultural Charles d'Orléans is an ideal subject for this sort of endeavor; while this book does not answer Wallace's call for comparatist historiography, it does attempt a comparatist literary history. In the chapters that follow I hope to make visible several such "obscured or unconnected relations" and developments in English poetics, and to reconsider how we place this poet and these translations (meanwhile reconsidering *how* we might go about placing other complex or liminal texts, translations and not).

---

9. *Chaucerian Polity,* xiii.

The Chapters

Chapter 2 begins by introducing the main social and literary contexts in which Charles wrote. This chapter sets the poetry against—in but not of—the *translatio,* that loosely defined but influential set of medieval theoretical paradigms for translation. The chapter asks how the work stands in its moment as a large, early, lyric translation and describes how the English and French poems generally differ. The social, biographical, and historical contexts are introduced, and the work of selected translation theorists, from Alfred the Great to Rita Copeland, is brought to bear to place the poetry as translation. The deracinated Charles and his writerly position are portrayed best, perhaps, in the cover to this book (also found in figure 1). That illustration, folio 73 of BL ms. Royal F 16.ii, depicts Charles, imprisoned in the Tower of London. English royal iconography dominates—note the large coat-of-arms supported by lions in the lower half of the page, the flags atop the turrets, and the beautifully detailed skyline of London. The well-armed English guards surround Charles the ermine-clad writer, who also looks (wistfully?) out a Tower window. The political context for Charles's writing is more prominent here than it is in other illustrations in the same manuscript, the first folio of which traditionally portrays Charles in a courtly setting.[10] The poem illustrated here, "Des Nouvelles d'Albion," is in fact a ballade written to the duc de Bourgogne who helped arrange Charles's release in 1440. It is perhaps he, or one of his high emissaries, who is depicted at the left of the scene arriving, meeting Charles, handing him something (a book? his ransom?), and leaving with him, again heavily guarded. But in fact Charles did not spend much time in the Tower; we can best read this illustration less as a literal depiction of historical fact and more as a Tudor-era representation of his perceived position in England: a French writer of royal blood, but entirely surrounded by images of the power of the English Crown. Charles's central position as poet was, in other words, always affected by his position as foreign prisoner, and the *translatio* included in this case the writer's actual body as well as the body of his work.

Chapter 3 questions, and I hope demystifies, the apparent paradox of a translated subjectivity. In what ways does this lyric "I" establish distinct English and French incarnations? A self-translation, the poetry and its curious historical contexts also invite reconsideration of recent ideas about

---

10. Reproduced in Backhouse, "Founders of Royal Library," plate 17.

early modern imitation, alterity, and "self-fashioning." Key questions in the move from "medieval" to "Renaissance" poetics involve intertext: how is a poet to fashion the lyric self with the words of another? What is the poet's right relation to past poetry? Any translation is an interpretation, of course, wherein interpretive distances of various kinds must be bridged or elided, foregrounded or ignored, foreshortened or fudged. The translator's problem has often been seen as one of historical distance and/or of psychological distance, of "getting into the head" of the prior poet or even in some sense becoming that prior poet.[11] But in self-translation one would assume a certain relief from such problems of writerly identity. After all, in self-translations one merely translates one's own words—one is one's own source—so the relation to the source would no longer involve bridging interpretive distances or navigating alterities of culture, nation, biography, temporality. One might naturally assume that self-translations would be very close to identical. Charles's work, however, exposes that assumption as incomplete at best. For like Luc Santé, Julien Green, Ennius, Beckett, and any number of other multilingual writers in any period, Charles turns out to be a different poet in his different languages. Furthermore, as the paradigms of medieval *translatio* were losing their power over secular translation, and as Renaissance paradigms of *imitatio* were taking hold (a moment Karlheinz Stierle, for one, has identified as an essential turning point in early modern literature),[12] here appears a large, carefully wrought body of bilingual lyric that seems to defy both sets of norms for, and beliefs about, intertext. When Charles departs from the goals and motives of the *translatio,* he comes to explore the writing self—the speaking and writing lyric "I," the self-translating persona—whose texts in the two languages differ significantly from one another. Charles self-represents in multiple contexts (manuscript, cultural, political), and the writerly "I" or lyric subjectivity is thereby multiplied, complicated, and enhanced.

Chapter 4 then takes a long view, asking what has become of those multiplied self-representations across five and a half centuries. This part of the

---

11. For instance, Seneca discusses the various ways of being changed by what one reads and imitates and treats the problem of identity with the prior poet; he counsels a living, fleshly identity rather than a dead image or lifeless picture. "Etiam si cuius in te comparebit similitudo, quem admiratio tibi altius fixerit, similem esse te volo quomodo filiam, non quomodo imaginem; imago res mortua est" (*Epistulae morales* LXXXIV.7–8). The Loeb editors, incidentally, remind us that parts of this epistle appear in the preface to an important medieval text, Macrobius's *Saturnalia.*

12. "*Translatio studii* and Renaissance," in *The Translatability of Cultures,* ed. Wolfgang Iser and Sanford Budick (Stanford University Press, 1996), 55–66.

book discovers a number of primary documents connecting Charles to the foundation of the early English canon, documents that his four most recent bibliographers have not noted.[13] Several early English canon-founders (George Ellis, Joseph Ritson, Horace Walpole, and Thomas Park, among others) were aware of Charles's poetry, and their ambivalent and even contradictory statements about it reveal a good bit about the construction of literary values in our early canon. At least one influential editor, Thomas Park, connects Charles's poetry with Renaissance rhetorician and poetic theorist George Puttenham. (But Park makes that connection, one that still seems entirely valid, before Burckhardt, Michelet, and Pater have constructed the period wall between "medieval" and "Renaissance.") Charles's poetry has been positioned quite differently in the French and the English critical traditions; the details of its curious reception and marginalization provide an illuminating example of how canons may operate to include or to exclude poets based on (in Bourdieu's term) "cultural capital," on shifting aesthetic sensibilities, or on nationalistic and biographical grounds. While critics after Bourdieu might locate the canon's power in school and syllabus, this chapter identifies some additional factors that may bear on "cultural amphibians"[14] or multicultural authors and texts, texts that invite but that may or may not find multiple readerships over time.

Chapter 5 takes up Charles's own end-of-life effort to find a permanent and worldwide readership for his poetry. Grenoble ms. 873, a remarkable and largely unread and unstudied manuscript, has not been edited since 1842.[15] It is a selected works—that fact itself indicating a newly assertive and self-conscious authorial position—but with a twist: Charles has the selected lyrics rearranged, translated into Latin, and placed in facing-column French-Latin format in a large, illuminated vellum book. Grenoble 873 is an overt bid to create a "world lyric" book that will withstand the erosions of time, a bid rather like that of sixteenth-century print-lyric

---

13. Deborah Nelson, *Charles d'Orléans: An Analytical Bibliography* (London: Grant and Cutler, 1990); Edith Yenal, *Charles d'Orléans: A Bibliography of Primary and Secondary Sources* (New York: AMS Press, 1984); Claudio Galderisi, *Charles d'Orléans: Plus dire que penser: Une lecture bibliographique* (Bari: Adriatica Editrice, 1994); and Jean-François Kosta-Théfaine, "Charles d'Orleans: Bibliographie récente," *Le Moyen Français* 38 (1996): 144–50.

14. Thanks to Anne Lake Prescott for this apt and colorful term, for her careful reading, and for scholarship that informs this book much more than particular footnotes can show.

15. Aimé Champollion-Figeac, ed., *Poésies du duc Charles d'Orléans . . .* (Paris: J. Belin-Leprieur, 1842).

authors. The choice and rearrangement of particular poems to be presented here reveal, furthermore, a new emphasis on political and nationalistic concerns and a new willingness to use lyric poetry and the lyric book as a way to foreground those concerns. When compared with the other copies of his poetry he probably supervised during his lifetime, this striking production reveals the distinct values guiding the English, French, and Latin versions. Chapter 5 addresses the *ordinatio* that structures and presents the translation of the lyrics into Latin, a translation that openly states its aim at a pan-European poetic immortality.

The topics of chapters 4 and 5—Charles's poetic afterlife and his placement in literary canons—are necessarily linked with the issue of periodization, which is the topic of chapter 6. Chapter 6 takes up the issue contrastively, asking how we can place the work against the background of writers usually categorized as "medieval" or as "Renaissance." Although in French Charles is considered a latest-medieval poet, in English no such easy categorization is possible. There are a number of "Chaucerian" aspects to his work, as one might expect, but the English sequence establishes a distinct lyric subjectivity and persona of a kind we normally associate with poets appearing much later in our tradition. His approach to the erotic, his use of puns, wordplay, and rhetorical devices, his formal complexity and experimentation, his stance or voice: all these place him well outside the fifteenth-century literary milieu in which he found himself in England. His English poetry in several respects resembles the work of Renaissance poets like Wyatt, Sidney, and even Donne as much as it resembles the poetry of his near-contemporaries Gower, James I, Lydgate, or Hoccleve. As usual, Charles's oddly placed poetry leads us to reexamine the very frameworks we use: when we allow for the blinders of Middle English orthography, the characteristics of this poetry challenge period divisions and labels, both long-held ("medieval," "Renaissance") and recent ("early modern"). We might recall that period categories are at best useful tautologies, and we might also acknowledge David Wallace's point that "no magic curtain separated 'medieval' London and Westminster from 'Renaissance' Florence and Milan"[16]—nor, I would add, from "Renaissance" Chambord and Blois, as is evident in the life and work of this one poet. After all, Charles's life encompasses both "medieval" and "Renaissance" encounters and practices. Son of Louis d'Orléans and Valentina of Milan, and nephew of Charles V, he is born into the great feu-

---

16. *Chaucerian Polity,* 1.

dal houses of Valois and Visconti; yet his own nephew is perhaps the quintessential Renaissance king, François I. Not just in genealogy but in literary-social contacts, Charles's life spans the too-artificial gap we have created between "medieval" and "Renaissance": earlier in his life, Charles was captive in the home of the duke of Suffolk, whose wife was Alice Chaucer, granddaughter of the poet; at the end of his life, Charles was creating "world lyric books" for posterity, overseeing poetic translations, and conducting literary *puys* or salons at Blois. His poetics encompasses both aspects, too, for in this one body of poetry we see the verbal wit and *sprezzatura* of the Renaissance lyric mode challenging the framework of medieval set-pieces. He writes his early poetry in the world of de Pisan and Chartier; not long after his death, the poetry is held in the libraries of people like Henry VIII and Catherine de Medici. Charles's life and oeuvre, in other words, when viewed in their multiple contexts, remind us of the fundamental continuities between "medieval" and "Renaissance" literature and life: that "no magic curtain" exists except in our own schemata. The work invites us to reconsider our traditional literary period boundaries from a bicultural perspective.

Clearly, Charles's poetry presents a number of less-usual critical and literary-historical problems. Students of this poetry have benefited greatly from the more traditional thematic and formal approaches of, for example, John Fox, Alice Planche, Gilbert Ouy, and Daniel Poirion, whose work is foundational. But since Charles's poetry intersects with most of the reasons his century is important to current scholarship, I have asked in this book another set of questions. The book pretends neither to explain all of these intersections nor to exhaust the poetry's theoretical possibilities, nor even to answer all of its own questions, but hopes rather to excavate and present this significant corpus—to recover the literary body of Charles, if you will—in a preliminary act reminiscent of that initial physical recovery of 1415. This book is the first on Charles's lyric poems since 1969 (John Fox's *The Lyric Poetry of Charles d'Orléans*)[17] and the first, in fact, to take the whole corpus in its multiple contexts. The book unashamedly attends to the poems themselves (most to the English poems, which tend to provoke more questions), but the poems in their contexts are also the focus for reconsidering some conventionally held views of, and approaches to, the poetry of the period(s). Instead of proving any particu-

---

17. Oxford: Clarendon, 1969.

lar thing or things about this poetry, the method and thus the shape of the book are deliberately interrogative. Each chapter, as the above summary indicates, introduces some of Charles's poetry and treats a critical, theoretical, or literary-historical issue that the poetry and contexts illuminate or problematize, or for which the poetry invites a different kind of critical attention than the more-often-read authors tend to receive. Each chapter pursues an aspect of Charles's work outward, and a following chapter likewise unfolds to pursue a contiguous aspect. The method is exploratory, adding and contextualizing evidence, rather than teleological or deductive (preselecting and excluding evidence). I would hope above all to provide information that suggests future questions and research. Informed by the recuperative work of recent scholarship in the fifteenth and sixteenth centuries, the book finds in these translations a telling site of cultural contest and literary experimentation. Charles's curious trilingual oeuvre is a large, important, underdiscussed body of work appearing at a significant point in the history of English literature. By assessing and contextualizing the poetics of these translations, we might bring Charles's poetry into a happier, and enduring, English captivity.

2

Translatio, Translation, and Charles d'Orléans's *Paroled* Poetics

The 141 parallel English and French poems attributed to Charles d'Orléans (1394–1465)[1] pose to students of lyric translation a fascinating, instructive set of theoretical and historical questions: what was the status of translated authorship? What do the translations reveal about the state of (and the relations between) two changing vernaculars and the two literary traditions in question? How did the translations square with the dominant cultural model for change, the *translatio?* Even to call these particular texts translations, as I do here for convenience, raises useful debate. To term them "parallel texts" might be better for theoretical and practical reasons. First, the term *translation* carries theoretical expectations that tend to block new readings of this poetry. Second, more practically, it is rarely certain for any given poem in this oeuvre which version was written first, and some few scholars still question the authorship of the English sequence.[2]

I shall assume on the weight of the evidence to date[3] that Charles d'Orléans is the author of both French and English versions. The English sequence, found in the large vellum manuscript now called BL ms. Harley

---

1. English poems cited are from Mary-Jo Arn's edition, *Fortunes Stabilnes;* French poems are from Pierre Champion's edition, *Poésies;* and all translations are mine unless otherwise noted. A version of this essay appears in *Exemplaria* 8, no. 1 (1996): 169–92.

2. William Calin, "Will the Real Charles of Orleans Stand! or Who Wrote the English Poems in Harley 682?" in *Conjunctures: Medieval Studies in Honor of Douglas Kelly,* ed. Keith Busby and Norris J. Lacy (Amsterdam: Rodopi, 1994), 69–86, provides a clear, recent argument against Charles's authorship; yet Calin offers his approach because "the philological and textual evidence proves to be inconclusive" (70).

3. As reviewed by Arn, "Charles of Orleans." On whether the English or French versions came first, see Steele and Day, eds., *English Poems,* xxvi–xxvii; and Hans Meier, "Middle English Styles in Translation: The Case of Chaucer and Charles," in *So Meny People, Longages, and Tonges: Philological Essays in Scots and Mediaeval English Presented to Angus McIntosh,* ed. Michael Benskin and M. L. Samuels (Edinburgh: Authors Press, 1981), 372.

682, names him as its subject, first-person narrator, and specifically, as its author, since it was

> Wrete . . .
> As on the thriteenthe day of Novembre
> Bi the trewe Charlis duk of Orlyaunce.
>
> (ll. 3042–44)[4]

If what the text tells us is not literally so, an as-yet-unidentifiable English translator took care to remain anonymous—entirely invisible, actually—and thus to preserve the appearance of Charles's authorship of these poems. Translators, like compilers and commentators, generally announced themselves as such, distinguishing themselves from the *auctor*[5]—as did the translator of Charles's poems into Latin, Antonio Astesano.[6] Astesano's standard translator's disclaimer,

> Si quid in hoc libro quod dignum laude putaris
>   Invenies, ipsi laus sit habenda duci;
> Si vero offendes aliquid quod crimine dignum
>   Exstet, ego culpam solus habere velim
>
> (ll. 45–48)

[If you find anything in this book that you deem worthy of praise, the praise must go to the duke himself; if indeed you come upon anything that is worthy of reproach, I alone would wish to incur the blame]

goes on to stress the duc d'Orléans's ownership of the poetry:

> Verum his omissis verbis, lege carmina lector
>   Quae sunt maiori prodita ab ingenio;
> Et tibi persuade quod Karolus ipse loquatur
>   Aurelianensis talia verba movens
>
> (ll. 49–52)

---

4. See also lines 5–6, 2720, and 4788 for self-naming in the sequence.

5. On the distinctions among *scriptor, compilator, commentator, actor,* and *auctor,* see A. J. Minnis, *Medieval Theory of Authorship,* 2d ed. (Philadelphia: University of Pennsylvania Press, 1988), 73–74 and 94–95.

6. Astesano devotes dozens of Latin verses in his translator's preface to Charles's works in ms. Grenoble 873; if such a preface existed in Harley 682's famous missing first quire, it would have to have been extremely short.

> [In truth, reader, after you have left these words (i.e., the preface) behind, read the poems and persuade yourself that Charles of Orleans himself speaks, issuing such words.][7]

Likewise, even if a translator, and not Charles himself, performed the translations into English, Charles is still, as its inscribed author, essentially connected with the English work—these are truly "his" texts, more than they are anyone else's that we can name with certainty. For the purposes of this study, then, Charles's authorship (in one sense and another) is not at issue. The remnant authorship questions, like the intriguing biographical questions that surround this figure, will yield in this book to questions of poetic language, cultural practice, and literary history. Of special interest here is the English side of the bilingual parallel corpus, a 6,531-line experimental lyric sequence that is England's largest and earliest surviving self-contained, author-assembled body of personal lyric.[8] Secular translations this large and this carefully presented are rare in the fifteenth century, and this chapter focuses on the English poems as atypical, as divergent from the usual early modern norms of translation.

One usual explanation for these unusual poems, one to dispose of quickly, is that the prince-poet Charles d'Orléans, captured at Agincourt in 1415 and captive in England until 1440, had twenty-five years on his hands and simply passed the time versifying.[9] Those of us who readily

---

7. He also explains the genesis of the translation, and calls Charles the "auctor" of the poetry.

> In versus igitur librum hunc transferre latinos
> Institui: auctoris motus amore fui;
> Qui meus est dominus.
>
> (ll. 23–25)

> [I have taken it upon myself, therefore, to translate this book into Latin verses; I was moved by my love for the author, who is my lord.

Thanks to Lia Rushton, whose understanding of these lines informs mine, for transcribing and translating them.

8. Copied parts of which are found in at least eleven manuscripts extant. Julia Boffey in *English Courtly Love Lyrics* calls the relative manuscript presence of this oeuvre "vast" (74).

9. For example, Robert Louis Stevenson's influential *Familiar Studies of Men and Books* (New York: Dodd and Mead, 1887), 246, explains that Charles merely "whiled away the hours of captivity with rhyming. Indeed there can be no better pastime for a lonely man than the mechanical exercise of verse. Such intricate forms . . . seem to have been invented for the prison and the sick-bed."

accept Charles's authorship shouldn't necessarily also accept that explanation: Charles was quite active during his captivity,[10] and the quantity and the quality of this bilingual oeuvre, with the efforts its author made at every stage to bring it forth as it is,[11] make the work seem quite unlike a late-courtly pastime sprung from a poetics of personal boredom.

At first glance, in fact, the apparent replicativity or equivalence[12] of the French and English sequences would seem consistent with a poetics of medieval *translatio*. As Karlheinz Stierle puts it, *"Transferre, translatio* . . . [is] a central category of political and cultural theory"[13] and one that implies what he calls a vertical axis of translation—translation takes, passes on, replicates something it has inherited. Replicativity, equivalence, fidelity: these medieval translation norms assert continuity across chasms of time, culture, and language and reflect a deeply conservative epistemology. Indeed, by 1440, translation of this kind had long been a chief means of culture building. In England, *translatio imperii* and *translatio studii* had been joined in nation building since Alfred the Great. Alfred saw translation as a way to restore to England not only intellectual and spiritual her-

---

10. For specifics, see Pierre Champion, *Vie de Charles d'Orléans,* 2d ed. (Paris: Honoré Champion, 1969), 668–72; and Enid McLeod, *Charles of Orleans: Prince and Poet* (London: Chatto and Windus, 1969), 129–244. For one account of the relationship between Charles's poetry and his travels while in England, see Ann Tukey Harrison's "Charles d'Orléans: The Reluctant Traveler," *Fifteenth Century Studies* 10 (1984): 79–90.

11. For details see Pierre Champion, *Le Manuscrit autographe des poésies de Charles d'Orléans* (Paris, 1907; rpt. Geneva: Slatkine, 1975), and his *Librairie de Charles d'Orléans* (Paris, 1910; rpt. Geneva: Slatkine, 1975), lx, lxi, lxiii.

12. By equivalence I mean not Jakobsonian equivalence (although the two concepts are not unrelated), but simply what contemporary translation theorists like Douglas Robinson, *The Translator's Turn* (Baltimore: Johns Hopkins University Press, 1991); Willis Barnstone, *The Poetics of Translation: History, Theory, Practice* (New Haven: Yale University Press, 1993); André Lefevere, *Translating Literature* (New York: Modern Language Association, 1992); and André Lefevere and Susan Bassnett, eds., *Translation, History, Culture* (London: Pinter, 1990) mean: the persistent assumption that a translation can be the same as its source text. Both BN f. fr. 25458 and Harley 682 are lyric sequences framed with dream-narrative sections, so are in some rough sense "equivalent." On the differences in content and theme between the two, see Steele and Day, eds., *English Poems,* xxi, xxvi, xxix–xxxiv.

13. *"Translatio studii* and Renaissance," 56. Stierle points out several of its medieval expressions: Otto von Freising's *Chronica sive historia de duabus civitatibus* (1143–46); Hugh of Saint Victor's *De Arca Noe morali;* Vincent de Beauvais, *Speculum historiale;* Chrétien de Troyes; Marie de France; and others. See also Werner Goez, *Translatio imperii: Ein Beitrag zur Geschichte des Geschichtsdenkens und der politischen Theorie im Mittelalter und in der frühen Neuzeit* (Tübingen: Mohr, 1958); and Étienne Gilson, *Les Idées et les lettres* (Paris: J. Vrin, 1932), for foundational critical treatments of the idea in our century.

itage but political power as well.[14] Closely connected with such restoration was *translatio studii,* the transfer of knowledge from one (generally older, more highly valued) culture to another. *Translatio studii* involved the close, faithful translation of sacred and serious texts—of matter that matters—from the "high" language into the vernacular(s). Medieval translations claimed a position of faithful servitude to their master sources—thus the importance of replicativity, equivalence, fidelity.

Early theorists may have differed about degrees and kinds of fidelity in translation (e.g., word for word, sense for sense) but did not generally challenge the underlying assumption that a translation should replicate its source.[15] Even after the great vernacular translation explosions of the

---

14. From Alfred's translation of the *Pastoral Care:*

> It often comes into my mind what wise counsellors (clergy) there were once throughout England . . . and how the kings . . . obeyed God and his messengers; and how they maintained peace and morality and authority within the nation, and also expanded their territory within it; and how they succeeded both in war and in wisdom . . . and how people from outside came into this country and sought wisdom and teaching; and how now we must acquire them from outside, if we will have them at all. . . . I also remembered how I saw before it was all savaged and burned, how the churches stood throughout all England filled with treasures and books, and also of great multitudes of God's servants, but who knew very little use of the books, for they understood nothing of them, nor might, because they were not written in their own language. As if they said: our ancestors, when they held these places before us, loved wisdom, and by means of that they acquired riches, and bequeathed them to us. Here one may still see their track, but we know not how to follow their footsteps. And thus we have now neglected both wealth and wisdom, because we would not bend our minds to the trail. . . . Thus it seems to me better . . . that we also translate certain books, those that be most necessary for all men to know, into the language we are all able to understand . . . so that all the young who are in England free men . . . be set to learning . . . until they know well how to read written English. . . . Then I began to translate into English the book that is called in Latin *Pastoralis* . . . sometimes word for word and sometimes sense for sense . . . and to each bishopric in my kingdom I will send one.

Thanks to Carter Hailey, University of Virginia, for reminding me of and for translating this native example. See also *King Alfred's West-Saxon Version of Gregory's Pastoral Care,* ed. Henry Sweet, 2 vols., Early English Text Society, o.s. 45 and 50 (London, 1871; rpt. Millwood, N.Y.: Kraus Reprints, 1988), 1:2–9.

15. Cicero, *De optimo genere oratorum* 14 and 23; Horace, *Ars Poetica* 133–34; Jerome's famous distinction between word-for-word and sense-for-sense (Letter to Pammachius); Boethius's second commentary on the *Isagoge* of Porphyry; John Scotus Eriugena's preface to his translation of Pseudo-Dionysius the Areopagite's *De caelesti hierarchia;* a twelfth-century commentator's words on Boethius's *De Arithmetica* (ms. Bern 633, fol. 21, col. a); Roger Bacon in *Opus Tertium;* Burgundio of Pisa's prologue to the translation of St. John Chrysostom's commentary on the Gospel of John; Henricus Aristippus's preface to his translation of Plato's *Meno,* among others. It is not a coincidental pun that faithful translation was expected of those translating sacred material, but the principle of fidelity was applied just as fully to philosophical material, in the service of *translatio studii.*

Renaissance, England's strongest critical challenge to equivalence, Dryden's, was circumscribed by the older parameters of *translatio*. Dryden sketched translation's acceptable boundaries as degrees of equivalence: paraphrase (word for word) and metaphrase (sense for sense). Beyond equivalences, the translator risks "[losing] his name."[16] Yet a translator who revives ancient authors (says Dryden in reviving the *Heroides*) may safely depart from fidelity only "to write as he supposes that [source] author would have done, had he lived in our age and country" (1:239). Thus even Dryden's liberalized seventeenth-century definitions excuse just such infidelities as permit the elision of historical difference—just such discontinuity as would support the continuity of a concept as tenacious as *translatio*.[17]

Recent theoretical approaches to *translatio* give greater attention to discontinuities in translation. Rita Copeland, for example, challenges the idea that medieval translation acted mainly as a restorative or replicative force. Medieval translations, Copeland argues, can instead be part of the age's dialectic between rhetoric and hermeneutics. Translations, like commentaries and *accessus,* can displace rather than serve their source texts, and can act to alter texts according to prevailing ideologies.[18] More generally, cultural and poststructuralist theories also challenge older assumptions about equivalence in translation. Cultural theorists tend to stress the power struggles, the material conditions of production, or the cultural appropriations and impositions involved in translation.[19] Poststructuralists might instead focus on the doubled gaps between *signifiant* and *signifié,* on the comparative differences between signs-within-sys-

---

16. "The third way is that of imitation, where the translator (if now he has not lost that name) assumes the liberty, not only to vary from the words and sense, but to forsake them both as he sees occasion; and taking only some general hints from the original, to run division on the groundwork, as he pleases." From the "Preface to the Translation of Ovid's Epistles," in *Essays of John Dryden,* ed. W. P. Ker, 2 vols. (New York: Russell and Russell, 1961), 1:237.

17. Thomas Greene, *The Light in Troy* (New Haven: Yale University Press, 1982), specifies several kinds of imitation that acknowledge to different degrees historical difference: dialectical, heuristic, eclectic. These operate, necessarily, in relation to older texts and apply less well to self-translations.

18. Rita Copeland, *Rhetoric, Hermeneutics, and Translation in the Middle Ages* (Cambridge: Cambridge University Press, 1991), 3, 4, 7; chaps. 3 (63–66), 6, (151–78), and 7 (179–220) especially.

19. "When . . . the violence of imperialism straddles a subject-language, translation can become a species of violation," writes Gayatri Spivak in "Imperialism and Sexual Difference," *Oxford Literary Review* 8 (1986): 234. For a Foucauldian update and extension, see Lawrence Venuti's "Genealogies of Translation Theory: Schleiermacher," *Traduction Terminologie Rédaction* 4, no. 2 (1991): 125–50.

tems, or on the doubled instabilities of meaning involved in translation.[20] Like Copeland, cultural and poststructural theorists tend to assume discontinuity rather than equivalence in translation, and instead of defining and judging the terms of equivalence, tend to perceive their task as analysis of discontinuity. Stierle, in fact, claims that "horizontal" translation, the sort of translation that operates mutually across cultures rather than in a vertical pattern of fidelity, is the mark of the Renaissance; he locates the change from vertical to horizontal models of translation in the work of Petrarch. "The experience of the co-presence of cultures," he says, "is perhaps the most important aspect of what we call Renaissance."[21] Charles, however, is not the same sort of translator as Petrarch, nor the same sort of poet, yet the "co-presence of cultures" that marks horizontal, Renaissance translation is indeed vibrantly manifest in Charles's self-translations.

I would suggest that neither older nor newer views will entirely suffice for the case at hand. *Translatio* of some more specific sort likely plays a part in these translations, but what sort? and what part? Whether we theorize translation as replicative, rhetorical, or hermeneutic, as restorative or opportunistic, as serving cultural stasis or cultural change, in the case of Charles d'Orléans's lyric translations, it is the departures from the habits and practices of medieval *translatio* that signify. Both in the larger design of the work and in the small-scale methods, these lyric translations alter the usual intersections of translation with *translatio*.

Translatio Studii and the Social Politics of Language

Although Charles d'Orléans had lifelong interests in medicine, philosophy, and religion[22] and a considerable library of Latin and French sacred

---

20. Jacques Derrida et al., "Table Ronde sur la traduction," in *L'Oreille de l'autre: Otobiographies, transferts, traductions* (Montreal: VLB, 1982), 125–212. See also A. C. Ingberg, "The Enigma of the Translator: A Poststructuralist Reading of Theories of Translation," Ph.D. diss., Purdue University, 1986. Better still, J.-F. Lyotard, "The Different, the Referent, and the Proper Name," *Diacritics* 14 (1984): 4–14. The title of *Translating Poetry: The Double Labyrinth,* ed. Daniel Weissbort (London: Macmillan, 1989) indicates the issue's complexity.

21. "*Translatio studii* and Renaissance," 64; general discussion is on pp. 63–65.

22. Champion, *Librairie,* xxvi–xxix, for a list of books he brought back from England; "sa librairie nous le montre encore curieux de médecine" (l); l–lii as well. Cf. McLeod, *Charles of Orleans,* 165–66; Champion, *Vie,* 214–16, but more interestingly, 223–34.

texts and intellectual and medical treatises,[23] he did not use translation to bring across a specific intellectual heritage. The poems are secular, of course, and while there are serious, meditative poems in the sequence, more of them are witty and entertaining. The translation occurs not from an ancient classical language, but between contemporaneous vernaculars. (One could argue that to translate from French to English, that is, from a high-status to a lower-status vernacular, is perfectly consonant with the direction and impetus of *translatio*. But Charles actually went to some trouble to resist the direction and impetus of *translatio* by having his lyrics "translated up," so to speak, into Latin,[24] an unusually assertive action that claims a high-classical permanence and value for lyric.) The matter translated and the languages involved indicate something animating the translations other than what we have generally thought of as *translatio studii*.

Indeed it is curious that Charles felt a need to move between the French and English vernaculars at all. After all, French was still a dominant language in England; book import records and library lists confirm that readers in England preferred French literature.[25] If the translations into Latin imply a Latin-literate European audience and a status and permanence

---

23. Champion, *Librairie*. For his and his royal son's libraries, see also Pascale Thibault, *La Bibliothèque de Charles d'Orléans et de Louis XII au château de Blois* (Blois: Les Amis de la Bibliothèque de Blois, 1989); for his brother's library, see Gustave duPont-Ferrier, *Jean d'Orléans, Comte d'Angoulême d'après sa bibliothèque (1467)* (Paris: Félix Alcan, 1897); for a nephew's, see Edmond Sénemaud, *La Bibliothèque de Charles d'Orléans, Comte d'Angoulême, au château de Cognac en 1496* (Paris: A. Claudin, 1861). For the libraries of his third wife, Marie de Clèves, and of his brother, the Bastard of Dunois, see Champion's *Librairie*, appendix 1 and appendix 3, respectively. The Orléans family had already been prominent bibliophiles for three generations.

24. In Grenoble ms. 873, discussed by Marco Balzaretti, "Antonio Astesano traduttore di Charles d'Orléans," *Studi Francesi* 29 (1985): 58–62, and treated in chapter 5 below.

25. E. Armstrong, "English Purchase of Books from the Continent, 1465–1526," *English Historical Review* 94 (1979): 268–90; M. J. Barber, "The Books and Patronage of Learning of a Fifteenth-Century Prince," *Book Collector* 12 (1963): 308–15. For an old-style view, see H. R. Plomer, "The Importation of Low Country and French Books in England, 1480 and 1502–3," *Library*, 4th ser., 9 (1929): 164–68. See also Calin, "Will the Real Charles," 83–84, on the relation of the two languages. That Gower wrote the *Cinkante Ballades* in French indicates that French was likely perceived as the preferred medium for lyric writing by the generation ahead of Charles. Julia Boffey, *English Courtly Love Lyrics*, 9, 29, 74, and passim, stresses the predominantly French character of fifteenth-century English lyric; see also John Scattergood, "Literary Culture at the Court of Richard II," in *Reading the Past: Essays on Medieval and Renaissance Literature* (Portland, Oreg.: Four Courts Press, 1996), 114–27, but especially 119–21.

unusual for medieval secular lyric, the Harley 682 English poems imply a current, vernacular audience with a taste for English lyric that couldn't be satisfied with the widely available French lyrics. Although we know little about Charles's immediate audience,[26] if we assume for the lyrics an English readership equally at home in French and English, for which there is good evidence,[27] then we have to ask what sort of *translatio* is required here and what the English lyrics bring across, or translate, or offer an audience, that the French lyrics do not.

Since lyric is in some sense "contentless," as compared to the usual sorts of medieval *studia* to be translated or even as compared to medieval romance,[28] the translator perhaps instead intended a *translatio poesis*—that is, to bring across a lyric poetics meant to instruct and a heritage of lyric practice meant to delight, both of which were available in French (but neither in English).[29] But a lack of overt poetic commentary in these texts fails to confirm a deliberately literary *translatio poesis* at work in Harley 682, and in fact what is achieved in English is in significant respects unlike Charles's French poetics. The historical contexts, though, would support a more personalized *translatio poesis*. Because of Charles's superior status as prince, any French-to-English translations could resemble the acts of a superior cultural missionary or ambassador more than those of a humble servant of *translatio*. After all, Charles was in the north at Pontefract, Fotheringay, and Bolingbroke castles for a total of fourteen years—seven

---

26. An anagram poem ("Alas mercy where shal myn hert yow find") containing the name of an Englishwoman, Anne Molins, may indicate a coterie English readership. See also Samuel Moore, "Patrons of Letters in Norfolk and Suffolk, c. 1450," *PMLA* 27 (1912): 188–207 and 28 (1913): 79–105.

27. Malcolm Parkes, "Literacy of the Laity," in *The Medieval World,* ed. David Daiches and Anthony Thorlby (London: Aldus, 1973), 555–78. Manuscript evidence indicates that French poetry was much more popular in England than has been usually granted and that its appeal persists into the Tudor period, as well: see Steven W. May's "Manuscript Circulation at the Elizabethan Court," in *New Ways of Looking at Old Texts,* ed. W. Speed Hill (Binghamton, N.Y.: Medieval and Renaissance Text Society/Renaissance English Text Society, 1993), 273–80. Even if we think of the audience most conservatively, as an audience of one, the poet himself, we still have to explain the efforts and successes of this large body of bilingual poetry.

28. See Calin's notion of "courtly adaptation" in *The French Tradition and the Literature of Medieval England* (Toronto: University of Toronto Press, 1994).

29. Machaut, Deschamps, Oton de Granson, Christine de Pisan, Alain Chartier, et al., wrote and theorized lyric and lyric sequences; Deschamps's *Art de dictier,* for one, maps French lyric practice. Chaucer, Gower, Lydgate, and company neither wrote so much English lyric nor theorized lyric. Further discussion of the respective literary fields into which Charles's French and English works fell appears in chapters 4 and 6 below.

years in lonely Lincolnshire—where such an elegant figure might well have thought himself a cultural paragon.[30] But his status as prince was undercut by his position as prisoner. His financial straits and the changing legalities of his hosts' payments from the Crown complicate any interpretation of his translations as the missionary largesse of a superior being.[31] Given Charles's peculiarly dual position—cousin and battle-spoil of king Henry V, both superior in rank to and subject to (as prisoner of) his host-captors—one can imagine the sort of social delicacy required of both host-captors and the honored guest-prisoner. The usual critical view of "courtly," aristocratic, or "at court" poetry, then, as arising from the sociopolitical necessities to curry favor at court[32] would need to be subtilized in light of these translations and their contexts. It seems reasonable to imagine Charles's impulse to share his rich native poetic tradition by translating it (or having it translated) for the enjoyment of a group who could find in it both the familiar and the new: a style of poetry familiar from popular French lyrics, but essentially new to the English language and literary system.[33] Add to this mixture the politics involved in choice of languages: perhaps the captive saw that one way to ingratiate himself with his captors was to use the language for which they were beginning to claim a new status. This was, after all, the age when Henry V established English, not Latin or French, as the language of government, fully (finally) actualizing Alfred's early understanding of the political importance of the ver-

---

30. For a dark account of conditions in late-medieval Lincolnshire, see Graham Platts, *Land and People in Medieval Lincolnshire* (Lincoln: History of Lincolnshire Committee, 1985), especially chapter 9, "Culture in Medieval Lincolnshire" and 262–80; alternatively, the University of London, Institute of Historical Research, *Victoria History of the Counties of England: Lincolnshire* (London: Archibald Constable, 1900–1906).

31. On and off, Charles had to pay his own keep for what ended up being most of the twenty-five years. See Champion, *Un Inventaire des papiers de Charles d'Orléans (1444)* (Paris: Librairie Ancienne Honoré Champion, 1912), and McLeod, *Charles of Orleans,* 161–62 especially, and for more background, xiv–xv, 101, 144–45, 148, 151–52, 156–59, 179, 187, 219, 242–43, and accompanying notes.

32. R. F. Green, *Poets and Princepleasers* (Toronto: University of Toronto Press, 1980); J. E. Stevens, *Music and Poetry in the Early Tudor Court* (London: Methuen, 1961); extending the notion into the Renaissance are Stephen Greenblatt, *Renaissance Self-Fashioning* (Chicago: University of Chicago Press, 1980); and Catherine Bates, *Rhetoric of Courtship* (Cambridge: Cambridge University Press, 1992).

33. For some of the ways in which Charles's poetry stands out against fifteenth-century England's rather flat lyric landscape, see Mary-Jo Arn, "*Fortunes Stablines:* The English Poems of Charles of Orleans in Their English Context," *Fifteenth-Century Studies* 7 (1983): 1–18, and chapters 3, 5, and 6 below.

nacular.[34] There was reason enough between 1415 and 1440 for the number-one French political prisoner to want smooth relations with the English powers. What more diplomatic, even complimentary act of translation, and what better exercise of poetic ingenuity, than to create something new in the host-captors' language? To translate in these contexts may have balanced compliment and condescension (although there is no real evidence for either). Charles may have been asked to render the verses in English; he may have decided that given his position, it was politic to do so; he may have asked some unknown translator to do so. Some combination, then, of social expedience and an encounter of poetic sensibilities may explain the genesis of these quasi-parallel texts. In any case the translations were more likely conceived as local, personal attempts to please than as part of *translatio studii*'s wider intellectual attempts to enlighten.

But if Charles's translations attempted a conscious linguistic ingratiation or a conscious poetic *translatio,* one would still reasonably expect conscious statements of poetic purpose, like those in the Latin translation of Charles's poems.[35] Such statements, however, are distinctly absent in Charles's English poems. When the lyric speaker does tell us why he writes, it has nothing to do with *translatio* (*studii* or any other sort), nothing to do with the social politics of language, and everything to do with the personal consolations of writing itself: writing is "the leche to all his soore felyng" (l. 837). The speaker says he is "wrytyng to sett [himself] in gladnes" (l. 1900). Although Charles had access to and interest in more traditional sorts of *translatio studii* material, in this sequence the *studii* part—the matter that matters—is a deeply explored and translated lyric "I."

Translatio imperii and the "Caitiff of Fraunce"

As for *translatio imperii:* it is clear that Charles d'Orléans both knew and applied in French poems a classic *translatio imperii* statement—and equally clear that he chose not to place the English translation in its ser-

---

34. Christopher Allmand, *Henry V* (Berkeley and Los Angeles: University of California Press, 1992), 414, 419–25. The decree is a surprisingly democratic and unsurprisingly nationalistic one that both opens government to vernacular readers and claims the native supremacy of that vernacular.

35. Or like the *translatio* declaration in the prologue to *Cligés.* Antonio Astesano, translating Charles's lyrics into Latin in Grenoble ms. 873, explains his motivations and attempts to place Charles's lyrics in an illustrious line; for discussion see chapter 5 below.

vice. Charles's bibliophile parents owned several copies of Sallust, one of which was probably used in educating Charles and his brother Jean d'Angoulême.[36] In fact the young Charles, displaying his preferences early, wrote some poems in their instructional copy of Sallust; but young Jean more appropriately wrote in it lists of Roman rulers and kings of France. "Ita imperium semper ad optumum [*sic*] quemque a minus bono transfertur," says Sallust (*Bellum Catilinae* 2.6; "thus empire is always transferred from the less good to the best"), and Charles only later responds with a set of poems that can be read as a sort of miniature *Salluste moralisé*.

Complainte I ("France jadis on te soulait nommer") shows that Charles and his cousin Henry V have Christianized Sallust in order to interpret the battle of Agincourt similarly: "Je reconnais," said the victorious Henry in 1415,

> que Dieu m'a donné la grâce d'avoir eu la victoire sur les français, non pas que je la vaille:[37] mais je crois certainement que Dieu les a voulu punir. Et s'il est vrai ce que j'en ai oui dire, ce n'est merveille. Car on dit oncques plus grand désordre de voluptés, de péchés et de mauvais vices ne fut vu, comme ceux qui règnent en France aujourd'hui. C'est pitié de l'ouïr recorder et horreur aux écoutants. Et si Dieu en est courroucé ce n'est pas merveille et nul ne s'en doit ébahir.

> [I recognize that God has given me the grace to have had a victory over the French, not that I deserve it; but I certainly believe that God wanted to punish them. And if what I've heard said about it/them is true, it's no wonder. For it's said there's never been seen a greater chaos of voluptuaries, of sins and bad vices, as those that reign in France today. It's pitiful to hear it reported, and horror to the hearers. And if God is angry, it's no wonder, and no one should be disconcerted by it.]

Charles's poem's ironized refrain ("Treschrestian, franc royaume de France!"), the second stanza's direct questions

---

36. Champion, *Librairie,* 96–100, discusses the manuscript, BN ms. Lat. 9684, and the additions to it. A telling illumination from BN ms. Lat. 5747 *(Jugurtha)* anachronistically depicts Sallust instructing the Orléans children. Champion includes the illumination as plate 1 in his *Vie de Charles d'Orléans.* For discussion of the politics of selection in Charles's lyric books, see chapter 5 below.

37. Note the modesty topos qualified with the subjunctive. Modernized by and cited in Champion, *Vie,* 153; also Fox, *Lyric Poetry,* 17–18; both cite chronicler Le Fèvre de Saint-Rémy, 1:260.

> Scez tu dont vient ton mal, a vray parler?
> Cognois tu point pourquoy es en tristesse?

[Do you know where your ill comes from, truly? Do you know at all why you are in woe?]

and the nation's enumerated sins

> Ton grant ourgueil, glotonnie, peresse,
> Couvoitise, sans justice tenir,
> Et luxure

[Your great pride, gluttony, laziness, envy, greed without justice, and wantonness]

make it clear that France is the "minus bonum" from whom the glories of victory are withheld—with "Dieu" as the added agent, of course. Intermediary political poems pray for peace (LXXV, LXXVI) and one gloating ballade (CI) shows that Charles doesn't mind applying Sallust to any victor, according to the fickle fortunes of war.

> Comment voys je ses Anglois esbays!
> Rejoys toi, franc royaume de France.
> On apparçoit que de Dieu sont hays,
> Puis qu'ilz n'ont plus couraige ne puissance.
> Bien pensoient, par leur oultrecuidancc,
> Toy surmonter et tenir en serviage,
> Et ont tenu a tort ton heritaige.
> Mais a present Dieu pour toy se combat
> Et se montre du tout de ta partie;
> Leur grant orgueil entierment abat,
> Et t'a rendu Guyenne et Normandie.

[How I see these English scattered! Rejoice, free/noble kingdom of France! It's evident that they're hated by God, since they no longer have courage or power. They thought indeed by their arrogance to overcome you and hold you in servitude, and wrongly held your heritage. But now God fights for you and shows himself entirely on your side, has fully beaten back their great pride, and has returned to you Guyenne and Normandy.]

The ballade's third stanza even applies the concept to England's internal affairs. This is eerily perspicacious, since in 1454, about a year after this poem was probably written, the Wars of the Roses began in England.

> N'ont pas Anglois souvent leurs rois trays?
> Certes . . .
> Et encore le roy de leur pays
> Est maintenant en doubteuse balance:
> D'en parler mal chascun Anglois s'avance;
> Assez montrant, par leur mauvais langaige
> Que voulontiers lui feraoient oultraige.
> Qui sera Roy entr'eux est grant desbat;
> Pour ce, Fraunce, que veulx tu que te dye?
> De sa verge Dieu les pugnist et bat
> Et t'a rendu Guyenne et Normandie.

[Haven't these English often betrayed their kings? Of course . . . And still the king(ship) of their country is now weighing in a doubtful balance: each Englishman steps forward in speaking ill of him/it; showing enough by their bad language that they'd gladly do him harm. Who will be king among them is much in dispute; for this, France, what do you want me to say? From his authority with his rod God punishes and beats them and has returned Guyenne and Normandy to you.]

But while Charles writes a fair amount of political poetry in French in which he does transfer the moral bounties of empire to the victorious, while he knew his Sallust, and while he had histories of Rome and France in his possession in England,[38] he does not put translation in service of *translatio imperii.* The political poems do not appear in parallel English versions.[39] Obviously, "Comment vois-je ces Anglais esbahis!" is not a

---

38. Champion, *Librairie,* xxv–xxix.
39. Many are verse letters sent to Bourbon or to Burgundy during the later captive years when it seemed that Burgundy could arrange his release (which in fact he helped do). Complainte I ("France jadis on te souloit nommer") actually appears in the Royal F 16.ii manuscript, owned by Henry VII and VIII. The manuscript placement and provenance of the political poems are fascinating and are treated in part in chapter 5.

good candidate for a tactful translation project into English, given the situation; Charles does, however, have this poem and other politically charged poems translated into Latin late in his life. From the English version, though, Charles even excises twenty of the twenty-six mentions of France that appear in French versions.

Again, I speculate that the selective topicalities of the various translations result from the odd political doubleness of his position as prince and captive. If Charles's position made it delicate for him to translate as a cultural paragon or literary missionary, it would have made it impossible for him to translate into English verse the glories of Gaul. Instead, Charles wisely assumed in life, and perhaps by omission in verse, a distinctly conciliatory position during his captivity. He communicated with Burgundian, French, Armagnac, Lancastrian, and Yorkist factions;[40] he proposed and later helped arrange the marriage of Margaret d'Anjou and Henry VI;[41] he helped negotiate treaties at Gravelines, Calais, and Tours.[42] The acute awareness of his own position we see in his letters[43] may have guided what he chose *not* to translate. What he does choose to translate (or have translated) may indicate, as I have said, his awareness of an English audience's lyric tastes and sensibilities—sensibilities English poets hadn't yet acted on in any notable way.[44] In any case *translatio imperii* stops for Charles d'Orléans at Blois, or at least at Calais (no doubt where he too might rather have stopped in 1415). Instead of directing translation toward the exteriorized, historical concerns of *translatio imperii*, Charles's English work directs translation inward toward an immediate poetic subjectivity. Especially as contrasted with mainstream

---

40. His second wife was Bonne d'Armagnac. In 1433 he proposed to Henry VI a peace summit among all these factions and a few others (Champion, *Vie,* 205–7); a similar initiative in 1434 also failed (208). For the later, successful negotiations and his deliverance, see 272–312.

41. Champion, *Vie,* 349; McLeod, *Charles of Orleans,* 267–70.

42. McLeod, *Charles of Orleans,* 194–204, 220–21, 224–44, 267–70; Champion, *Vie,* 154–312, but especially 272–312.

43. Especially in verse letters to Burgundy and Bourbon; see also Champion, *Inventaire;* and Fox, *Lyric Poetry,* 17 and n. 4.

44. Whether art more reflects or shapes its readers' sensibilities is a larger question than this study can tackle, and is probably best left to the chaos theorists. Gower, for one, perceived French as the proper medium for a lyric sequence *(Cinkante Ballades)* and reserves English for his sustained narrative verse *(Confessio Amantis).* John Quixley did translate Gower's *Traitié pour essampler les amantz marietz* into English around 1402, probably for his daughter's marriage—an instructive, occasional work not at all the same sort of lyric project at issue here. For details see Henry MacCracken, *Quixley's Ballades Royal (?1402)* (Leeds, 1908; rpt. *Yorkshire Archaeological Journal* 20 (1909): 33–50).

translatio practices, these parallel texts emphasize the sequence as witty, personal, secular, vernacular lyric. Not serving faithfully (or even hermeneutically) a revered Source, Charles takes as his source his own exactly contemporary, vernacular texts,[45] and thereby implicitly claims for his poems an independent value, an *auctoritas*—both an authority and an authorship—not usually accorded translation even today and not accorded vernacular lyric in England until a century later. The energy of translation is directed toward a poetics of the interior, of the self—a new sort of development in English lyric poetics in 1415.[46] The translations alter *translatio studii*, avoid *translatio imperii,* and so make space for *translatio sui* or *suater*[47]—at least on the large scale.

The Prisoner *Parole*d: Discontinuity and Lyric Authorship

The small-scale translation habits, however, may better indicate what sort of *translatio* is being performed here, what sensibilities are engaged, what is being brought across and how.[48] I see Charles's English poems as experiments—some of them quite successful—in meter and rhyme, in diction and wordplay, in rhetoric, in genre, in persona, and more. Harley 682 ends with a whole section of new, English-only poems that continue and extend the practice of those with French analogues. So, paradoxically, these experimental translations may perform a most traditional function of translation—that of building a poet's skill.[49] But Charles builds his skill in

---

45. Except Ballade 59, a translation of Christine de Pisan's "Seulete je suis." For an account of this, see Sergio Cigada, "Christine de Pisan e la traduzione delle poesie di Charles d'Orléans," *Aevum* 32 (1958): 509–16.

46. See Albrecht Classen, *Die Autobiographische Lyrik des Europäischen Spätmittelalters* (Amsterdam: Rodopi, 1991), 269–345. Classen entitles his third chapter "Selbstbehauptung und Restitution eines verwundeten Ichs: Dichtung als Therapie."

47. Or *translatio Caroli,* if you read lyric as if it were psychologically autobiographical. For those kinds of readings see Classen, *Autobiographische Lyrik;* and Rouben Cholakian, *Deflection/Reflection in the Lyric Poetry of Charles d'Orléans: A Psychosemiotic Reading* (Potomac, Md.: Maryland Press, 1984). Chapter 3 below further distinguishes such psychological and biographical readings from readings that interrogate an early modern poetic subjectivity.

48. Perhaps *translatio* in its rhetorical sense, as Bernard de Chartres or Geoffroi de Vinsauf meant it, metaphor as stylistic principle or technique. Geoffroi de Vinsauf, *Poetria Nova,* 765–915, ed. and trans. Margaret F. Nims (Toronto: Pontifical Institute of Medieval Studies, 1967), 43–49; for Bernard, see Michelle A. Freeman's introduction to her *Poetics of "Translatio studii" and "Conjointure,"* French Forum Monographs, 12 (Lexington, Ky., 1979).

49. What Copeland, following Pliny the Younger, calls *exercitatio* (*Rhetoric, Hermeneutics, and Translation,* 31).

English verse not by traditional means—not, that is, by faithfully adhering to principles of translation equivalence, as would just about everyone until Wyatt. Although the sequences may seem to be closely equivalent in content, in their inner workings and in their positions within distinct literary systems they are quite different. More than a century ahead of even Dryden's limited permission for discontinuity in translation, Charles's ostensibly replicative parallel texts escape *translatio*'s bonds of equivalence and draw considerably for their effects on linguistic and cultural discontinuities. This pair of poems, Ballade X/Ballade 10, is at least partially representative of the sequence's generative translations.

Ballade X

A Ma dame je ne sçay que je dye
Ne par quel bout je doye commencer
Pour vous mander la doloreuse vie
Qu'Amour me fait chacun jour endurer.
Trop mieulx vaulsist se taire que parler, 5
Car proufiter ne me peuent mes plains,
Ne je ne puis guerison recouvrer,
Puis qu'ainsi est que de vous suis loingtains.

Quanque je voy me deplaist et ennuye,
Et n'en ose contenance moustrer, 10
Mais ma bouche fait semblant qu'elle rie,
Quant maintefoiz je sens mon cueur plourer.
Au fort, martir on me devra nommer,
Se Dieu d'Amours fait nulz amoureux saints:
Car j'ay des maulx plus que ne sçay compter, 15
Puis qu'ainsi est que de vous suy loingtains.

Et non pourtant, humblement vous mercie,
Car par escript vous a pleu me donner
Ung doulx confort que j'ay a chiere lie
Receu de cueur et de joyeux penser, 20
Vous suppliant que ne vueilliez changier,
Car en vous sont tous mes plaisirs mondains,
Desquelz me fault a present deporter,
Puis qu'ainsi est que de vous suy loingtains.

Ballade 10

Madame a trouthe not wot y what to say
Nor bi what ende that y shulde first bigynne
The wofull lijf vnto yow to biwray
Which shertith me more nerre than doth my skyn
Hit forto speke as welle lo may y blyn   495
Forwhi bi speche not kan y be the nerre
What helpe god wott as shulde y bi hit wyn
Syn hit is so that y am from yow fare

What y now se hit noyeth me mafay
But y for drede my countenaunce forpeyne   500
As with my mouth to shewe a laughtir gay
When that myn hert as wepith me withinne
A martir me to calle hit were no synne
If Cupide make a seynt as of louer
For paynys thikke endewre y lo not thynne   505
Syn hit is so that y am from yow fer

But neuyrtheles y humbly thanke yow ay
For yowre writyng my woo hathe pesid syn
With swete comfort y took the selvyn day
The whiche y more sett by then alle my kyn   510
That neuyr fro my brest as shall hit twyn
Which chaungith not y pray yow as y dare
For now my blis on hit is to missyn
Syn hit is so that y am from yow fare

My ledy hert is lightid vnto tyn   515
Bi comfort loo but absence doth me war
That more y lust to wayle then laughe or gren
Syn hit is so that y am from yow fare

(ll. 491–518)[50]

---

50. I omit Arn's editorial capitalization and punctuation, since her reasons for adding them do not pertain here (clarity of text and syntax) and since one of her reasons in fact works against the interpretive position I take here. Arn says, "I have chosen to capitalize [the nouns] wherever I saw in them a possibility of personification" (*Fortunes Stabilnes,* 127), a legitimate editorial intervention; as a noneditorial interpreter, I am arguing that there is less personification here than one would expect, and that the actual lack of capitalization in the manuscript supports that notion.

We should first dispose of the few important respects in which this parallel pair is not representative of Charles's larger sequence. Here, for example, the French is already a *décasyllabe,* while in most other pairs a French *octosyllabe* is expanded (and altered) to become English pentameter. With the extra foot, Charles often indulges in what Jacques Barzun calls the French preference for the filled line, seen even here (where syllable count does not change between versions) in the chevilles, "lo" and "ay," at lines 495, 505, 507, and 516.[51] Another typical metrical filler that the English poems generally use to better effect is *reduplicatio,* or doubling. Charles often doubles words to fill a line and/or satisfy a rhyme, but in so doing changes patterns of imagery and adds concreteness. There is no such effect here from the poem's only doubled phrase, "laughe or gren" (l. 517). Still another translator's resource he oddly did not choose to exploit here as fully as he might have (and as he does in other English poems) is what I call syntactic mimesis, the strategy of representing or enacting content in syntax. It is a practice that becomes frequent among Renaissance poets: Sidney, Spenser, Donne, and especially Milton deploy it skillfully.[52] But the practice indicates a concern for form and wordplay that does not manifest itself elsewhere in fifteenth-century English lyric as far as I can find. In this particular case—I mean here the refrain—we should call it something else, perhaps syntactic antimimesis or syntax of frustration, since the poet does in syntax what he laments in content he cannot do. The French phrase keeps the lovers close ("de vous suis loingtains," ll. 8, 16, 24) in a sort of wish-fulfillment by syntax. But the English version, "syn hit is so that y am from yow fare" might as easily have been "syn hit is so that *y from yow am* fare," with the additional advantage of stresses on "y" and "yow." Better, why not "that *from yow y am* fare," keeping stress on absence, on "from," but joining "y" and "yow" in the line if not in life? Charles does show elsewhere a care for the placement of words in lines, so this refrain is perhaps not ideally representative of his methods.

But in several other important respects, the gaps between these parallel

---

51. *An Essay on French Verse* (New York: New Directions, 1990), 80. This is also a characteristic of Tudor poetry.

52. Sidney's anadiplosis (*Astrophel and Stella* 1, ll. 1–4) and syntactical delay of naming (5, 6) to create momentum and suspense; Spenser's morally mimetic syntax ("I that doe seeme not I, Duessa am," *Faerie Queene,* I.5.231); Donne in, among others, "Lecture upon the Shadow" (l. 1), "The Ecstasy" (ll. 15–16, 19–20), and "Nocturnal on St. Lucy's Day" (ll. 17–18, 45); Milton's wily enjambments and inversions, syntactically managed choriambi and trochaic substitutions (*Paradise Lost* IV.183, 187, 190, 191) and famous asyndeton (II.621, II.948–49), for example.

texts illustrate quite well Charles d'Orléans's poetics of translation. Both poems treat the problem of absence, a prime mover of his larger lyric sequence, and both poems interrogate the respective resources of speech and writing to resolve this problem. But the English poem complicates the relation among presence, absence, writing, and speech.[53] The French poem is pretty clearly concerned with writing, not speech. In the French version the word "mander" (l. 3) implicitly insists on letter writing, while only "plains" (l. 6) can be oral or written. The English poem, though, will come to rely on its first stanza's more noticeable fictive orality. The English opens with a confessional, conversational "Madame a trouthe" and phrasing that draws attention to sound: "not wot y what." The line rings the colloquial presences of speech, not the epistolary distances on which the later content and envoi will insist. The nonequivalent choice of "biwray" for "mander" at the third line serves rhyme but also adds to the first meaning of to divulge or reveal, since "biwray" can mean to speak ill of or to malign. The translation change thus adds to the English version an implicit commentary on the nature of the "wofull lijf." The problem of absence seems both more acute and more specific in the English. Where the French seeks to "profiter" (l. 6), a fairly general word, the English specifies the need to "be the nerre" (l. 496). The English speaker seems less optimistic about the possibilities, effects, even the use of speech at every stage: I don't know what to say, or how to start, might as well cease, can't be near you this way anyhow. Finally line 497 asks a frustrated rhetorical question not present in the French: "what helpe, god wot, as shulde y by hit wyn?" The parallel French line 5, though, is an almost nonchalant idiomatic subjunctive. Compare the smooth, nearly indifferent generalities of the French lament to the self-questioning and project-questioning agon of the English. The English speaker seems already to be present—speaking, not proposing speech—and yet presently doubting the power of this speech to effect the presence his speech itself (ironically? or in wish-fulfillment?) implies. By stanza 3 we shall see how the English poem's internal logic in resolving its complications differs from that of the French poem.

The second stanza, meanwhile, illustrates one of the English sequence's frequent tactics, the extension of metaphor into conceit. Both second stanzas use a religious metaphor, but the English version seizes opportunities

---

53. For an elegant view of some other aspects of two of these, see A. C. Spearing, "Prison, Writing, Absence: Representing the Subject in the English Poems of Charles d'Orléans," *Modern Language Quarterly* 53 (1992): 83–99.

to expand and emphasize it, beginning with "mafay" (l. 499). The heart weeps alliteratively and perhaps almost iconographically (l. 502), the lover is a "martir," and it would be a "synne" (l. 503).[54] The French analogue accepts a lesser martyrdom with a briefer metaphor,[55] but the English demands the full agony of lover's sainthood. Wordplay "thick and thynne" (l. 505) relies not on the conceptual cognition of "je ne sais compter" (l. 15) but on a sensory comparison, which helps draw attention to the English poem's more forcefully expressed pains, and thus to the altered and extended conceit. The sensory emphasis as well as the omission of an allegorical figure (l. 494) helps the lines find a balance between image (locally figurative) and allegory (a universal representational network)—the weighted balance of lyric scale—extended metaphor or conceit. This altered balance, too, is representative of the larger sequence: to be etymological about it, metaphor-*metafora-translatio* becomes more in the English poems than ornament or stylistic device. A translation discontinuity here entails a methodological shift that ramifies beyond the local instance. Where the French sequence takes allegory as its main figurative method and chief among its organizing principles, the English sequence moves definitively away from abstraction and allegory toward concreteness, metaphor, and real lyric conceit.[56]

Greater concreteness in the English text also results in a poem that links thematically to the larger sequence better than does the French, when the poet replaces line 4's Cupid allegory with a vividly imaged expression of the lover's experience (l. 494). The delightful clause "Which shertith me more nerre than doth my skyn," by the way, earns Charles d'Orléans a *Middle English Dictionary* entry for using *shert* as a verb, a liberty he likewise takes with "blyn" at line 495. There may also be some thematically relevant wordplay beneath the phrase: *shirting* is amusement, delight, plea-

---

54. There may also be a bilingual phonetic pun on *ceint-saint* (ll. 14 and 504 respectively), a sort of interlingual play Charles does indulge in elsewhere. Thanks to R. A. Shoaf for pointing this out (Virginia Medieval Symposium, November 20, 1993).

55. Sometimes a French text will use but drop a metaphor-loaded word, as in line 7, where the English analogue extends and plays with the French-dropped word. Here neither poem pursues the possibilities for metaphor in "guerison," although medical metaphors and puns abound elsewhere in Charles's work.

56. For a related view, see Ann Tukey Harrison, *Charles d'Orléans and the Allegorical Mode* (Chapel Hill: University of North Carolina Department of Romance Languages, 1975); for an opposing view, see Fox, *Lyric Poetry,* 52–90, especially 84–90. Hans Meier reaches slightly different conclusions but likewise notes greater concreteness, colloquialism, emotionality, and intimacy in the English Roundel 35, a translation of Chanson XXXV ("Middle English Styles," 372–75).

sure; *shirten,* the verb, means to jest or to play, and as a reflexive verb, to amuse oneself (a meaning perhaps hinted at but not supported here by the position of "me"); *shirtinge* is abridgement or making short. Phonetic resemblances, of course, are everywhere in language and should not by themselves make us feel certain either of authorially intended wordplay nor of Charles's readers' reception of any such wordplay. But the poet insists throughout the sequence on the inseparability of pleasures and pains, and on the precarious life that he says will be ended, shortened, without his beloved. The poet is also an incorrigible punster in both English and French, and often between the two. Mary-Jo Arn has discussed the prominence of phonetic motives in Ballade 6; it is clear that Charles, an accomplished musician, was interested in bringing phonetic resources to bear on his poetry.[57] So the multiple soundings in *shert* may very well reach down to the work's deeper themes. However, whether or not we want to dive for paronomasia, it is sure that these lines (and many other translations like them) change the tone of, and add concreteness and thematic interest to, the English sequence.

Here they also help the poem's internal logic. At lines 508–11, again, the English version is concrete and colloquial where the French is abstract and lofty. Line 20's "reçu de coeur et de joyeux penser" is smooth, but the English detail at 510–11 offers even more than its clearer picture of how the lover feels since he received her letter. Lines 508–11 respond better to line 494 above than does the French analogue. The speaker has received a letter from his love, "the which y more sett by than all my kyn / That never from my brest shall it twyn." The English speaker seems considerably more attached to this inscribed absent-presence, first of all, but more significantly, the letter has by stanza 3 taken the place next to his heart of the pains that had "sherted" him in stanza 1. Writing has replaced the woe

---

57. Recall especially that Eustache Deschamps, maître d'hôtel at Charles's parents' court, insisted that poetry was "musique naturele" and "paroules metrifiez" in his 1396 *L'Art de Dictier. Oeuvres complètes d'Eustache Deschamps,* ed. Gaston Raynaud, 11 vols. (Paris: Librairie de Firmin Didot et cie., 1891), 7:266–92. See also Arn's article, "Charles d'Orléans: Translator?" in *The Medieval Translator 4,* ed. Roger Ellis and Ruth Evans (Exeter: Exeter University Press, 1994). For coupling theory's phonetic-equivalence possibilities, see John Hopkins, "Coupling Theory and the Translation of Poetry: A Haiku Example," *Pacific Quarterly Moana* 5, no. 1 (1980): 47–51. On Charles's musical talents and background, see Champion, *Vie,* 14, 25–27; on music in his poetry, see Alice Planche, *Charles d'Orléans ou la recherche d'un langage* (Paris: Editions Honoré Champion, 1975), 87–95; also Nigel Wilkins, "Music and Poetry at Court: England and France in the Late Middle Ages," in *English Court Culture in the Later Middle Ages,* ed. V. J. Scattergood and J. W. Sherborne (London: Duckworth, 1983), 183–204.

in a very personal, physical way, and the concrete English images figure the replacement much more vividly.

This significant discontinuity is the more instructive because it also enacts the poem's, and the sequence's, metastruggle—perhaps Charles's own struggle—both to establish and simultaneously to question the consolation of writing.[58] Recall the speaking doubt of speech, the self-questioning first stanza. Stanza 3's images return to those of stanza 1 in offering the "swete comfort" of writing, but in the all-new envoi, it is a partial comfort, though again, a punning[59] and very concretely troped one:

> My ledy hert is lightid vnto tyn
> Bi comfort loo but absence doth me war
> That more y lust to wayle then laughe or gren
> Syn hit is so that y am from yow fare.

Ultimately absence wins. It must, as in Petrarch and Sidney, to keep the sequence moving and the writer writing. But the poem has been written; does it ease the ache of absence? Charles reaffirms writing's consoling possibilities when he begins Ballade 21, "Honoure and prayse as mot to him abound / That first did fynd the ways of writing." Ballade 21, like several others,[60] goes on to discuss the practical and emotional consolations of writing, arguably the real subject of the larger sequence.

But a poem like Ballade 21, whose direction and tone are clear and united, is not so complex nor so representative of the larger sequence as is a tonally dissonant poem like Ballade 10. Ballade 10's playful sadness makes an odd combination, and a common one in Charles's oeuvre. The speaker really doesn't seem to know whether to "wayle then laughe or gren" (l. 517). Frequently related to the play of tone represented in Ballade 10 are what I call Charles's hiding games, which treat the enforced duplicities of the heart. In many poems he puts on a happy face, while his heart is breaking, or entirely gone, disembodied, or clothed in black.[61] The speaker adopts a paradoxical sincerity to explain his heart's necessary

---

58. Charles read Boethius (Champion, *Librairie*, 20–22; *Vie*, 232–33). For a look at Charles's revised conception of Fortune, see Arn, "English Poems."

59. The envoi's first line endows "lightid" with added double meaning by way of etymological wordplay: tin, *plumbum album*, is lighter than lead, *plumbum*, in both weight and color.

60. See, e.g., ll. 143–47, 1893–1902, 2680–82, and others discussed in Spearing, "Prison, Writing, Absence."

61. Ballades 6, 11, 18, 24, 25, 32–35, 37–39, 43, for example.

hypocrisies and tends to layer emotions upon each other and to conceal or deny the inmost among them. The translation choice of "forpeyne" helps accomplish this sort of layering and concealment *in parvo*. While the word means "for-pin," or constrain (and may be related to the word *forpyned* that Chaucer uses to mean tormented, suffering, wasted), "forpeyne" also carries a strong phonetic echo of the line's earlier phrase, "for drede." The ear expects "for drede . . . and for peyne," for dread and for pain. By means of that phonetically invited parallelism, "forpeyne" includes more richly layered (and more biographically resonant) senses of constraint imposed on pains.

This one pair of parallel texts indicates in microcosm (although imperfectly) Charles's understanding and use of the resources made available by the nonequivalences or discontinuities inherent in translation. Charles shows himself capable elsewhere (Ballade XII/Ballade 12, e.g.) of a nearly word-for-word fidelity. And in terms of surface content, the sequences appear generally replicative. But Ballade X/10, more typical of the works' particular translation practices, illustrates that lyric *translatio* involves much more than fidelity or equivalence in translation. Charles, even in writing parallel content, reveals a greater interest in, and capacity for, poetic experiment than in poetic fidelity,[62] and actually writes over seventy English poems independent of French analogues. Ballade 60, for example, a poem without a French analogue, is built on chiasmus. Chiasmus, a technique Charles uses only locally in his French verse, is one of several rhetorical tricks that appear more prominently in English than in French poems; in Ballade 60 it is a fully deployed structural device.[63] Although the French-only oeuvre is larger than the English-only, Charles's poetic experiments go further in English than they do in French.

Even this very brief, preliminary look indicates that translation in the lyrics of Charles d'Orléans approaches an experimental carrying-across that may resemble an early brand of Renaissance lyric *imitatio* more than what we generally think of as medieval *translatio*. This is so in the small-scale uses of discontinuity, in the large-scale value claimed for the lyric "I," in the authority claimed by a translator, and ultimately, in the translations' emergence as "originals." The distinction in French between *original* and *originel*—that which originates versus that which is of, like, or from an origin—is useful here in thinking of the originalities available to poet-trans-

---

62. See Fox, *Lyric Poetry*, 111ff. on the experimental nature of the verse.
63. Discussed in chapter 6 below; see also Ballades 99 and 105.

lators. Discontinuities in the parallel texts invite us to reconsider what "originality" means to us post-Romantics, what it might have meant in the fifteenth century, and what it would come to mean for Renaissance translators. The English sequence also dramatizes the latitude lyric translations could have despite apparently equivalent content and suggests some alternative relationships between translation and *translatio*. *Translatio* in the poems of Charles d'Orléans paradoxically consists in this: he translates himself into freedom from translation, *parole*s himself from the prison of one *langue* to the illusory liberties of lyric experiment in another.

3

Self-Translation, Writerly Self-Consciousness, and the Early Modern Lyric "I"

In translations like those of Charles d'Orléans that assert such a status and value for lyric and that are both *originelles* and *originales,* one might hope for open statements about a translator's and a poet's roles, for heightened text-consciousness or metatextuality, or for extra attention to the value, status, and nature of the lyric speaker, the "I." On the first count, visibility, Harley 682 disappoints: it never declares itself a translation and never tells how or why it has been translated.[1] On the latter two counts, text-consciousness and self-consciousness, however, Harley 682 more than satisfies. Charles's English poems are highly text-conscious, and they devote themselves attentively to the writing self or subject—the lyric "I" or persona. These essential features of Charles's lyric "I," self-consciousness and text-consciousness, and Charles's particular expressions of them (his "poetics of subjectivity," if you will) are the main topics of this chapter, which explores the particular means by which the poet displays the translating/translated lyric "I."[2] Like any "I," poetic or biographical, Charles's "I" often reveals and defines itself in dialogue with other entities.[3] Since Charles's "I" is especially interesting when it is in conversation with parts of itself, I only sketch here a few of the more traditional dialogue poems and reserve a larger section for the "lyric self and its heart." And since

---

1. Visibility becomes an important issue in sixteenth- and seventeenth-century translation. See my "Thomas Watson and Renaissance Lyric Translation," *Translation and Literature* 5, no. 1 (1996): 3–25. Lawrence Venuti, whose definitions are less applicable to early modern texts, discusses visibility in translation more generally in "The Translator's Invisibility," *Criticism* 28 (1986): 179–212.

2. Chapter 6 treats Charles's poetic subjectivity or "inwardness," to use Maus's term, as part of a problem for our discipline's habits of periodization.

3. For theorizing of this basically Hegelian notion, see Charles Taylor, *Sources of the Self* (Cambridge: Harvard University Press, 1989), among others writing on this topic recently.

39

Charles's English poems, much more than his French poems, foreground the "I" and tensions between the speaking self and the writing self, the chapter also treats the English envois (many of which are English-only) and several other poems that express a noticeable textual self-consciousness. The chapter's last section examines the last poem in the English sequence as a valedictory expression of the poetic subjectivity at work here.

Recent discussions of early modern poetic subjectivity can reflect light on Charles's "I." Joel Fineman, H. Marshall Leicester Jr., and A. C. Spearing, although they are writing on poets as various as Shakespeare, Chaucer, and Dante, have pointed out theoretical considerations that apply particularly well to Charles's "I." Fineman, for instance, emphasizes epideictic mode as the primary factor shaping the lyric "I"; epideixis is of course prominent in both the English and French versions Charles creates. Fineman argues, however, that in the sonnets Shakespeare "invents a genuinely new poetic subjectivity" by disrupting epideictic mode in certain ways and by attending to eye, ear, and text; I would mention that Charles in 1440 equally disrupts the epideictic mode and attends in some of the same ways Shakespeare does to textuality and the writing "eye"/"I."[4] Leicester, taking another line of argument, writes perceptively of the "impersonated self" in Chaucer and insists on the distinctions between poet and speaker, and between voice and presence: "what I mean by impersonated artistry—and indeed what I mean by voice—does not necessarily involve an external self." The writing "I" for Leicester is a function of language:

> Although any text can be read in a way that elicits its voice, some texts actively engage the phenomenon of voice, exploit it, make it the center of their discourse—in fact, make it their content. This sort of text is *about* its speaker. . . . The [individual *Canterbury Tales*] are examples of impersonated artistry because they concentrate not on the way preexisting persons create language but on the way language creates people. They detail how a fictional teller's text im-personates him or her by cre-

---

4. Fineman, *Shakespeare's Perjur'd Eye: The Invention of Poetic Subjectivity in the Sonnets* (Berkeley and Los Angeles: University of California Press, 1986), 1–2. For similar arguments based on essentially the same material, see Fineman's *The Subjectivity Effect in Western Literary Tradition: Essays toward the Release of Shakespeare's Will* (Cambridge: MIT Press, 1991).

ating a personality, that is, a textual subject that acts like, rather than is, a person.⁵

This theoretical position applies clearly to Charles, the translating "I" whose impersonated selves are quite different in the two languages, and whose texts do make the speaker and his voice the center of the discourse. Leicester's terms, like A. C. Spearing's analysis, can help us avoid the biographical fallacy of equating actual lives with poetic personas while nevertheless connecting text and writer. Spearing uses the term "poetic subject" further to distinguish the "unitary psychic substance" of real past selves from the constructed speaking position of poets who begin in this period of literature to represent themselves as subjects (agents in) and subjects (topics of) their fictions.⁶ Spearing's term, like Leicester's, does not encourage one to blur art and life in the way, say, Greenblatt's term "self-fashioning" does. Lyric self and lyric "I," the phrases used most often here, acknowledge the potential blurring of speaker and poet (which I think is a real though often unfortunate phenomenon of poetic reception to be considered) while stressing the constructed and textual nature of the "I" speaking in a poem.

Early modern poetic subjects necessarily fashion themselves by engaging with prior texts. An author's particular poetics of *imitatio,* or more simply, the way the author chooses to treat other poetry and which poetry he chooses to treat, seem to determine what sort of a lyric self the author fashions. This general truth about early modern lyric is easiest to see in translations, where the intersection of imitation and self-fashioning is more obvious: the translator-poet necessarily takes another's words to construct the lyric persona, "I," self, or subject. Is a translated lyric "I," then—its rhetoric of self based so intimately on the words of another, its subjectivity born from alterity—inherently paradoxical? Must poetic subjectivity arise from a self's negotiations within political and courtly parameters, as some historicist critics might hold? Or, as a Romantic laureate

---

5. Leicester, *The Disenchanted Self,* 10–11.
6. "The Poetic Subject from Chaucer to Spenser," in *Subjects on the World's Stage: Essays on British Literature of the Middle Ages and the Renaissance,* ed. David G. Allen and Robert A. White (Newark: University of Delaware Press and London: Associated University Presses, 1995), 13–37. See also Spearing's "Poetic Identity," in *A Companion to the "Gawain"-Poet* (Woodbridge, Suffolk: D. S. Brewer, 1997), 35–51. For a similarly helpful set of distinctions applied to the Renaissance sonnet sequence, see the introduction to Thomas P. Roche's *Petrarch and the English Sonnet Sequence* (New York: AMS Press, 1989).

advises, can poetic self-fashioning take place ex nihilo, from emotion and memory alone ("spontaneous emotion recollected in tranquility")? Between Greenblatt and Wordsworth there are other ways to understand the translating/translated lyric "I" and its apparent paradoxes: lyric selves, at least in the fifteenth and sixteenth centuries, are fashioned not only in the context of early modern courts but also, and perhaps chiefly, with respect to *imitatio*. Seth Lerer's *Chaucer and His Readers: Imagining the Author in Late Medieval England,* for instance, demonstrates that some fifteenth-century poetic subjects construe themselves in complex imitative and emulative relations to Chaucer, or rather, in complex relations to an *idea* of a Chaucerian poetics. Early modern poetic theorists themselves tell us imitation is central to poetics (though they do not always agree on the specific role it is to play).[7] Before Romantic notions of originality and spontaneity, before "emotions recollected" and sublime landscape reveries became prime sources of poetry, a poet's use of prior words in making a poetic self was central to his or her poetics. (This is one reason Harold Bloom's *Anxiety of Influence,* for instance, is less applicable to fifteenth- and sixteenth-century texts: its assumptions about a writer's relations to prior materials differ radically from the assumptions of fifteenth- and sixteenth-century writers themselves, and the result is a kind of "presentism" that fails to help us understand the older subjectivity.) And while post-Romantic critics may assume too much a life-art connection or an emotional intentionality—assuming, that is, that poetry is all about expressing the feelings of a unique biographical Self—historicist criticism, in focusing on sociopolitical contexts (as this book does in other chapters), may fail sufficiently to emphasize the power of literary-historical, linguistic, and aesthetic imperatives over fifteenth- and sixteenth-century literature. But the apparent paradox of a translated subjectivity is no paradox at all once we assume that language and literary tradition and readership, not the idiosyncratic psychological desires of a particular personality, are the factors that most shape this lyric "I." We might thus approach Charles's poetry, and by extension other translations and other early modern poetry, not as memoir, not psychologically (approaches I find generally anachronistic, too speculative, and even antiliterary), but with attention to the multiply constructed nature of the textual "poetic subject." Charles's

---

7. Puttenham, for example, comes to the issue on the first page of his 1589 *Arte of English Poesie:* "without any repugnancie at all, a Poet may in some sort be said a follower or imitator . . . and Poesie an art not only of making, but also of imitation" (I.i; in G. G. Smith, ed., *Elizabethan Critical Essays,* 2 vols. [London, 1904; rpt. 1937], 2:3). See also James I, William Webbe, Sir John Harington, and other Renaissance critics.

translations make it clear that the same biological person, the poet, may construct very different poetic subjects or lyric "I"s in the different languages. This chapter, then, concentrates on the construction of the writing subject, the literary persona itself, as an act neither of autobiography nor entirely of political self-fashioning, but as an act primarily of literary representation.

Critics have long named some of the ways of constructing new poetry upon old: intertextuality, influence, allusion, answer poems, parody, formal imitation; Thomas Greene, for example, more precisely identifies creative imitation, heuristic imitation, and dialogic imitation as specific ways European Renaissance poets found to recycle poetry.[8] Translation is generally thought to be one kind of writing separable from these other kinds of generative intertext because the new texts keep closer to the old, or because translation is thought to be by definition more replicative than those other kinds of intertext. Charles's oeuvre proves such thoughts limited and shows that translation, even when conditions seem perfect for keeping new and old texts close, is not necessarily replicative, nor so easily separable from other ways of making poetry.[9]

The prior poetry Charles uses is his own—his poetic self-fashioning in one language thus being an imitation, in some sense, of the "other side" of his poetic subjectivity.[10] In this rare early case of self-translation, should-

---

8. See also Jean-Claude Carron, "Imitation and Intertextuality in the Renaissance," *New Literary History* 19, no. 3 (1988): 565–79; G. W. Pigman III, "Versions of Imitation in the Renaissance," *Renaissance Quarterly* 33 (1980): 1–32. Critical accounts of poetic imitation abound: a convenient list is in the *New Princeton Encyclopedia of Poetry and Poetics,* ed. Alex Preminger and T. V. F. Brogan (Princeton, N.J.: Princeton University Press, 1993), s.v. "imitation."

9. For a new taxonomy of the many ways of using prior poems involved in early modern lyric translation, see my brief proposals in "Thomas Watson." For Watson, translation is the favorite brand of imitation and is inseparable from poesis and the creation of the lyric persona. For Edmund Spenser, on the other hand, translation in *The Ruines of Rome* is the first and main step in re-creating and then altering Du Bellay's lyric personae. For Thomas Combe, for example, translation is intimately linked with the Horatian idea "ut pictura, poesis." I shall consider the lyric selves and translation habits of these and other fifteenth- and sixteenth-century English translators from French in a book-length study now in its earliest stages.

10. It is wrong to assume that all the French poems were written before all the English poems. In fact there are dozens of English poems without French analogues, and vice versa. There is very little hard evidence about the order of composition (see Arn's introduction, *Fortunes Stabilnes,* 37–38), but we should keep in mind that the process is most likely not unidirectionally French-English, that some English poems may well have preceded French versions, and that composition and revision may have been simultaneous or bidirectional as well as unidirectional. The safest (and most interesting) way to approach this problem is to assume nothing and to treat the poems as bilingual parallel texts. There is one poem, Ballade 59, "Alone am y and wille to be alone," imitated from Christine de Pisan's "Seulete je suis."

n't the French and English lyric subjectivities be largely the same since, in terms of content at least, they are largely parallel texts from the same author? As it turns out, no: the English lyric self differs noticeably from the French lyric self, and the differences reveal themselves fairly early in the sequence, as we saw in the preceding discussion of Ballade X/10. *Translatio sui,* then, is not a simple matter of replicating an identity or a subjectivity. Furthermore, since the differences between these two self-translated lyric subjects cannot be attributed to the Otherness of prior culture or authorship—that is, the same poet is creating the two distinct lyric selves at about the same time—our critical assessment of the translation must take psychobiography not as meaningful variable but as constant. Nor will historical distance account for the differences. The poet's personal psychology, cultural background, reading habits, and so on, may be surrounding contexts for the poetry but will not finally explain the originating differences between these two lyric selves.[11] Thus, this study of early modern self-translation insists on the constructed nature of the poetic subject and on aspects of its construction other than the personally biographical or psychological: its linguistic, sociopolitical, generic, and literary-historical aspects.

We should notice the rather singular writerly position Charles occupied and indeed was depicted as occupying. Many illustrations of early writers show them either presenting a book to a patron or to a circle of readers/listeners, as Salter and Pearsall note. Other illustrations show a writer as teacher, reporter or recorder of events, preacher, or dreamer. Frequently the author is solitary, reading or writing at a desk.[12] However, the illustration in BL ms. Royal F 16.ii shows a process and a context for Charles's writing (see fig. 1). Charles is shown at work at a large table. He is guarded and observed, but one feels the figures watching him write in his Tower room are not really a literary audience for his work. (One guard even

---

11. Chapter 2, of course, argues for the divergent sociopolitical contexts as factors at least partially shaping the different versions in the three languages.

12. Elizabeth Salter and Derek Pearsall, "The Role of the Frontispiece," in *Medieval Iconography and Narrative,* ed. Flemming Andersen, Esther Nyholm, Marianne Powell, and Flemming Stubkjaer (Odense: Odense University Press, 1980), 100–123. This illustration of Charles is a bit unusual in that its narrative runs from right to left. Salter and Pearsall's eight categories of illustrations depicting authors are found on pp. 115–16. The depiction of the writer's position that is closest to Charles's is "author as protagonist in a famous scene from his life," exemplified by manuscripts of Cicero and Petrarch.

appears to lean, bored perhaps, on his weapon. The sequence *is* long.) The poet is isolated in powerful English walls. If we read the illumination as one of Sixten Ringbom's "continuous narratives," in which different phases of a story or a series of events are depicted in a single frame, we see Charles also looking longingly out a window (one thinks of his poem "En regardant vers le pays de Fraunce"), and eventually (partially through his writing?) gaining release.[13] The poem accompanying this picture, "Des Nouvelles d'Albion," is in fact an epistolary ballade to the duc de Bourgogne, who was important in Charles's ransom negotiations; one wonders if the red-mantled figure who arrives and then accompanies Charles out through the portcullis could be Burgundy or one of his emissaries, perhaps Hugues de Lannoy. The phrase "gaining release from his writing" may have been literally as well as figuratively true. His writing is not depicted as typically instructional or presentational, but rather as ambiguously instrumental. Nor is his writerly position typically figured: it is not social or static but solitary and in motion, in process. We last see his back turned, riding out with entourage in the illumination, as indeed the speaker of the sequence says farewell to the English reader in the evocative final poem.

Furthermore, this lyric self, as Spearing has remarked, distinguishes itself from that of other late-medieval poets by adopting an unusually direct stance. Charles d'Orléans (and, Spearing notes, James I, another foreign prisoner-poet) write "not as servants of Cupid's servants but as lovers themselves."[14] In addition to this direct, experiential stance for its lyric self, Charles's English approaches to the problems of lyric address and textuality resemble the approaches of poets like Wyatt, Spenser, Sidney, and Donne.[15] Shifting apostrophe, dialogue, and other devices in the English poems tap the rhetorical and performative dimensions of lyric more than do the relatively static and abstract French poems. The self-conscious, text-conscious lyric persona reveals itself throughout the sequence, but most clearly in the material selected for discussion here: the English heart poems and the English envois.

---

13. "Some Pictorial Conventions for the Recounting of Thought and Experiences in Late Medieval Art," in Andersen et al., *Medieval Iconography and Narrative,* 38–69.

14. "Prison, Writing, Absence," 84.

15. For discussion of other proleptic features of Charles's English sequence, and on the complex position of the translations in the fifteenth-century literary landscape, see chapter 6 on periodization and translation.

En-voi(x) de Poète

In the English sequence, translation figures largely in one particular tactic of varying lyric address and self-positioning: the addition of an envoi. About a fourth of the French ballades lack envois,[16] but all of the English ballades have them,[17] a fact that is one of the most resonantly signifying nonequivalences between these parallel sequences. Some critics have interpreted the fact of added English envois as evidence for authorship[18] or for generic intention. Martin Camargo, for example, interprets the added envois as evidence of the English ballades' fundamentally epistolary character. A conventional envoi (the half-stanza send-off to the letter-poem's recipient, usually a sovereign or otherwise powerful reader) can—but does not have to—signal epistle or epistolary mode. Camargo's epistolary claims work quite well for the narrative frames and for the six poems he identifies as letters.[19] As for most of the ballades, however, it is important not to confuse mode and genre, or worse, form and genre: envoi does not epistle make, as Charles's sequence (like Villon's ballades) illustrates beautifully. Although several French epistles with traditional envois show Charles in perfect control of the standard forms, he does not translate these;[20] he translates away from, not within, the conventions of epistolary envoi. The poems that use the envoi to epistolary purpose are not translated. In fact it is clear that Charles has other purposes in mind for the lyric envois, especially in English. This poet often uses envois not only to flatter, to beg, to say farewell, or to reprise a theme, but also to roll the credits—to heighten interest in the English "I" and in the poem itself. Rather than operating as functional-epistolary conventions, the English envois serve lyric subjectivity in its attention to textuality and thus construct an especially writerly poetic subject.

---

16. Ballades I, IV, V, VI, X, XI, XV, XIX, XX, XXVI, XXXIII, XXXV, XXXVI, XXXIX, XLIV, LI, LVIII, LXXI, LXXIV.

17. Except Ballades 75–81, which form a dramatized narrative element in the frame story.

18. Red herrings; see Steele and Day, eds., *English Poems*, xxiv and xxvi–xxvii.

19. *Middle English Verse Love Epistle* (Tübingen: Niemeyer, 1991), 98–105, 110–20. Camargo discusses the ballades on pp. 106–9. Yvonne LeBlanc notes that even in the French sequence, "the relative anonymity" of some pieces or the lack of naming makes them less epistolary; *Va Letter Va: The French Verse Epistle, 1400–1500* (Birmingham, Ala.: Summa Press, 1995), 13–14.

20. Ballade LXXXIII to Bourbon contains a conventional mention of the messenger, "I am giving this letter to Guillaume Cadier." Ballade LXXVII mentions the route and *destinataire:* "Va ma ballade prestement à St.Omer . . . au duc . . ." Ballades XCI, XCII, XCIX, C, CI (in a way), and CIV use the most conventional formula, "Prince . . ." or a variant of it.

Any envoi provides closure for and separates itself from the lyric body that has come before. In certain of Charles d'Orléans's envois, the moment of closure and separation is also one in which a change of address challenges the conventional relationships in which the lyric speaker participates, adapting them to a poem's particular purposes. The stanzas often ostensibly address a given person or thing, while the envoi redirects the reader's attention to a powerful "real" reader. Sometimes the powerful reader addressed in the envois is Cupid, sometimes Venus, sometimes God, and, predictably, is very often the lady.[21] Charles borrows the conventional formulas of address to a sovereign power for these envois, appropriately reconfiguring them. Ballade 3, for example, a reflective poem on the dangers of love at first sight, turns at the envoi, but instead of asking for the good will of a prince, begins "O God of Loue, ne takith displesyng . . ." Ballade 22, a fairly generalized lament for the plight of the lonely lyric "I," turns at the envoi to ask the lady for help; in case there is any doubt as to which sovereign power the envoi intends, Charles inserts an almost conversational reminder, "I mene but yow, my maystres and lady." Ballade 24, another such lament, turns at the envoi to address either Cupid or Atropos, love or death, so desperate is the lyric speaker: "O make me, Loue, so happe to purchase / Thou-wotistwhat, to sett me in gladnes / Or Antropos [sic], thou brest my lyvis lase." The changes of address at the envois remind us that what has come before has been a subordinated performance, or more precisely, that the poem has been expressly performed for the benefit of whatever sovereign reader is named in the envoi. The lyric persona turns often, in other words, to face changing addressees; this restless apostrophe adds needed variety to a fixed-form sequence and tends to keep attention centered on the one constant position, that of the lyric "I." In Charles's translations, these restless turns in apostrophe are often clever and even witty; of most concern here is that they draw particular attention to the speaking self and the writing self and alter the relative positions of speaker, writer, and reader(s).

Charles expands the list of conventionally addressed sovereign readers—Cupid, Venus, God, the prince, the lady—to include other powers. In Ballade 9, for example, the stanzas praise his lady's beauty, goodness, and so forth, in conventional terms and in the third person.

Fresshe bewte riche of yowthe and lustynes
The smylymg lookis casten so louely

---

21. Ballades 6, 27, 29, 34, 46, 47, for example.

> The plesaunt speche governyd bi wittynes
> Body welle shape of port so womanly
> The high estat demenyd so swetely
> The welle ensewridnes of word and chere
> Without disdeyne shewing to lowe and hye
> For whiche alle folk hir prayse and so do y
> Alle thewis goode this hath my lady dere

Already the sequence's ostensibly primary addressee, the lady, is set outside the text, hearing herself spoken of: "For whiche alle folk hir prayse and so do y / Alle thewis goode this hath my lady dere." Then, after three such refrains, at the envoi the lyric speaker turns to address a sovereign social power, the company, thus adding to stanzas that otherwise could have been read as a private, even meditational hymn of praise, a certain social and performative dimension.

> Ye ladies and alle faire bothe lowe and hie
> That hereth this my preysyng my lady
> I yow biseche to take no displesere
> Y say hit not to yowre disprayse forthy
> But me to shewe hir servaunt to y dy

As an epideictic performance, the poem has to please others in addition to the primary reader, the lady. We secondary readers may or may not imagine ourselves part of the company, but as Fineman and Aristotle before him have theorized,[22] it is a general effect of epideixis that all eyes are on the "I."

The stanzas of Ballade 64, similarly, look like high praise of the primary reader, the lady; the envoi's shifted address changes the poem into an appeal to a higher power, Cupid.[23] Such redirected appeals place both speaker and primary reader under the deity's jurisdiction, in this case creating a court-of-love dynamic in the poems and deposing the lady as sovereign addressee in favor of Cupid. Several of the more serious poems (e.g., Ballades 28, 55, 57) address God, not the god of love, in the envoi, making the preceding stanzas seem retrospectively prayerlike. Charles is

---

22. "As early as Aristotle . . . it is recognized that the rhetorical magnification praise accords its object also rebounds [sic] back upon itself, drawing attention to itself and to its own rhetorical procedure" (*Shakespeare's Perjur'd Eye,* 5).

23. Ballades 12, 24, 41, 49, 64, and 69 also appeal to Cupid as God of Love.

most willing to hybridize conventions, but the lyric "I" seems to be the one unshakable position.

Ballade 21, another example of epideixis complicated, begins as a general meditation on the value of writing: "Honure and prays as mot to him habound / That first did fynde the wayes of writyng . . ." The poem turns at the envoi to personalize the preceding generalities, to redirect the lady's understanding of them, and to refocus attention on the experience of the "I" or persona.

> But what Madame crist ewre me so that ye
> May vndirstonde as bi my mouth telyng
> What y haue dewrid in tymys quantite
> Only for loue and feithfulle trewe servyng

What the poetic subject has endured is the point, and it is made through a consideration of writing.

More generally speaking, it is not just thematic hierarchies of power but hierarchies of readers that are shaken and altered in the English envois. There comes a moment when all readers of an address-shifting poem realize that they too have been deposed as sovereign addressees. To write such an envoi draws an inner circle of primary readers and thus an outer circle of later readers who, voyeurlike, witness first the poem and then the address to the envoi's new sovereign power, and thus finally are more acutely aware of the variability of lyric address possible within one brief ballade. We respond twice: first to the lyric, then to the redirected lyric, with a greater awareness of the speaker's directing voice. Shifting address at the envoi takes what is already a moment of heightened attention—of closure, of separation—and retrospectively reinforces the lyric "I."

"To Hear with Eyes": Orality and Textuality in the Envois

In addition to altering the relative positions of speaker, poet, reader, and text—a sort of a general action of lyric address even in the ballades mainly addressed to the lady—address changes in the envois supplement certain other important effects particular to the English sequence. The flexible envoi draws a distinct line between the fictive orality of the stanzas and the writtenness of the entire poem. Most envois, like that of Ballade 21 noted above, remind readers at the end that the purportedly spoken thing we have just imagined—or the thing that Charles's audience might have just heard spoken—is in fact a document (though not necessarily a letter), a written thing. The voices we hear in Charles's sometimes acute efforts at imitating speech and conversation are not present voices at all, we are suddenly and frequently reminded, but marks of absence on a page.

A major theme of Charles's sequence is to question the value of speech and writing in easing the problem of absence, as Spearing has demonstrated.[24] This will become a theme voiced by sixteenth-century lyric selves, as well: "As good to write as for to lie and groan," Sidney's Astrophel will lament (*Astrophel and Stella* 40); "Come, let me write. 'And to what end?' . . . Thus write I while I doubt to write," wrangles Astrophel with his wit (34; see also 35 and 44). Likewise, one conventional sort of envoi in Charles's sequence, the self-addressed-stamped "go little bille" topos, draws particular attention to the poem, to the speech-writing issue, and to the lyric speaker.

Ballade 91, of which there is no French version, addresses the lady in three stanzas but only obliquely refers to her in the envoi (which is addressed to the poem itself):

Go litille bille, crist sende the bettir grace
Then wolde some whiche haue of me no price.

The poet replaces himself with his poem in hopes that the text will be better prized than he has been. The envoi's passively accusatory "some" may refer to (and vaguely reproach) the lady addressed in the stanzas or some other nonappreciator. Charles's English lyric self displaces his personal anxieties onto expressed concerns for his mediating text, another move found in Renaissance sonnets. We might think here of Spenser's lady, who, when she receives a poem from the speaker, gives no "bettir grace" to his "innocent paper" and in fact sets it afire, according to *Amoretti* 48; that poem brings to life poets' worst fears for the reception of their texts. Spenser's metatextual worries often resemble those in Charles's envois. But Sidney, for example, will develop more hopefully a similar impulse to send his poem as proxy: "I am not I, pity the tale of me" ends a sonnet (*Astrophel and Stella* 45) whose poet well understands that love-fictions may substitute for lovers and in fact may be better received. Charles, like the sonneteers he anticipates, knows that richly performative lyrics, "litille billes," may receive "bettir grace" than a poor poet. Self- and text-referen-

---

24. "Prison, Writing, and Absence."

tiality have good persuasive potential, in other words, in 1440 as in 1595. The envoi to Ballade 120 provides another example:

> Goo poor bille good fortune be thi gide
> Forblot with teeris of myn eyen twayne
> For me to ioy my sorowis and to hide
> How it may be owt sleying me in payne.

First, this envoi stands out visually and aurally from its preceding stanzas, which are almost fully anaphoric.[25] The poem is "forblot with teeris," a conventional detail that calls attention to its "poemness" and to its mediating role as a textual bearer of both literary marks and human tears—both fiction-made and real sorrows. This metatext, like the cross James I draws in his work (a reminder of the writerly "I" that, as Spearing says, "is carefully designed to create the effect of living evidence"),[26] reminds us that both lyric speaker and lyric poet make their marks on the envoi.

These uses of the "go little bille" topos—closure, displacement, metatext—seem conventional enough at first glance. But Charles's translations reveal uses of the device particular to the English oeuvre. In Ballades 31 and 19, the "go little bille" topoi call attention not just to the fact of writing but to the ballade's mediating function, its intended reconnection not with future ages but with a very present lady. Ballade 19 does not contain an envoi in French; the English version's new self-address,

> Go rewdisshe bel complayne my ponysshement
> But welaway y wolde if that y shulde
> For forgetyng to knowe my iugement
> As bi the mouthe y levyr had yow told,

---

25. Nearly every line begins "So" and is built on contrastive and additive structures, as the first stanza illustrates:

> So fresshe bewte so moch goodlynes
> So skace of grace so large of crewelte
> So moche vertue and so moche gentilnes
> So long this straunge so bareyne of pite
> So lusty yowthe so replete of bounte
> So litel mercy and so gret disdayne
> So fervent love then as hit cawsith me
> How may it be owt sleying me in payne.

26. "Poetic Subject," 19.

ends a ballade that tells us it is a response to the lady's request for a poem from him.

> Most goodly yong o plesaunt debonayre
> Yowre sendyng which me gaf comaundement
> A balad forto make ye speke so fayre
> That with glad hert y shew here myn entent
>
> (ll. 762–65)

The envoi, like the ballade itself, continually questions the orality and writtenness of the lovers' communications. She has spoken fair (l. 764) either by messenger or by letter; "sendyng" (l. 763) allows both possibilities. The refrain, though, is a witty, sexy double-entendre, "As bi the mouth y levyr had yow told." Her fair speech has been persuasive enough to lead him to write the ballade now before us, but in writing it he reminds her and his other readers that writing is not as pleasurable as speaking (or other oral communiqué):

> And eek to write me noyeth double fold
> For gyf y myght bi othir wey or went
> As bi the mouth y levyr had yow told.
>
> (ll. 775–77)

Words answer words—the written poem originates in and demands oral responsiveness. The "rewdisshe bel" is not only to go and find out how the lady judges his text— and him—but to suggest more satisfying, more present means of oral response, love-talk and kisses. In Ballade 51, likewise, the speaker wishes for a presence and intimacy, but sends a mediating, absence-marked text:

> Go belle and say that here my trowthe y plight
> Had y my wisshe y were without candille light
> Even with the verry sorse of womanhed.
>
> (ll. 1806–8)

In other poems, too, even when the speaker addresses the lady, he is highly conscious of his mediating text. In Ballade 38, though he cannot see her, he takes consolation in the fact that his writing will. Memory and text work together: "wherefore remembrance biseche thee / This poore balade to take it my lade" (Ballade 43). In Ballade 39 the speaker grouchily commands his poem to tell the lady he is true: "go thou dark fordullid rude meture." The same word, "meture" or measure, appears in Ballade 93, now used to pun, or if not quite to pun, to touch at several meanings:

> Now gode swetehert biholde this scripture
> And find a bettir moyan for us twayne
> Bi whiche that y may chaungen this meture
> As now in wele and now in woo again.

He hopes to change his "meture," his tune, if his "meture," mediating text, may lead to a better, more present connection between them, a closer "meture" or measure of distance between them. He hopes she can find a better "moyen" (mean, average, meeting of the "meture" of distance between them) and "moyen" (means, way) for them to be together. Presence and absence, speech and writing, kisses and poems, poet and speaker: Charles's shift of address to the *bille* forces the contrasts and places the English text as witness, explicator, mediator, translator between these spheres.

Like the envois of Ballades 19, 51, 91, and 120, the envoi of Ballade 31 reminds us of the poem's textuality while making an imaginative gesture to a moment of speaking and presence. But where Ballade 19's refrain ("As bi the mouth y levyr had yow told") is witty and counterfactually wishful, Ballade 31's is wistful, recalling an actual, precise, and powerful moment of speaking, "when she me gafe this name as lo my loue." In both the French and English versions of 31, the wistful recollections achieve a certain distance by placing the lady as a third-person "she" instead of a directly addressed "you." Both French and English refrains are reminders of the lady's prior act of speaking, naming him her love, but the short French line, "Quant me donna le nom d'amy," does not enjoy the same songlike, alliterative pause caused by the English cheville, "as lo." The French line relies on consonantal chiasmus—/m/d/n/, /n/d/m/—for its ripple and midpoint caesura. The English is assonant and hesitates later in the line. Furthermore, the French envoi addresses not the letter itself but Loyauté, another conventional abstraction from the French allegorical tradition.

> Loyauté, veuilliez asseurer
> Ma Dame que sien suy, ainsy

Qu'elle me voulu commander
Quant me donna le [nom] d'amy.

This difference between English and French is entirely typical of the larger sequence: the French follows its tradition, from which the English departs; where the French is abstract, the English is concrete. And in this case the new concreteness is specifically text-conscious. The text enjoys a more prominent English appearance. The envoi,

Go belle for trouthe ensewre thou my maystres
That y am hiris in alle maner prove
As she comaundid me to my gladnes
When she me gafe this name
As lo my loue,

addresses the letter that is to address the lady; the only references to the sequence's primary reader are secondary, distant, in the past and future tenses, mediated by the ever-present text. Both versions are to be messengers of proof of the real meaning and validity of the lover's feelings, but where the French sends an allegorical and abstract "Loyauté," the English envoi makes the poem itself the tangible messenger who acts for the sake of "trouthe." Again, words answer and validate words, but the English poem creates a greater tension between the poignantly distant moment of speaking and the concrete presence of the absence-mediating text. This may remind us of the similar but more nearly synaesthetic tension between speech and writing Shakespeare builds when he gives texts a mediating role:

O let my books be then the eloquence
And dumb presagers of my speaking breast
Who plead for love, and look for recompense,
More than that tongue that more hath more expressed
O, learn to read what silent love hath writ:
To hear with eyes belongs to love's fine wit.

(Sonnet 23)

Likewise, Charles d'Orléans's English envois frequently create on the silent page a speaking voice that asks (as the French poems do not so much

Early Modern Lyric "I"   55

do) to be "heard with eyes." The technique evokes the present speaking voice, at very least a reader's subvocalization.

The "go little bille" topos also reminds the reader of the materiality, of the writtenness (and of the writer) of what has come before. Charles's envois direct readers' attention to the text, which is a frequent opening gambit in Renaissance sonnets, drawing immediate attention to textuality.[27] His text-self-consciousness, however, tends to come at a recapitulative rather than at a predictive or instructive moment—in the envois rather than in the opening lines, which tend to cling to the fictions of speech. The English openers tend to be dramatic: "Now what tyding, my lady and maistres? How farith our loue, y pray yow hertily?" (Ballade 14), "I yelde my silf to yow! Saue me my lijf!" (Ballade 102), and Ballade 10, "Madame a trouthe not wot y what to say," discussed at some length above. Opening as frequently as he does—about every third or fourth poem, overall[28]—with convincing fictions of presence and speech adds considerable tension, given the poems' return in the envois to their final reminders of textuality.

Again, certain Renaissance sonnets end also in reminders of textuality, but these often have a longer-term goal in mind than Charles appears to have. Shakespeare, for example, closes a few poems by reminding readers of the writtenness and lasting value of the lyric preceding (Sonnet 18.14, "So long lives this, and this gives life to thee," and Sonnet 19.14, "My love shall in my verse ever live young").[29] However, Charles d'Orléans's translated envois and their text-consciousness do not claim such immortalizing power for his verse: this is curious and worth a moment's pause. The claim of durability or immortality tends to accompany printed translations and to imply that translators are aware or hope that by this means poems can live for yet another culture or readership.[30] Does the claim appear more

---

27. Drayton opens *Sonnets to Idea* with "Read here sweet maid the story of my woe," alerting the reader up front to his lyric text- and self-consciousness; Daniel's second *Delia* sonnet begins, "Go wailing verse, the infants of my love"; Spenser opens *Amoretti* with a slow, nearly cinematic zoom on the lady reading his poetry: "Happy ye leaves whenas with lily hands . . . Happy ye lines . . . Happy ye rhymes," focusing increasingly close attention on the poem.

28. More in the later and less in the earlier poems.

29. This is less so in Shakespeare's Sonnet 17; see also Spenser's "One day I wrote my name upon the strand" and any number of other Renaissance lyrics that promise fame to lady and poet in the *exegi monumentum* tradition. See, among many others who have written on the topic since, O. B. Hardison's foundational *The Enduring Monument* (Chapel Hill: University of North Carolina Press, 1962; rpt. Westport, Conn.: Greenwood, 1973).

30. Translators' prefaces frequently state or imply this: Caxton's and Copeland's prefaces would be typical examples.

vibrantly in the print than in the script age? Perhaps, but continuity, if not permanent fame, is the basis of the whole long preprint tradition of the topoi of *translatio studii.* The claim of poetry's lasting value is not exclusively print-based—it is classical too—but it might be a claim that appears when cultures value literary continuity over the fortunes of war or when writers see literature as one stable response to the human problems of mortality and mutability. Despite Charles's preprint position, he was well placed as a translator—not to mention as a reader of Boethius, as the owner of a large classical library, as a student of history, and as a victim of war and fickle fortune—to make claims not only for the continuity of *translatio* but for the eternizing powers of poetry. Yet his English poetry contains no such open claims. (In fact Charles playfully asserts that "Fortunes stabilnes" is its instability, an early English expression, perhaps, of a variant of the proverbially Gallic idea: *plus ça change, plus c'est la même chose.*) On the other hand, the very creation of such extensive translations—into English, the language of the conquerors, and later into Latin, the eternal language—could be said to claim the poetry's lasting value. Recall that Astesano's Latin preface to Grenoble ms. 873, the elaborate vellum production containing French-Latin lyrics in parallel columns, does make such claims; that manuscript itself is a bid for world renown and permanence. Although the English poems voice no longing for the more durable, worldwide, Latinate audience Astesano seeks, and although they never announce a medieval *translatio* nor a classical or Renaissance *exegi monumentum,* they do (like Shakespeare's couplets and Sidney's, Daniel's, and Spenser's references to their poems) turn back toward the lyric and remind us of the poem itself and the poet's presence behind the lyric speaker. At the English envois, and particularly at a "go bille" envoi, Charles moves decidedly away from his French sequence and away from conventional uses of topos and envoi: he steps out from behind his speaker to remind us not of poetic fame, but of his created text, of his (and our) separateness from the textual world, and of the layered absences present beneath his insistent lyric "I."

The Lyric Self in Conversation with Others: Dialogue Poems

In addition to Charles's English envois, two other chief patterns of shifting address in the translations, the dialogues and the heart poems, sharpen the presence of the English lyric self. Charles's dialogues and heart poems stress the dissociation between writing and speech, and between fictive and nonfictive worlds. Dialogues (to be treated only briefly here) and heart poems tend to go about their dissociative business in opposite ways but with oddly similar results for the poetic subject. Briefly, in several English dialogues, the poet first creates a fiction of dramatic speech, usually including a conflict or tension between two speaking entities; then alters the "horizons of expectation"[31] for the various medieval dialogue types he uses; and with the help of translation, emphasizes to an unusual degree the speaker's prominence and the greater extremity of his struggle. (Some of the ballade-dialogues, Ballade 65 and the Ballade 75-76-77 set, for example, do not involve the sort of lyric ventriloquism I want to stress here but instead dramatize the framing narrative.) Dialogues bring an external voice into conversation with the lyric speaker; they dramatize an overheard moment, placing readers as voyeurs and eavesdroppers on a fictional encounter. This is the technique of a Sidney, a Donne, a Browning. Of course medieval debate poetry provides Charles with a healthy antecedent tradition; and as is the case with the envois, Charles playfully alters the traditions.

Although Ballade 70, for example, appears to be a fairly conventional prosopopoeic dialogue with Venus, it is surprising for its imbalance of address. The poem doesn't afford the reader the expected pleasures of dialogue: a questioner and an informer, a description of an imaginary figure descended to earth, some wisdom pleasingly spun out.[32] Charles is fully capable of writing dream-vision narrative: the memorable narrative prosopopoeias in the "Vision in Complaint" (2540–2715) and "Love's Renewal" (4736–5351) more than satisfy readers' generic expectations for this sort of dialogue. The lyric dialogues, however, alter these horizons of expectation. Charles creates in Ballade 70 a rather lopsided lyric dialogue that focuses almost entirely on the speaker's plight.

In the forest of noyous hevynes
As y went wandryng in the moneth of may
I mette of loue the myghti gret goddes

---

31. Hans Jauss's term in "Literary History as a Challenge to Literary Theory," in *Toward an Aesthetic of Reception,* trans. Timothy Bahti (Minneapolis: University of Minnesota Press, 1982).

32. See Spearing's *Medieval Dream-Poetry* (Cambridge: Cambridge University Press, 1976); or J. Stephen Russell, *The English Dream Vision* (Columbus: Ohio State University Press, 1988). The long tradition includes Boethius, Alain de Lille, Dante, Chaucer, Lydgate, and in his narrative verse, Charles.

> Which axid me whithir y was away
> I hir answerid as fortune doth convey
> An oon exylid from ioy be me loth
> That passyng welle alle folke me clepyn may
> The man forlost that wot not where he goth
>
> Half in a smyle ayen of hir humblesse
> She seide my frend if so y wist ma fay
> Wherfore that thou art brought in such distresse
> To shape thyn ese y wolde my silf assay
> For here-tofore y sett thyn hert in way
> Of gret plesere y not whoo made thee wroth
> Hit grevith me thee see in suche aray
> The man forlost that wot not where he goth
>
> Allas y seide most souereyne good princesse
> Ye knowe my case what nedith to yow say . . .

But say he does. In fact, the speaker and Venus expend nearly all their energies describing the speaker, with special emphasis on him at the crucial and contextually varied refrain, "The man forlost that wot not where he goth." In both English and French (Ballade LXIII) the lover is blind; the French, atypically, has a nice detail lost to the English.

> Aveugle suy, ne sçay ou aler doye;
> De mon baston, affin que ne fourvoye,
> Je vois tastant mon chemin ça et la
>
> (ll. 25–27)

In describing the speaker tapping his cane about, the French version offers an imaged, miniature-narrative elaboration of "Aveugle." The English speaker "Al fer myswent with [his] staf grapsyng wey," a less delicate riff on blindness than the quick rhythms and midline near-rhymes of "mon bâton, afin" and "tâtant . . . mon chemin." But in English the speaker's state is (typically) much more desperate. The English version adds line 2421, "That no thyng axe but me a grave to cloth," making us wonder if Venus might offer her gown to shroud the moribund (but revivable) lover.

Ballade 72, likewise, departs from its generic origins with a similar imbalance of address in favor of the lyric speaker, who again is more desperate in the English version. Ballade 72 is a "parlement of fowlis" dream-vision with dialogue, but one that speaks the speaker's prominence. First, the birds' speech is reported rather than direct: "An oost of fowlis semblid in a croft / Myn neye biside and pletid ther latyne" (ll. 2464–65). Instead of birds singing the joys of new love, or a speaker who hears and reports their songs, the speaker's woe takes a one-sided control of what is more usually a sing-and-speak exchange. The speaker weeps and says,

> Ye birdis ought
> To thanke nature . . .
> That han yowre makis . . .
> Where y sorow the deth of my maystres . . .
>
> (ll. 2474–77)

This poem compresses and distorts the Valentine's Day parlement-of-birds convention in order to write more vividly the speaker's woe. Translation supports this intensified focus on the lyric speaker: the French speaker's "Lors en moillant de larmes mon coessin, / Je regrettay ma dure destinée" (ll. 16–17) becomes a much more vivid "Tho gan y reyne with teeris of myn eyne / Mi pilowe and to wayle and cursen oft" (ll. 2471–72). In French, the speaker moistens a pillow in a present-participle phrase; he emphatically soaks it in English with a main verb's rain of tears. Enjambment in English reinforces the effect of uncontrollable emotion, words spilling across the line-break like tears onto the pillow.[33] The poet has also used doubling *(reduplicatio)* in English not just for metrical filler but with the result of specifying the rather general "regrettay." In "wayle and cursen oft," the speaker both wails and uses language to utter, probably loudly, his regrets. Then too, the abstract French refrain, "Sur le dur lit d'Ennuieuse Pensee," typically lacks both an intensifier ("so") and the possessive adjective ("my") that personalizes the English refrain, "Vpon my bed so hard of noyous thought." These translation differences remind us that the poet is willing to use the conventions of dialogue to create an English lyric speaker more woeful and more prominent than his French counterpart.

In a fascinating dialogue manqué, Ballade 79, in which Cupid has relinquished his power over the speaker and reluctantly returned his heart to him, the speaker prepares to take his leave, but bursts into tears and is unable to speak.

---

33. Note also the interesting use of the verb *to rain* as transitive.

> Love gan perceyve my carfulle countenaunce
> And seide my frend y pray thee hertily
> If there ben ought as vndir my puysshaunce
> To doon thee ese ne spare it not hardily
> But then y was so woofulle and heuy
> That y to him oon word koude spake agayne
> Oon word no nor half oon verily
> That of wepyng y koude me not restrayne.
>
> (ll. 2918–25)

The lyric subject speaks a lover's speechlessness, which is not only a playfully paradoxical mimesis, but which reminds us that a speaking subject is distinct from a speechless lover. Especially at lines 2923–24, where it looks as if we may hear the "one word" he would say to Cupid, the speaker simulates the hesitancy of great emotion—"that I to him one word could speak again— / One word—no—nor half one, truly." Line 2924, with only nine syllables, needs a long pause before "no" to sound right. The poet's controlled, word-filled poem recreates an uncontrolled speaker, bereft of words. And as usual, the English version describes the speaker's woe more vividly. The French poem opens, "Quant j'euz mon cueur et ma quittance, / Ma voulenté fu assouvie...," which becomes in English, "When that I had myn hert and my quytaunce / Mi gost therwith was woxen light trewly...." The French terms are abstract and cognitive; will submits to reason, after all. A calmed will is a more reasoned, controllable result than an emotive, inexplicably spiritual yet also bodily "gost woxen light."[34] At 2932–33 the French is spare: "J'avoye la veue esbluye / Et ne cessoye de pleurer," while the English is more descriptive, "Myn eyen so fordreynt in teeris ly / That of wepyng y koude me not restrayne." That last line, the refrain, implies that the English speaker tries and fails to stop an emotion from displaying itself. The French imperfect verbs merely record that he did not cease weeping, but the English line records the speaker's inner struggle—not at all the smooth farewell expected when departing in courtly dialogue. In several dialogue poems, then, Charles first creates a fiction of dramatic speech, alters the horizons of expectation for the dialogue types, and, with the help of translation, emphasizes to an unusual degree the poetic subject's struggle.

---

34. "Gost" meant a number of things, involving body and soul: spirit, good or evil (*MED* 1a, 1d); the Holy Ghost (1b); the evil spirit possessing a lunatic (1c); a villain, scoundrel, or incarnate devil (1e); the soul of the deceased, the spirit of Christ descending into hell (2a); a damned soul or an emaciated or tortured person (2b); a dead body or corpse (2c); and so forth.

The Lyric Self in Conversation with Itself: Heart Poems

Charles's heart poems also create fictive speech and conflict, alter the outlines of generic convention, and stress the extreme sufferings of the lyric speaker. However, instead of bringing outer voices—Venus or Cupid—into a textual dialogue, the heart poems move in the opposite direction, externalizing inner voices. The many English heart poems (Ballades 33, 34, 37, 43, 47, 48, 49, 51, 55, 56, 71, 74, 82, 96, 99, 102, 103, 106, 107, 112, not to mention a number of roundels) externalize and reify an internal part of the lyric self (the heart) and elevate its autonomy beyond that of the very speaker from whom it has been dissociated.[35]

Not that a lover speaking of or to the heart as if it were a separate entity is unusual in early literature: the heart was prominent in the medieval courtly and allegorical vocabulary of the *Roman de la Rose* tradition. It is a convention often taken to extremes—abstracted and allegorized in medieval literature, reified and polished in the Renaissance (though this is too glib a period distinction to be accurate, as R. F. Green shows).[36] Although many medieval poems split and allegorize the parts of the self (eye and heart dialogues, body and soul debates, and so on),[37] what is special here is that the split self receives such sustained attention as an expressive agent of subjectivity used as a rhetorical (rather than an allegorical)

---

35. There are no French poems parallel to Ballades 74, 96, 99, 102, 103, 107, and 112.

36. Allegorizing the heart is chiefly but not exclusively a medieval move: Spenser, too, would allegorically but iconographically externalize the heart in representing Amoret's tortured state (*Faerie Queene* III.xi–xii). Likewise, the heart as love-token had been literalized in gifts and poems before the Renaissance; R. F. Green, in fact, attributes the origin of the expression "wearing one's heart on the sleeve" to Charles, specifically to his lines 3983–88 ("Hearts, Minds, and Some English Poems of Charles d'Orléans," *English Studies in Canada* 9, no. 2 [1983]: 147). Sidney, however, ties the convention in poetic love knots with "My true love has my heart and I have his." On the love-games of emblematized and literalized hearts and tokens, see Stevens, *Music and Poetry,* 209–11; and especially Green, who illustrates many early literalizations of the lovers' hearts. On medieval heart-and-eye poems, see Thomas L. Reed, *Middle English Debate Poetry and the Aesthetics of Irresolution* (Columbia: University of Missouri Press, 1990), 140, 158, 165, and 142–43. On medieval hearts, see James Holly Hanford, "The Debate of Heart and Eye," *Modern Language Notes* 26 (1911): 161–67, which focuses on the *Disputatio inter cor et oculum* (reminding us that the tradition was pan-European). The point here is that Charles's French poems generally stay within medieval allegorical conventions for the courtly heart, while the English poems alter them.

37. For examples see Michel-André Bossy, ed. and trans., *Medieval Debate Poetry: Vernacular Works* (New York: Garland, 1987). For fascinating generic and modal analysis of these forms' links with dramatic and satiric modes of representation, see Jean-Claude Aubailly, *Le Monologue, le dialogue, et la sottie* (Paris: Champion, 1976). For discussion of late-medieval English debates as finally unresolved dialectics, see Reed, *Middle English Debate Poetry.*

feature of the sequence. Especially in the English version, the separated, reified heart may coexist with medieval allegorical traditions[38] and may anticipate Renaissance conventions of a literalized "heart" as token,[39] but the overall effect is something different from both of these.

Ballade 37, for example, includes some traditional personifications (Hope, Daunger) but ends in a vivid description that relies for its final effect in English on the sudden coming-to-life of what could have been taken as a static trope. The poem begins

> Bvt late agoo went y my hert to se
> As of his fare to haue sum knowlechyng
> I fond him sett with Hope in compane
> That to him seide these wordis comfortyng,
>
> (ll. 1309–12)

a sort of conventional promise that Hope and the Heart will be rendered as speaking entities in a miniature allegory, as is the case in the French version (Ballade XXXVII). But by the end of the English poem, hope is an emotion that has vascular effects on a particular physical heart. "My sabill hert with hope now blusshith reed," adds the English-only envoi, in a conceit that figures blood rushing back to the speaker's woe-blackened heart. Elsewhere the speaker admonishes the heart ("To longe for shame . . . / Myn hert y see thee slepe . . . / Awake this day awake! O verry fy!" Ballade 48), and in Ballade 33 negotiates with a hard-bargaining heart:

> [*Lover.*] Myn hert, if so that y good tidyng here
> To tell hit thee what woll þou geve me say
> [*Heart.*] They mowe be suche þat y wolde bye hem dere
> They mowe ben suche y sett not by an ay.
> [*L.*] As for reward, thou shalt but litill pay
> [*H.*] Then say hem me y pray the hertily . . .[40]

---

38. In Ballades 43 and 71 the heart tends to appear in a more traditional or semiallegorical way.
39. The refrain of Ballade 96 expresses its theme, the heart-exchange, "As take myn hert and lete yowris bide with me." In Ballade 107 he sends out his heart to "logge in the fresshe manar / Of the body of hir so ingoodly / Alway to dwelle though y be here or whare" (ll. 6086–88).
40. The heart often "prays heartily," a rather lame pun.

Next the speaker thanks and rewards the heart with ephemeral gifts of the lady's favor ("How how myn hert opyn þe gate of thought / And resceyue into thee a swete present / The which my bestbilouyd hath to thee brought," ll. 1222–24). But the speaker worries about the heart's obsession, describing its separate speaking voice in the night:

When y am hushte hit mervayle to me is
To here myn hert how that he talkith soft
And so with loue does faster his woundis
With newe and newe hath hurtis to him brought.

(ll. 1734–37)

He chides it, threatening to beat it if it doesn't calm down ("Be nyse, myn hert, as purse is of an ay . . . Ye must be betyne, by Seynt Gyle, / To titill fitill fitill thus alday," ll. 4193–96). He rebels against it ("Thou shalt no more rewle me my hert / I wol no more be to thee thral," ll. 4179–80). He blames it ("But what myn hert is most to blame parde / To do me loue þe which þat wilith me / Mi deth," ll. 6039–41); argues with it ("I seide him Loo myn hert me grevith sore/ That thou shuldist me mystruste in such manere," ll. 1970–71); and even inscribes it ("I writen haue within myn hert trewly / . . . This refrayt," ll. 1685–87). Ballade 43 takes the speaker-heart split further, splitting the heart or at least writing it as stubbornly alienated from itself:

Moche haue y spent of speche to his profite
But that to harke y trowe he is not he
Mi wordis alle nar worth to hym a myte
His will is sett in such perplexite . . .

(ll. 1522–25)

The will of the heart is set in such perplexity, and the speaker's relationship with the heart is more variable and agonic, to a greater degree in the English versions, which take fragmented subjectivity well beyond the French poems' allegorical conventions. In Ballades VI/6, for example, the speaking subject is divided, and eyes and heart also have a say. The eyes are spies in both French and English refrains ("Ainsi m'ont raporté mes yeulx," and "As me reportid hath myn eyen twayne"). In both languages, the heart claims ownership of the spying eyes at the end of every stanza.

Only the English speaker tries to regain control of the fragments of himself, however, because in the new envoi he gets his first chance to speak the refrain, effectively reclaiming his heart and eyes as a reunified speaking subject. Ballade 6 is the speaker's first report in the sequence of his woefully fragmented subjectivity, which is to say his first rhetorical manipulation of it. Listen as the fragmented speaker turns at the English-only envoi to blame the lady for the schism within.

> Not long a-goo y hyed me apase
> In secret wise myn hert forto counsayle
> Himsilf forto withdrawe as for a space
> Out of lovys paynfulle thought and trauayle
> To which he seide me nay sett there a nayle
> Speke me no more therof y hertly pray
> For god wot to loue y shalle me payne
> For y haue chose the fayrist that be may
> As me reportid hath myn eyen twayne
>
> Now pardone me y seide as in this case
> Forwhi y say hit for oure bothe avayle
> With alle the power that god welle in me hase
> That in goos trouthe thou dost me to mervayle
> Seest not thou welle that fortune doth vs fayle
> Hast thou good lust to lyue in sorow? Nay
> I-wis he seide y trust more to attayne
> I had a praty look yit yestirday
> As me reportid hath myn eyen twayne
>
> Allas seide y thou fonnyst as haue y grace
> That for oon look thi lijf lust to biwayle
> For countenaunce or lookis of hir face
> Knowist thou hir thought/ ye cast me lo a kayle
> O pese/ quod he now good y lust not rayle
> Nor bileue no word thou dost me say
> For trewely serue y shalle and nevyr fayne
> Of good which is the best/ leue this aray
> As me reportid hath myn eyen twayne
>
> O y-wis madame in this maner aray
> Myn hert and y thus haue ye brost atwayne

> But what swete hert as gide vs such a way
> As me reportid hath myn eyen twayne

Compare the French poem:

> N'a pas long temps qu'alay parler
> A mon cueur, tout secrettement,
> Et lui conseillay de s'oster
> Hors de l'amoureux pensement
> Mais [il] me dist bien fellement:
> "Ne m'en parlez plus, je vous prie;
> J'ameray tousjours, se m'aist Dieux,
> Car j'ay la plus belle choisie.
> Ainsi m'ont raporté mes yeulx."
>
> Lors dis: "Veuillez me pardonner,
> Car je vous jure mon serement
> Que conseil vous cuide donner,
> A mon pouvoir, tresloyaument;
> Voulez vous sans allegement
> En douleur finer vostre vie?
> —Nennil dya, dit il, j'auray mieulx:
> Ma Dame ma fait chiere lie;
> Ainsi m'ont raporté mes yeulx.
>
> —Cuidez vous savoir, sans doubter,
> Par un regart tant seulement,"
> Se dis je, "du tout son penser,
> Ou par un doulx acointement?
> —Taisiez [sic] vous, dist il; vraiement,
> Je ne croiray chose qu'on die,
> Mais la serviray en tous lieux,
> Car de tous biens est enrichie:
> Ainsi m'ont raporté mes yeulx."

Since the French version has no envoi, its projected, split subjectivities conduct their dialogue alone, without the final gloss and appeal to the lady in the English envoi ("Myn hert and y thus haue ye brost atwayne"). Furthermore, while the ballade is lightly witty in both languages, the English poem sets a significantly different tone for the speaker-heart relationship—a tone that will persist over the course of the otherwise quite varied English relationship. The French conversation's refined tone is such that it could occur between two lords, between courtly sparring partners who keep nevertheless a sense of courtesy and formality: "fellement" (l. 5), "ne m'en parlez plus, je voue prie" (l. 6), and the slightly testy but still formal "taisez-vous" (l. 23). The corresponding lines in English, however, use informal "thou" plus a good deal more slang. "Nay sett there a nayle," an idiom for "that's enough" from the rugged worlds of barrel-making and barrel-filling, is in no way part of the semantic codes of courtly love on which the French poems draw. "Nennil" (l. 16) in French may be a bit colloquial, but "m'a fait chiere lie" (l. 17) is a stock phrase from the standard medieval vocabulary of love, considerably more formal and more general than the specific "I had a praty look yit yestirday." Consider also "thou fonnyst"—you're kidding—and the vehement rhythms and line-breaks in the English conversation, "ye cast me lo a kayle."[41] The French speaker and heart engage politely in conventionalized sparring; the English speaker and heart engage in a rough verbal tussle, gloves off.

The concrete, colloquial English tone may be a result of Charles's effort to bring into the poems not a French poetics but the actual speaking voices he heard around him during his captivity. At least some of these differences are linguistic, resulting from the intersecting requirements of syntax, vocabulary, and meter. Perhaps, as Luc Santé said of himself, Charles almost becomes a different person, and thus a different poet, in the different languages. Did Charles captive in England feel freer of his position as head of the house of Valois, or freer of the old codified vocabularies of the French tradition? Or was he simply less well steeped in the less-well-established English codes? Charles's translations cross not only boundaries of language but of historical development in the two literary traditions, so they are well positioned for innovation and experiment. We may speculate about the reasons for it, but clearly, where the French split between speaker and heart is more conventionally formal, the English split is more intimate, colloquial, rough, and specific.

Most notably, the heart receives a distinct voice beyond the conventional, especially in the English versions. Ballade 33, for example, a pure dialogue poem, continues Ballade 6's tonal variance: it is as usual more colloquial and conversational than its French sibling.

---

41. In which I read "ye" not as a formal "you" but as a slangy "yeah, gimme a break."

[*H.*] But saist thou trouthe or dost thou mokke and play
[*L.*] I say the soth bi god what nede y lye

(ll. 1204–5)

These interjectory rhythms are quite unlike the smooth, formal French lines

Le cueur.—Dites vous vray, sans me moquer?
L'amant.—Ouil, je vous le certifie,

(ll. 14–15)

in which syntax (*sans* plus *infinitive;* the verb *certifier* that shelters before it its indirect and direct objects) permits a compression that the English—with its auxiliary-conjugated present ("dost thou mokke"), its metrically encouraged doubling ("mokke and play"), its two-word verb ("say soth" for "certifie")—does not have.

Even beyond the exigencies of the English language's necessarily looser, more distributive syntax, the poet does seem to work to create a conversational tone. Elsewhere in Ballade 33 there are Charles's usual English moves toward slang and specificity: compare "the swete" (l. 1216) with "dame" (l. 26); "se pener" (l. 20) is less detailed than "put his silf in such a payne and fray" (l. 1210); and "toute ma vie" (l. 24) is less specific than "unto that hour that y dy" (l. 1214). Most remarkable is the different pacing of the two sets of lines cited above (Ballade 33, ll. 1204–5 and Ballade XXXIII, ll. 14–15). The "but" signals a rapid conversational outburst that the next twenty single-syllable words maintain. The interjections "bi god" and "what neede y lye" respond indignantly to the heart's implicit challenge to the speaker's veracity. The louder English tones convey in a rush fluctuations of feeling between speaker and heart that are not at all present in the rather level, more evenly measured French voices. (These English tones will come to characterize the speaking voices in Wyatt, Sidney, even Donne.)

Although in both languages Ballades XXXIII/33 end in an improved relationship between heart and speaker—in the English-only envoi, the heart calls the speaker "frend"—in the overall sequence, the longer English path toward reconciliation is rockier. The English lyric self's experience seems more agonic, troubled, because the English heart's plight is more extreme and more concretely elaborated. Charles frequently uses the extra syllables available in English pentameter to add adjectival description: "my dullid hert" (l. 1545), "my woundy hert" (l. 1302), "my bolnyd hert" (l. 5968). Even beyond what could be discounted as metrical filler, certain poems also add to the English version memorable descriptions of the heart (e.g., Ballade 37's English-only "My sabill hert now blusshith reed"). While both English and French versions clothe the heart in black, the English heart is a living entity on its deathbed:

> For where as in an exstreme forto dy
> Myn hert lay he deed hit to him hent . . .
> Wrappid in blak
>
> (ll. 2904–7)

and

> As in extreme thus fond y hem [eyes and heart] to deyen . . .
> (l. 5708)

Charles's linguistic innovation in these two poems, the phrase "in extreme," shows how much more vividly the English heart suffers; to express this conception of the heart stretches even the language.[42] And in poems in which the heart is even more than a vividly rendered, separate entity—that is, where it attains a full voice and presence, a mind of its own (e.g., Ballades 43 and 112)—its out-of-body experiences further complicate an already complicated and prominent lyric "I."

This heart is not the inner mover of the speaker, nor of the poet. This is not the confessional heart that is of a piece with the lyric self it is to reveal. This heart is not the *sanctum sanctorum* of the lyric "I," the "heart's forest" to which Wyatt's speaker will flee in "The Long Love." Rather it is the heart of Charles's speaker that flees to the refuge of imagination in Ballade 43:

---

42. Steele and Day's note to this latter line refers to a similar use at line 6354 and points out that "in extreme" is not used in the French poems. "In fact there is no such phrase in French, and in English it is found first in 1546, under the more natural form 'in extremes.' The present use seems to be due to Charles." For investigation of some of Charles's other additions to the English language, see Autumn Simmons, "A Contribution to the Middle English Dictionary: Citations from the English Poems of Charles, Duc D'Orléans," *Journal of English Linguistics* 2 (1968): 43–56.

> Mi poore hert bicomen is hermyte
> In hermitage of thoughtfulle fantase.
>
> (ll. 1511–12)

And unlike Wyatt's obedient speaker ("What may I do when my master [love] feareth / But in the field with him to live and die?"), Charles's speaker abandons his heart and reproaches its loving in a refrain: "And yet y say him how it is foly." Given such a split subjectivity and a nagging speaker who so repeatedly rejects his heart's motions as futile, one might expect the poem to end on a note of renunciation, perhaps along the lines of rather different Wyatt lyrics that end, "Me lusteth no more rotten boughs to climb."[43] Instead, Charles puts the split subjectivity he has created to markedly rhetorical use: he reworks the conventional, persuasive appeal to a lady's pity by projecting this more vulnerable part of himself, the heart, and then threatening to abandon it if she will not respond as he wishes.

> This as for me y cast to leue him [the heart] quyt
> . . . .
> Without so be ye lust to him write
> Some praty word of yowre benygne bounte
> Forto alesse his gret aduersite . . .
>
> (ll. 1533–37)

Since the broken relationship between the speaker and his heart continues to be antagonistic to varying degrees, the later reconciliation is never stable. Even in the later poems, the speaker expresses despair in futile dealings with an intractable heart, displacing his trouble onto a reified fragment of himself. Although in "news" poems the speaker and the heart move from separate knowledge of the lady's feelings to shared knowledge, the heart still has a will of its own (Ballade 112). The distinct voice the heart is given, the speaker's attempts to control or console the heart, the threats of self-torture, the heart's rejections of and mistrust of the speaker (Ballades 55 and 56), the heart's speechless-fainting scene (Ballade 51), the heart's desire to die, the speaker's split life (Ballade 74)—these would con-

---

43. Sonnet 31 ("Farewell Love and all thy laws forever") and Song 203 ("Tangled I was in love's snare"), in Sir Thomas Wyatt, *The Complete Poems,* ed. R. A. Rebholz (London: Penguin, 1978; rpt. 1988), 87 and 262–63.

stitute a real psychomachia were they not so wittily conceived and deftly executed. As is evident from the tone and wordplay of the poems cited so far, we are dealing with a clever, winking poet here, one who writes an unstable subjectivity, an interestingly variable lyric self, a self whose construction is inflected by the media of its expression. The variance between the French and English lyric selves makes it clear enough that we are not reading a poet's operatic psychological autobiography.[44]

Nor are we reading a typical late-medieval English heart, which is often a generalized phenomenon, the destination of love arrows once they are past the eye. Sir John Clanvowe's *Boke of Cupid,* for example, leaves the heart as a physical entity within the lover's body and, literarily speaking, leaves it as part of the dream-vision context:

> I am so shaken with the feueres white,
> Of al this May yet slept I but a lyte;
> And also hit is vnlyke to me
> That eny herte shulde slepy be,
> In whom that loue his firy dart wol smyte.
>
> (ll. 41–45)[45]

Relations with the heart in Charles's sequence, however, are agonic, troubled, involving domination and submission, persuasion and resistance, pain and pity, vexed communications, enforced secrecy, and fragmentation. But ultimately the poet creates the autonomous heart to serve the speaker's appeals for sympathy for his struggles with a supposedly more vulnerable, if recalcitrant, part of him. The English poems' fragmented lyric subjectivity is performative, rhetorical, intended to appeal to a reader's enjoyment and a lady's desire: It's your fault my heart and I are broken up (Ballade 6). My heart controls me, but it's wasted on you (Ballade 7). I feel death so near my heart I can't write anymore (Ballade 26). My heart "hool is gyue vnto hir gouernaunce" (Ballade 42). I'll just abandon my poor old heart, he says, unless you write us a love letter (Ballade 43). What saves all this from sounding petulant and manipulative is the clever playfulness of the verses and their motions among and outside of lyric conventions for the heart. The later poems reconventionalize the

---

44. For the autobiographical view, however, see Classen, *Autobiographische Lyrik;* and Cholakian, *Deflection/Reflection,* who take Charles at his speaker's word.

45. *The Works of Sir John Clanvowe,* ed. V. J. Scattergood (Cambridge: D. S. Brewer, and Totowa, N.J.: Rowman and Littlefield, 1975). Scattergood discusses Clanvowe's many connections with France and French literature.

heart-self relationship—heart given as ransom, heart as messenger, heart trying to be tenant in lady—as if the poet has finished exploring or exploiting the speaker's interior split, or has tired of the game. The message is not so much "pity me" as a proto-Sidneyan "I am not I: enjoy the seriously clever tales of me." This of course is one of the chief self-fashioning messages of Renaissance sonnet sequences; the intense textual self-consciousness in this sequence is one of the challenges to its typical periodization in the English canon.

Overall the English poems present a variable, self-conscious relationship between the lyric speaker and the externalized agent he calls his heart. The heart poems explore the interior "I" in a larger rhetorical, persuasive effort. Translation has resulted in a lyric speaker whose departures from convention look well back on the allegorical hearts of the *Roman de la Rose* tradition and look well ahead to the agonic, rhetorically savvy personas we describe as characteristic of Renaissance lyric.

Textual Self-Consciousness and Closure in the Lyric Sequence: "Albe Y Fer Forget Me Nevyr"

The sense of an ending and the closural procedures that create it are important features of lyric in any age, but poetic procedures and readerly expectations for closure vary historically.[46] Charles d'Orléans's French poems use many accepted fifteenth-century procedures of formal closure: strong refrains, rondeau forms with their small circling closures, lines more frequently end-stopped in French than in English. In English, however, Charles seems more willing to experiment with closure, writing poems more clearly strophic than stichic, varying the functions of refrains, and creating his remarkable envois. Authors often put a point on closural matters in the last poem of a sequence, regardless of any fatigue they may feel. In this last poem of the English sequence, Charles does translate his conventional French "sense of an ending"[47] into something quite fascinatingly different. Ballade 121 has no corresponding French poem in BN f. fr. 25458,[48] so it is not a translation in that sense, but it does include a fair measure of what is at issue in establishing Charles d'Orléans's English lyric "I."

---

46. As Barbara Herrnstein Smith explores in *Poetic Closure* (Chicago: University of Chicago Press, 1968).

47. Frank Kermode's title in *The Sense of an Ending* (New York: Oxford University Press, 1967). Kermode discusses the position of the writer as a literal and metaphorical "solitary confinement," and writers' responses as creating a fictional space outside (155–80). Charles's literal confinement seems to have produced instead an exteriorizing of interior spaces.

48. The French poems just fade out with a set of rondeaux.

As for farewel/farewel/farewel/
And of farewel more then a thousand skore
Haue ye fare wel or more had y to dele
For forto say this partyng doth me sore
Hit doth hit doth hit nede no more ben sore
For though that y wolde kepe it close mafay
Mi bollid hert doth so his sikis rore
That mawgre me hit doth my wele biwray

What may y doon now levyng yowre presence
But drawe me sool my silven to complayne
In waylyng so the tyme of yowre absence
Which is to me god wot most grevous payne
And wol be to that y se yow agayne
Which let ben swete as sone as that ye may
For the sighis that doth ellis on me rayne
As maugre me thei wol myn hert biwray

But thynk yow eek that it is passyng hard
Vnto an hert ful of aduersite
To hide his payne that is so sore bistad
So blynd is loue and wenyth othir be
This sey y lo my selven wel bi me
That sore y drede syn y am yeven a way
Lest that my bollyng sighis on [me] preve
As maugre me that hit my loue biwray

But in good trouthe the deth hit were me levyr
Then hit were wist wherfor that y yow pray
Albe y fer forget me nevyr
To eft sone that y may yow more biwray

(ll. 6504–31)

In one sense this ballade is a conventional valedictory poem (his ultimate expression of the moment of impending absence), suitable to close a sequence. In another sense, the poem's exclamatory and interrogative voice is typical of the English poetry overall and thus closes it consistently. More importantly, the poem is the site of Charles's last implied questions not only about the nature of love but about the lyric relations among speaker, readers, and text. Its position in the sequence implies answers to one of the persistent questions about the lyric self: its relation to the poet's biography. A reader looking for a biographical "I" might expect such a valedictory poem to precede a group of poems "about" a real absence, as is implied in the latter sonnets of *Astrophel and Stella,* for example, but no such poems follow here. Norma Goodrich, who tends to seek the biographical, reads the poem as if it were Charles, not Charles's speaker, writing,[49] and stanza 2 can provide some support for such a reading. However, Goodrich does not treat the question of textual presence, Charles's consciousness of which has been clear in nearly the whole sequence and is present in the rest of Ballade 121. The most direct impending absence, as we find in turning the last page of this book of poems, is textual. If the speaker can be equated at all with the poet here, it is primarily in the sense that the poet is saying farewell to us his readers.[50] To end the sequence in this sort of valediction is sharply to remind us that not only lovers but poets say farewell, and that while the sequence has treated presence and absence between lovers, the other important presence that Charles has taken such pains to emphasize throughout the lyrics—textual presence—is about to end. This particular valedictory poem, in true Charles fashion, insists on its own speechlike presence and on the prominence of the text and its conflicted poetic subject. Tensions between heart and speaker, between presence and absence, speech and text, all characterize this closing poem.

The poem opens with repetitive exclamatory assertions of its occasion—six *farwel*s in three lines—and stresses "levyng yowre presence" (l. 6512) and "wayling . . . yowre absence" (l. 6514). The repeated *farwel*s and "hit doth hit doth" (l. 6508) imply the tumbling rhythms and repetitions of emotional speech, entirely characteristic of this poetic subject. The sense of enforced secrecy that has been a consistent feature of the sequence is also much in evidence here.[51] The speaker claims he wants to hide his feelings (even as he reveals them) but that his heart roars out in spite of him. "For though that y wolde kepe it close mafay / Mi bollid hert doth so his sikis rore" (l. 6510). In stanza 3 the speaker asks the lady to consider how

---

49. Norma Goodrich, *Charles, Duke of Orleans: A Literary Biography* (New York: Macmillan, 1963), 102.

50. On the other hand, the life circumstances may indeed be brought to bear here in another way: the manuscript is marked for illumination but is not illuminated, which may signal a hasty departure or some other biographical circumstance intervening in the construction of this particular farewell.

51. Stevens, *Music and Poetry,* 216–18, notes that secretiveness is a typical part of love gaming in music and poetry between Chaucer and Wyatt, but in Charles it becomes prominent and here paradoxical.

hard it is to hide one's feelings. "Bithynk yow eek that it is passing hard / Vnto an hert ful of aduersite / To hide his payne, that is so sore bistad" (ll. 6520–22). The envoi takes the idea to its extreme: he would rather die than have his feelings known. Of course the mild paradox in this stance has been evident throughout: the poet takes great trouble to reveal to the readers how very much the speaker claims to want to conceal. "Who can tell his love loves but little" is a common ploy among Renaissance poets telling their love, and this is perhaps Charles's idiosyncratic anticipation of that trope. I take both of these moves as variants of *occupatio* specialized for the particular rhetorical thrust of love lyric.

The envoi, if read both along the lines of its fictional occasion (a lovers' parting), and along the lines of its larger poetic context (as the last poem in a sequence), takes on double meaning.

> But in good trouthe the deth hit were me levyr
> Then hit were wist wherfor that y yow pray
> Albe y fer forget me nevyr
> To eft sone that y may yow more biwray
>
> (ll. 6528–31)

It can be—just as the entire sequence can be, just as much early modern lyric can be—both "about" a love and "about" poetry. Its occasion can be taken as the parting of speaker and his love and/or the parting of poet and reader. The last two lines, especially, encourage the latter reading and are really a winking invitation and promise from the poet who here steps out from the lyric persona. The three previous refrains, "That mawgre me hit doth my wele biwray," "As maugre me thei wol myn hert biwray," and "As maugre me that hit my loue biwray," stress the speaker's oft-expressed wish to hide his feelings, and his familiar anxiety that his sighs, his heart, his looks "biwray" him in both senses, reveal and betray. He'd rather die than have it known, says the envoi. Then, the poem's and the sequence's final line, "To eft sone that y may yow more biwray," reverses the direction of the speaker's three preceding refrains, and the poet steps forward to ask for remembrance and to promise more poetry. This last line tacitly acknowledges that his hiding games have been just that, games; he finally admits that he knows his repetitions of "I mustn't reveal how much I love you" already have revealed it, of course, and that there is still more to reveal (or to play at concealing). The last lines promise intimacy and a future poetry that will reveal more (perhaps more protestations that he wishes to hide his overwhelming feelings?): "Albe y fer forget me nevyr / To eft sone that y may yow more biwray."

"Albe y fer forget me nevyr" could be the motto of the entire sequence, for it contains the wish of all poets, perhaps of all people, that their presence be remembered and cherished even in their absence. It explains the consolation of writing and the wish thereby to transcend distance, time, even death. Having to pause for a fair beat at the end of this line gives it extra weight and resonance. This short, strong line, a catalexis rare in the sequence, is unamended in the manuscript, and it stops the reader short, suspends us at "never . . ." At this point—really for the only time in the sequence, for recall that Charles never claims either the continuities of the *translatio* nor the permanence of poetic fame—the poetry holds out the possibility of poetic remembrance (to be forgotten never) and the possibility of more poems to be written (to reveal more). This poetic subjectivity asks for, and depends on, a personal hearing rather than a public memorial. Soon to be absent and silent, Charles's speaker asks for remembrance and the hope of exchanging future words. Emerging from a conjunction of conflicts between nations, between languages in flux, between political and personal identities, between changing literary traditions, Charles's "I," like so many early modern lyric personas, presents itself in struggle and suggestively postpones its own silence, even in the end. Ballade 121's envoi makes a deliciously complex ending to poem and to sequence, an ending that reaffirms the self-awareness and mercurial powers of Charles d'Orléans's English lyric "I."

4

Translation, Canons, and Cultural Capital: Manuscripts and Reception of Charles d'Orléans's English Poetry

"Albe y fer forget me nevyr." What cultural support was there for remembering Charles's poetry after 1440? How have we subsequently remembered or forgotten these texts, or, to put it another way, what value, what canonical weight has been attached to these texts over the course of six centuries? Pierre Bourdieu's term "capital culturel" describes the socially constructed value or attractiveness or canonical weight of texts; John Guillory, borrowing Bourdieu's term, locates in the school and in the syllabus the institutionalized power to include or exclude texts in canons.[1] My analysis of this telling case of canonical marginalization locates that power instead in the hands of anonymous scribes, early modern printers, and eighteenth-century editors in particular (with the added agencies of early modern book collectors and antiquarians, nineteenth-century critics, and modern anthology-builders). What makes this case particularly provocative is that it revises some of our recently formed understandings of the workings of the literary canon. If we accept, for example, that hegemonic processes of canon formation have favored dead white male aristocrats (and in New Critical or post-Romantic canons, the dead white male *lyric* poets), then we have to wonder why this dead white male aristocratic lyric poet has been so systematically marginalized. If we think of class, race, gender, and genre as chief canon-shaping categories, then Charles of Orleans would seem to have been a nearly perfect candidate for high canonicity. Along other lines, too, if we think that the shape of late-medieval literary canons is

---

1. Guillory, *Cultural Capital: The Problem of Literary Canon Formation* (Chicago: University of Chicago Press, 1993). For Bourdieu's further discussion of the intersections of the aesthetic with the sociocultural, see *Les Règles de l'art* (Paris: Seuil, 1992).

irregular because of the period's irregular manuscript survivals—we can only canonize the extant, after all—then this large body of work, which survives in three languages in at least eleven manuscripts, would seem to have been ideal canon-fodder. Yet, especially considering the overwhelming size of his extant corpus relative to other fully canonized fifteenth-century authors, Charles's work has hardly made an appearance in our literary lists. It is remarkable that a poet with all the right tickets has not been admitted. This case leads us to question what factors in addition to class, race, gender, and genre might affect the cultural capital and canonicity of literary texts. The following pages contain a necessarily preliminary set of answers. The chapter tries to assess the presence, the evaluations, devaluations, and revaluations of this poet and his texts by tracking specific mentions of him and copies of his work over the course of five and a half centuries in both French and English literary canons.

First, Julia Boffey is not exaggerating to call the relative manuscript presence of these poems "vast." Certainly, much codicological work remains to be done on Charles's manuscripts, and it is not my purpose here to do that work. But a reinterpretation of the manuscript evidence we already do have reveals that Charles's poetry was read by a much broader early modern readership and over a much longer period of time than has usually been assumed to be the case. These were not just private texts read in localized manuscript circles. Furthermore, despite the initial spread of the poetry into a relatively broad readership, early modern attitudes to Charles-the-person seem to have impeded the literary reception of Charles-the-poet. Although Charles persists in the English literary imagination as a historical figure, some residual anti-French sentiment may have attached itself to the poetry, reducing its cultural capital and impeding its acceptance into canons of literature. Finally, I trace here, in material Charles's bibliographers have not noted, some specific fluctuations in English opinions of the poetry. A brief review of Charles's many appearances in French canons provides background for the lengthier examination of his fewer appearances in English canons in the eighteenth and nineteenth centuries. This bicultural review of the editorial and critical fortunes of the poetry shows how, over the course of several centuries, matters historical, social, political, aesthetic, and technological impinged on this poetry, marginalized it, shaped and repositioned it in the developing English canons.

Manuscript Presence in England, Fifteenth through Seventeenth Centuries

Of course, as Neil Ker points out, "the fallacious test of surviving books"[2] can only lead to a tentative set of inferences, and what follows pretends to no more authority than any other such interpretive reconstruction. That said, what we can infer from the presence of his surviving manuscripts in England indicates that Charles d'Orléans's poetry (both English and French) was read in England more widely and for a longer time than is usually thought. As Julia Boffey notes, late-medieval lyrics appeared incidentally, almost haphazardly in miscellanies, often filling an empty page between two treatises or appearing singly and in small groups scattered through generically mixed anthologies.[3] By contrast, "the surviving body of English poems connected with Charles is, in comparison with all other English lyric oeuvres, vast: a complete collection in BL ms. Harley 682, and eleven later copies."[4] Charles is also the only major poet writing English lyric before what we usually mark as the Renaissance who carefully collects and arranges his poems by genre and language, who earns a reputation as a lyric author, and whose authorial acts foster a subjectivity new in English lyric, as we have seen.[5] Boffey reminds us that "the available evidence suggests that no English authors prepared or polished their courtly lyrics in this way."[6]

But was this relatively vast, generically selected, carefully authored oeuvre read in England outside a coterie readership before the first known

---

2. *Medieval Libraries of Great Britain: A List of Surviving Books* (London: The Royal Historical Society, 1941; rpt. 1964), xi.

3. *English Courtly Love Lyrics,* 6–7, 11, 19–27.

4. *English Courtly Love Lyrics,* 74.

5. Gower writes his *Cinkante Balades* in French, without an individuated lyric subjectivity to speak of; the work appears in one manuscript, the Trentham ms. See *Complete Works of John Gower,* ed. G. C. Macaulay, 4 vols. (Oxford: Clarendon, 1899; rpt. Grosse Pointe, Mich.: Scholarly Press, 1992), 1:lxxix–lxxxiii. The poems are on pp. 335–78. John Quixley's translation into English of Gower's *Traitié pour essampler les amantz marietz,* circa 1402, also appears in only one manuscript. See MacCracken, *Quixley's Ballades Royal.* Quixley likely translated the poems for his daughter's marriage—an instructive, occasional work rather than the sort of literary project at issue here.

6. *English Courtly Love Lyrics,* 63. Charles's contemporaries knew him as a poet; figure 1, a reduced image of a manuscript illumination in BL ms. Royal F 16.ii, shows him writing at a desk; he refers to himself as the author and subject of his poetry in lines 5–6, 2720, 3044, and 4788 of the English poems. "The only situation in which self-referential detail might be fitting is in a *cycle* of lyrics . . . and the *single surviving example* of such a cycle in English, the poems . . . in BL MS Harley 682, indeed contains several such autobiographical hints" (Boffey, *English Courtly Love Lyrics,* 62; emphasis added).

printing of it, the Roxburghe Club edition of 1827? We have generally assumed not. We have known of these manuscripts, have studied them individually,[7] but have not yet interpreted the whole of the material evidence to assess the poetry's felt presence in England. The material evidence of the manuscripts leads me to conclude that the texts enjoyed a much wider readership in England than has been previously thought. In fact, manuscript studies reveal that Charles's poetry was read well into the Renaissance, and that it was owned not only by the very most powerful people in England but also by a middle-class or commercial readership. This extension of what is usually thought of as rarefied coterie poetry into classes other than the aristocratic warrants further investigation, for even what evidence we have runs counter to some critical thinking about early modern lyric poetics as necessarily restrictive and restricted.[8]

Charles's poems were owned by the top household in sixteenth-century England, the Tudors. This is no real surprise—the interconnected English and French royal family trees and the continuing English royal taste for French cultural artifacts would explain it well enough, even without the particular evidence in this case. British Library ms. Royal F 16.ii, a luxurious illuminated manuscript containing French and English poems, may have been prepared as late as 1501–2, as a gift for Prince Arthur.[9] Janet Backhouse dates the manuscript earlier but has pointed out several specific connections between the Tudors and this copy of Charles's poetry (for example, the appearance of the Tudor greyhound and the Beaufort portcullis among its border illustrations).[10] Bernard André, *orator regis* to

---

7. Champion, *Manuscrit autographe.* J. P. M. Jansen, "Charles d'Orléans and the Fairfax Poems," *English Studies* 70 (June 1989): 206–24, and "The French Manuscripts of the English Poems of Charles of Orleans," *Notes and Queries,* n.s. 35 (December 1988): 439–40. R. H. Robbins, "Some Charles d'Orléans Fragments," *Modern Language Notes* 66 (1951): 501–5. See also Nelson, *Charles d'Orléans;* Yenal, *Charles d'Orléans;* and Galderisi, *Charles d'Orléans.*

8. Meale points out that "the major difference between the book-trade in England and that abroad (for instance in fourteenth- and early fifteenth-century France and later fifteenth-century Burgundy)" is that it draws from a broader social base and is not reliant exclusively upon court patronage systems ("Patrons, Buyers, and Owners," 202).

9. British Museum, Department of Manuscripts, *Illuminated Manuscripts in the British Museum,* with notes by George F. Warner (London, 1899), treats it and includes color plates. See also Warner and Julius P. Gilson, eds., *Catalogue of Western Manuscripts in the Old Royal and King's Collections* (London: Trustees of the British Museum, 1921), 2:203–4. For a recent study, see Backhouse, "Founders of Royal Library." Backhouse revises Warner's dating of this manuscript, for she thinks that it may have been commissioned earlier than 1501, by Edward IV in fact, but that the Tudor librarian kept the project alive.

10. Backhouse, "Founders of Royal Library," 34–39 and plates 15–19.

Henry VII and tutor to Prince Arthur and to Prince Henry (later Henry VIII), was involved in creating this manuscript.[11] Later in the century this vellum manuscript appears in Henry VIII's Richmond library, as does another early printed collection including Charles's lyrics.[12] The poems evidently retained their appeal for the very most influential readers of the early and middle sixteenth century.

But lesser mortals found Charles's verse appealing as well, judging from the margin markings in Harley 682, the primary complete manuscript in English. This major manuscript was read at least until the early seventeenth century, since six names in three different sixteenth-century hands permit us to trace if not the certain ownership of the manuscript, at least some of the people who may have borrowed it or known its owners.[13] These are not famous folk; the names—Elizabethe Gelle, Tomas Wyssedune, John Halesby, Thomas Pryor, Rycardus Holt, and Yohanne Tredecrofft—do not appear in the *DNB* nor in county histories, and evidence from wills and parish registers has so far been inconclusive. More needs to be done on the names written in Harley ms. 682, but it seems reasonable to assume that none of these was a particularly prominent family name in early Renaissance England.[14] By the seventeenth century a minor collec-

---

11. For more on Bernard André and the early Tudor courts, see three articles by Carlson, "King Arthur," "Politicizing Tudor Court Literature," and "Reputation and Duplicity."

12. The *Jardin de Plaisance* (Paris: Vérard, 1501); H. Ormont, "Les Manuscrits des rois d'Angleterre au château de Richmond," in *Études Romanes dédiées à Gaston Paris par ses élèves français* (Paris: Émile Bouillon, 1891), 1–13. While *Private Libraries in Renaissance England,* ed. R. J. Fehrenbach and E. Leedham-Green, (Binghamton, N.Y.: Medieval and Renaissance Text Society, 1992–) so far does not note any direct ownership of entire copies, the many unidentifiable lyric entries ("a litel boke of poems," etc.) substantiate Boffey's point that the tastes of the court ran to Charles-like lyrics, and extend that point to apply to Tudor courts as well. See May, "Manuscript Circulation," and A. Marotti, "Malleable and Fixed Texts" and "Manuscript, Print, and the English Renaissance Lyric," all in Hill, *New Ways.*

13. C. E. Wright, *Fontes Harleiani* (London: Trustees of the British Museum, 1972). But see Arn, ed., *Fortunes Stabilnes,* 115–19, for a more thorough explanation. Arn also includes the English, Latin, and macaronic verses and other marks added in the margins.

14. Research results for the name *Gelle* are representative of the others: Burke's *Commoners. A Genealogical History of the Commoners of Great Britain and Ireland,* vols. 1–4 (1834–38, rpt. Baltimore: Genealogical Publishing, 1977) notes the 1634 marriage of Elizabeth Gell, daughter of Leonard Gell, Esq., of Norton, and an Elizabeth, sister of Rev. Robert Sanderson, Bishop of Lincoln. There are also Gell families of Derbyshire: Philip Gell, MD, father of Honor Gell, in Wirksworth, and William Gell, Esq., of Darley, who married an Anne Hussey of Lincolnshire, daughter of Elizabethan courtier Sir William Hussey. R. Sims's *Index to the Pedigrees and Arms Contained in the Heralds' Visitations, and other genealogical manuscripts in the British Museum* (London: John Russell Smith, 1849) notes five manuscripts relating to the Gell family of Hopton (Harley ms. 1093, fol. 83b; ms. 6104, fol. 87; ms. 6592, fols. 8.93b and 32b, ms. 1537, fol. 1; Egerton ms. 996, fol. 69b; I have not seen these). Some Gells turn up in Lancashire: Sir John Gell of Hopton, slain in 1627; earlier,

tor, Edward Stillingfleet (1635–1699), bishop of Winchester, owned the 1440 parchment manuscript.

Another major manuscript, Fairfax 16, indicates a broad and enduring fifteenth-, sixteenth-, and early-seventeenth-century readership for at least one, and possibly more, of the English poems of Charles d'Orléans. Fairfax 16, an anthology that is also an important Chaucer manuscript, contains as its fifth quire a set of twenty ballades. One of these is certainly by Charles,[15] and the other nineteen, although of unknown authorship, resemble Charles's lyrics to a fair degree.[16] The provenance of Fairfax 16, like that of Royal F 16.ii and Harley 682, can be traced well into the sixteenth century and proves it a text sought after in circles beyond the royal. Fairfax 16, a manuscript dated at circa 1450, ten years after Charles's return to France, was owned and probably commissioned by John Stanley, MP (Surrey) in 1445–46.[17] The Stanley family had close connections to Westminster Abbey in the late fifteenth and early sixteenth centuries, and Fairfax 16 may have been bequeathed to the abbey during this time.[18]

---

a Ralph Gell of Hopton, Lancashire, whose daughter Helena married John Wigley of Middleton, Darbyshire, some time before 1601 (Burke's *Commoners*). A John Gelle is listed in the subsidy rolls of Yorkshire (Yorkshire Archaeological Society Records series 16, 21, 74, 1894–1929). F. K. Hitching and S. Hitching's *References to English Surnames, 1601* (Walton-on-Thames: Bernau, 1910) lists Gell in two parish registers, St. Helen's and Worcester. The other names lead to similarly labyrinthine dead-ends.

15. "O thou fortune which hast the gouvernaunce," fol. 321, also appears in BN f. fr. 25458, Charles's autograph manuscript. Boffey, *English Courtly Love Lyrics*, 172, mentions that it also appears in Grenoble 873, but J. P. M. Jansen in "The French Manuscripts" disagrees; I found no English poems in Grenoble 873.

16. I cannot prove Charles's authorship of any of these nineteen poems; although some are impressionistically very Charles-like to the ear and mind (for example, poem 14, "Myn hertis joy, and all myn hole pleasaunce," and poem 16, "What schall I say, to whom schall I compleyn?"), others are not much like him, metrically and poetically speaking, and none appears in BN f. fr. 25458, the autograph manuscript. Without further evidence, one can most readily accept J. P. M. Jansen's attribution of the poems to the earl of Suffolk, William de la Pole, friend and captor of Charles (Jansen, ed., *The "Suffolk" Poems: An Edition of the Love Lyrics in Fairfax 16 Attributed to William de la Pole* [Groningen: Universiteitsdrukkerij, 1989], 13–30).

17. For an extended discussion of this manuscript and its history, see the John Norton-Smith's introduction to the Bodleian Library facsimile, *Bodleian Library MS Fairfax 16* (London: Scolar Press, 1979). John Stanley, who died in 1469, was not part of the famous Stanley family; he had lived in Cheshire and may have had contact with Suffolk in early 1450. Since Suffolk maintained his friendship with Charles d'Orléans even after 1440, Stanley could possibly have known Charles, although I have not found evidence for it. It may have been via Suffolk that Stanley knew of Charles.

18. Another sixteenth-century owner, Thomas Moyelle, was possibly connected by marriage to the Stanley family and may be the same Sir Thomas Moyle who was influential at the courts of Henry VII and Edward IV. See Norton-Smith's introduction to *Bodleian Library MS Fairfax 16*.

We also know that John Stowe used the manuscript either around 1560 to make his Chaucer edition of 1561, or for later work in the 1590s. Collector Joseph Holland (fl. 1580) saw and perhaps owned Fairfax 16. In 1650, bibliophile Charles Fairfax purchased the volume at Gloucester, and in 1671 sold it to the Bodleian Library.

At first glance, then, it would seem that by mid-Renaissance, the Fairfax 16 manuscript had gained a certain literary status; its ownership by Stowe and Holland and its purchase and sale by Fairfax seem to cast it as an antiquarian curiosity of sorts rather than as a popular, current set of poems, perhaps just as Stillingfleet's ownership of Harley 682 indicates its status as "dead" collectible. The material bibliography, however, shows that this interpretation of provenance may be incomplete and misleading.

What is especially notable about Fairfax 16—what helps correct and complete the interpretation of provenance—is its medium-quality, booklet production. Not a vellum treasure like Royal F 16.ii and several other Charles d'Orléans copies,[19] nor a smaller, simpler parchment elegance like Harley 682, Fairfax 16 has "lesser ornamentation" for the lyrics.[20] The manuscript was likely created from sample copies—"a nearly perfectly preserved example of a manuscript produced to order by a commercial scriptorium or bookseller."[21] The poems in quire V "may have been selected by a purchaser from a choice of small units."[22] Not unread, stale, late-courtly leftovers of interest only to collectors and royals, this poetry was in enough demand to be marketable to a relatively wide audience of lesser nobility, and probably to middle-class readers. As manuscript commodities, if Royal F 16.ii and Harley 682 are designer originals, Fairfax 16 is upscale department store prêt-à-porter.

Somewhere else falls the widespread and variable boutique chic of the scattered copies: Lansdowne 380, Harley 7333, CUL Additional 2585, the "Hearne fragment," and Harley 6916. These copies contain selections of

---

19. Charles on vellum: BN f. fr. 25458; Grenoble 873; BN f. fr. 1104 (Catherine de Medici's copy); Carpentras 375 (Marie de Clèves's copy); BN f. fr. 9223; on parchment, Arsenal 3457.

20. Boffey, *English Courtly Love Lyrics*, 41–42.

21. Norton-Smith, *Bodleian Library MS Fairfax 16*, vii. For general background on this point, see G. S. Ivy, "The Bibliography of the Manuscript Book," in *The English Library before 1700,* ed. Francis Wormald and C. E. Wright (London: Athlone Press, 1958); and H. S. Bennett, "The Production and Dissemination of Vernacular Manuscripts in the Fifteenth Century," *Library,* 5th ser., 1 (1946–47): 167–78. Recent work has called the commercial scriptorium theory into some doubt; see for example Robert Adams, "Langland's *Ordinatio*: The *Visio* and the *Vita* Once More," *Yearbook of Langland Studies* 8 (1995): 55–56.

22. Boffey, *English Courtly Love Lyrics*, 10.

both the French and English poems. Harley 6916 is something of a mystery manuscript, for while it is listed in the 1808 *Catalogus* (III.448), its provenance in England is uncertain and it is not noted in the *Fontes Harleiani*. Made of paper, it is thought to be a sixteenth-century copy of Charles's autograph or personal manuscript, BN f. fr. 25458, or some lost copy of it.[23] Even in the sixteenth century the poetry was being copied and dispersed according to the anthologizing habits of the previous century, habits that did not disappear with the advent of print. Lansdowne 380, similarly, was "transcribed by some person at the beginning of the sixteenth century."[24] Part II (fols. 147–217) contains "Balades plaisans et joyeuses" by Charles d'Orléans, though his name is not given, indicating the greater continuing interest during this period in copying the poems than in naming the poet qua poet—which may signal a tension between Renaissance England's anti-French sentiments and its enthusiastic, enduring interest in French lyrics. This part II of the Lansdowne 380 manuscript was owned by Sir Julius Caesar, Queen Elizabeth I's judge of the Admiralty and James I's and Charles I's chancellor of the Exchequer and master of rolls. Also owned by a later master of rolls, Sir Joseph Jekyll (1633–1738),[25] and perhaps by Archbishop Warham, was Harley 7333, but this manuscript is a bit different in that it is a "large vernacular manuscript begun in the mid–fifteenth century . . . [that] includes texts showing the influence of John Shirley . . . [and] was written in a house of Augustinian canons at Leicester,"[26] the Abbey of St. Mary de Pratis. But fragments of Charles's poems (unattributed) show up in the sixteenth century in Cardinal de Rohan's songbook and in English royal songbooks,[27] indicating a popularity and spread of the poems independent of their connection with

23. See Nelson's bibliography and Champion, ed., *Poésies*, 1:xxi. The *Catalogus* entry 380 reads: "Poesies [*sic*] de Charles d'Orléans, père de Louis XII, et de plusieurs autres auteurs" (*Catalogus librorum lansdowniae*, [*A Catalogue of the Lansdowne Manuscripts in the British Museum*] [London: R. and A. Taylor, 1819]. Champollion-Figeac, ed., *Poésies du duc Charles d'Orléans*, 456ff., says it is a miscellany about which Abbé de la Rue wrote.

24. *Catalogus librorum lansdowniae*, 3:110. Champion says the scribe was Thomas Kendell and that this manuscript was in England in the early sixteenth century (*Poésies*, 1:xxi n. 3). Champollion-Figeac, ed., *Poésies du duc Charles d'Orléans*, again, says that only forty-two ballades by Charles are here and that it resembles the manuscript at St.-Germain-des-Prés (I assume he means what we now call BN f. fr. 19139). I have not seen it.

25. Whose collection habits were influenced by his brother-in-law, Lord Chancellor John Somers (First Baron Somers, 1651–1716). At least some seventeenth-century collectors found the ballades pleasing or curious.

26. Ivy, "Bibliography of Manuscript Book," 65 n. 76; Boffey, *English Courtly Love Lyrics*, 128.

27. Boffey, *English Courtly Love Lyrics*, 76, 108–11.

a Valois prince. Harley 7333's clerical provenance and origin, its fragmented popularity, and especially its uneven quality set it apart: it is large and vellum, but Boffey calls it "workmanlike," a manuscript in which "modest ornament is the norm."[28]

Entirely without ornament, however, are the two most fascinating, elusive pieces of evidence for the rise and fall of Charles's textual presence in England, CUL Additional 2585 and Bodleian Rawlinson K 38/42 (the Hearne fragment).[29] CUL Additional 2585's two leaves contain four poems[30] evidently copied in the fifteenth century from Harley 682 or a lost exemplar. The Hearne fragment, circa 1440, has four other poems,[31] again evidently copied from 682 or a lost copy of it, and glosses in a later hand, indicating that Charles's English poems were in some demand from the start. The Hearne fragment helps date the fall of Charles's popularity, because it shows up as endpapers in a seventeenth-century book. By this time, in other words, these texts seem to have been tired hand-me-downs, ready to be recycled as pastedowns. Although Charles receives continuing mention as a historical figure in English literature, his poetry's material presence had clearly waned in England by the later Renaissance. Even in the absence of critical mention before 1740, we can intuitively reconstruct the trajectory of Charles's popularity: it makes sense that after the Elizabethan age, with whose poetry Charles's shares striking affinities, these poems' popularity should fade.

To summarize what can be gleaned from a review of the complex (and admittedly incomplete) manuscript evidence currently available: Charles d'Orléans's poetry is exceptional not just in surviving quantity, though there is certainly that, but because it is the first English sequence gathered on principles of genre, authorship, and language that continued to be read in England across two centuries of surprisingly broad readership. The material evidence reminds us that early Renaissance English readers still had a healthy appetite for reading, copying, and collecting what Charles's poetry offered, both in French and in English versions, although they did

---

28. Boffey, *English Courtly Love Lyrics*, 43.

29. First studied and printed by Robbins, "Some Charles d'Orléans Fragments." See Arn, ed., *Fortunes Stabilnes*, 122–23.

30. Ballades 59 and 60 and Roundels 5 and 6; Arn explains that the poems are laid out just as in Harley 682, and that the poems occupy recto-verso in the same way as Harley 682 and the other fragment.

31. Roundels 9, 10, 15, 16; 9–10 on a verso and 15–16 on a recto; imagine the page layout of these: missing poems 11–12 and 13–14 would have appeared on a lost leaf between the others.

not name him, or claim him, as their own. There is a discernable tension, furthermore, between responses to the poems and to the person, a tension that persists across several centuries of reception in England. This tension derives in part, I believe, from historical contexts beyond the immediate social and manuscript origins of the poetry.

Reception: England's Historical Responses to Charles

Despite the favorable initial climate of noble houses like Waterton's and Suffolk's, despite a manuscript presence that was wider and more lasting than we have thought, the French prince and his English poetry faced considerable hostility in fifteenth-century England. Powerful voices spoke out against France, against the French, and specifically against Charles d'Orléans. Anti-French sentiment, it seems, came to have long-lasting consequences for these translations' fortunes in England.

Although Charles had been the prize catch at Agincourt, as early as 1417 Henry V was warning Englishmen about him as a spy, as a potential escapee, and as an ally of the treacherous Scots:

> Furthemore I wole . . . that ye set a gode ordinance for my north marches and specialy for the Duc of Orlians. and for alle the remnant of my prisoners of france. and also for the king of Scotelond. for as I am secrely enfourmed by a man of ryght notable estate in this lond that there hath ben a man of the Ducs of Orliance in scotland and accorded with the Duc of albany. that this next somer he shal bryng in the mammet of Scotland to sturre what he may, and also that ther schold be founden weys to the havyng awey specialy of the Duc of Orlians. and also of the king as welle as of the remnant of my forsayd prysoners that god do defende. wherfor I wolle that the Duc of Orliance be kept stille withyn the castil of pontfret with owte goyng to robertis place or to any othre disport for it is bettre he lak his disport then we were deceyued.[32]

---

32. Robert is Robert Waterton, Charles's captor at Pontefract Castle, Yorkshire during 1416. Ms. Cotton Vesp. F. III, fol. 8; more easily available in electronic text in *An Anthology of Chancery English (1384–1462)*, ed. John H. Fisher, Malcolm Richardson, and Jane L. Fisher (Knoxville: University of Tennessee Press, 1984; digital text, University of Virginia Electronic Text Center), N70, ll. 1–9. I know of no historical evidence of such spying, but see McLeod, *Charles of Orleans,* chap. 11, 195–98, on surreptitious arm-squeezing during the visits of Burgundian Hugues de Lannoy.

And in 1419, Henry signed this reminder:

> And ferthermore we wol and also charge you that ye ordeyne that that be effectuelly done as in dede. that we wrote unto you as touching the Duc of Orliens as oure trust is to you. for the cas is so grete that ye ne couthe not ymagyn hit gretter.[33]

Henry V even included in his 1421 will a proviso that Charles not be released until the conquest of France was complete and asked on his deathbed (according to one chronicler, Monstrelet) that Charles not be released until Henry VI came of age.[34] Charles's most powerful enemy in England, Humphrey, duke of Gloucester, reminded Henry VI of his father's concern, and warned of Charles's "grete Subtilitie and Cauteleux disposition."[35] (The attitude of Humphrey, a grand bibliophile and founder of libraries, toward Charles could not have helped the spread and preservation of Charles's poetry.) A black mark at Suffolk's famous 1450 treason trial was his long, friendly association with Charles.[36]

Anti-Charles sentiment pursuant to anti-French sentiment should not strike us as unreasonable. It was, after all, with Charles's family, the Valois, that English kings had struggled for the rule of France and England; it was at Harfleur, at Agincourt, at Orléans itself, that so much English blood had been shed. England and France in the fifteenth century were in the nasty process of splitting a political and cultural marriage that had endured across four centuries, and Charles d'Orléans figured prominently in the final settlements.[37] Fine poet or not, generous and sociable translations into English notwithstanding, Charles could hardly have been lionized in England in quite the same way as native poets Chaucer, Lydgate, or Gower could, considering the historical and political contexts. We might well expect the literary-critical reception of the poetry to have been guided by these historical contexts, as was the case in France, and thus might also

---

33. Fisher, Richardson, and Fisher, *Anthology of Chancery English,* e-text, N72, ll. 2–3.

34. McLeod, *Charles of Orleans,* 158, 237, and 375 n. 63.

35. McLeod, *Charles of Orleans,* 237, citing Joseph Stevenson, *Letters and Papers Illustrative of the wars of the English in France during the reign of King Henry the Sixth, King of England* (London: Longman et al., 1861–64), II.ii.40–51.

36. McLeod, *Charles of Orleans,* 324–25 citing *Rotuli parliamentorum,* V.176–83.

37. Especially between 1436 and 1440. Champion, *Vie;* McLeod, *Charles of Orleans,* 198–99, 202–3, 206, 218–20, 225–30, 235, 237–38, 240–44; Rymer's *Foedera (Acta Regis . . .),* vol. 1 (London: J. and J. Knapton, 1731); also Rymer's *Syllabus in English of the Documents. . . ,* vol. 2 (London: Public Record Office; rpt. New York: AMS Press, 1973).

expect a much-diminished, chilly reception for the poems in England. Two marginalizing factors may have accrued from these unfavorable early political contexts—and interacted: (1) Charles continued to be better known in England as historical figure than as poet, and (2) the complete English poems did not appear in print in England until 1827, as far as we know.

Telling Absence from Print: Lyric Forms, Historical Contexts, and the English Cultural Imagination

Nationalistically born, Tudor-supported anti-French sentiment is too vague a notion and too gross a stereotype to account fully for the poems' long absence from print. After all, as Carol Meale has shown, French manuscripts continued to be in demand in England,[38] and the early English presses did put out a huge number of French titles, translated and not. One of the first things Caxton printed was a French phrasebook, and while language patterns were changing and are hard to define, French material was not suddenly inaccessible to English readers of printed matter—quite the contrary. More verse translations from French were made between 1476 and 1500 than from Italian: six times as many lines came from French, in fact.[39] However, notable for its absence from the long lists of French and French-born prayers, calendars, romances, treatises, and so on, is French *lyric* in print. I could not find a single *STC* entry between 1476 and 1558 that admits itself to be translated French lyric (although a few poems translated from French are nestled in the prose romances and shepherd's calendars). Perhaps generic vogue as much as nationalistic sentiment, or the two combined, kept Charles from print. Alain Chartier provides a useful parallel example: his *Curial* and *Breviaire des Nobles,* for example, came to England in 1483 and 1508, respectively, but the lyrics attributed to him, the *Pleasaunt and delectable demaundes,* were not printed in England until 1566. The Tudors did not dislike French lyric, as the Richmond castle list amply demonstrates, nor did they eschew French translations. But the early-sixteenth-century English printers (unlike their French counterparts)[40] evidently left lyric to thrive

---

38. Meale, "Patrons, Buyers, and Owners," 202–9, especially 207–9.

39. William Ringler, *Bibliography and Index to English Verse Printed 1476–1558* (London: Mansell, 1988), introduction, especially 6.

40. See Derek Pearsall, *John Lydgate* (London: Routledge and Kegan Paul, 1970), 6, who notes the "scattered and limited nature of book production in England" as opposed to that in France.

in the manuscripts[41] and even after midcentury turned their efforts not to lyric sequences but to lyrics in miscellanies. The competition between script and print; the volatile politics of the early Tudor courts; increased trade, affluence, and social mobility; the rise of vernaculars: all these probably exerted tremendous pressure on lyric as a genre within the English literary system. Poetic trends in the Renaissance would deal badly with older courtly forms in general—think of the lay and virelay, the villanelle and canzone—and with a French writer of ballades and roundels like Charles d'Orléans in particular. By mid–sixteenth century, Wyatt's mutations of Petrarch had proven themselves highly adaptable to the new environments of print and court. A verdant new form was flourishing: sonnets, and after 1582, sonnet sequences. The extinction of older forms was not, of course, immediate; ballades and roundels competed successfully in miscellanies through and after 1600. Luckily for Wyatt's fame, he wisely did not restrict himself to roundels and ballades but also wrote enough sonnets (and enough of these were picked up in early print venues like Tottel's *Songes and Sonettes*) to ensure his later survival in the canon. Unfortunate Charles, on the contrary, who seems to have suffered all his life from bad timing, did not write sonnets. Because the roundel, ballade, chanson, and so on (song forms) were ultimately displaced in the ecosystem of Renaissance literary preferences by sonnet, epigram, and elegy (inscribed forms), Charles's poems lost what we might think of as a Darwinian struggle for generic survival. Tottel's miscellany (an opening suggestion, really, for English lyric-in-print) and the other print miscellanies (explorations of that suggestion) are also arenas of generic, formal, and perhaps linguistic competition in which translation played a decisive part. But although detachable fragments of Harley 682 would have fit in perfectly well with the styles and forms and flavors of the early printed miscellanies, none appeared there, as far as I have found. By the 1590s, formally unified collections (sonnet sequences) dominated lyric print production, leaving Charles's ballade sequence behind in splendid vellum isolation.

The crucial fact that his English poetry was not printed shapes several centuries' cultural cognizance of Charles d'Orléans. He is known in print not as a poet but as a figure of history. The historical Charles is the one who persists, if unevenly, in English cultural perceptions over the cen-

---

41. On which see Marotti, *Manuscript, Print, and the English Renaissance Lyric* (Ithaca: Cornell University Press, 1995).

turies. A few samples of Charles's primarily historical presence in English literature will illustrate. Shakespeare gives Charles d'Orléans a cameo in *Henry V* in which he does make a lettered (though anachronistic) gesture—"I have heard a sonnet begin so to one's mistress," Charles wittily replies to the praises of a horse.[42] But "Orléans" in the Shakespearean vision is much more likely to be a historical feature than a literary one. *1 Henry VI* opens with Henry V's funeral; much of the play is set in Orléans and concerns the sieges, though Shakespeare, probably for his own purposes in the play, gets the history of Charles's ransom quite wrong.[43] *2 Henry VI* opens with Suffolk's importation of Queen Margaret and mentions the Orléans presence, but not the poetry. A century later, John Oldmixon's *Amores Britannici* mentions Charles's marriage to Isabella, widow of Richard II (as an "affront").[44] By 1862, Sir Henry Taylor's play *St. Clement's Eve* dramatizes the assassination of Charles's father.[45] But Taylor uses Charles's family story to speak not of literature but of cultural values: "whilst the Duke of Orleans represented the chivalry of the time...., the new Duke of Burgundy [he means Jean Sans Peur] was an equally genuine representative of its cruelty and pride."[46] Sir Thomas Park's sonnet on Charles, quoted later in this chapter, likewise creates a primarily historical, idealizing picture of loss, but adds mention of Charles as a poet. In the late nineteenth century, on the other hand, Oscar Wilde focuses on Charles's elaborately embroidered clothing.[47]

Charles and his histories thus seem to act in the English cultural imagination as mirrors (the way all histories, legends, interpretations, translations, perhaps act)—each age sees in the Valois prince's image what it wishes to emphasize. Early English writers, even dramatic ones like Shakespeare, concern themselves with his political, martial, and marital connections to England; an early Romantic, Thomas Park, uses him as a focus of historical landscape meditation; a Decadent writer like Wilde steers us to

---

42. III.vii.44–66, 87–120, 128–52 and IV.ii.1–5; see also IV.v.10ff.; IV.viii.70. Shakespeare's Charles stays scrupulously away from low humor in that scene.

43. III.iii.69–73, Joan's persuasive speech to Burgundy.

44. (London: John Nutt, 1703), 100, l. 32 and note.

45. *Works* (London: Henry S. King, 1877–78), 3:137–272.

46. Preface, 138–39. However, Taylor's notes do discuss Charles d'Orléans's imprisonment and poetry, and print a French stanza, 270–71.

47. "[A]nd the coat that Charles of Orleans wore, on the sleeves of which were embroidered the verses of a song beginning 'Madame, je suis tout joyeux,' the musical accompaniment of the words being wrought in gold thread, and each note, of square shape in those days, formed with four pearls" (*The Picture of Dorian Gray* [New York: Signet, 1962], 170).

the luxurious surfaces of a perceived medieval courtliness. Charles's unpublished poetry, though better known in pre-1650 England than we have thought, was still less well known over time in England than his well-documented, oft-rehearsed historical and national actions. His image and life story seem to have been readily appropriable to varying tastes.

An important biographical or historical origin, then, cannot assure the naturalization of poetic translations, any more than unfavorable historical contexts like Henry V's nationalism can eradicate them. But political hostility (these days, ask Solzhenitsyn or Rushdie) and the book-buying public's preferences in genre (these days, for paperback romances vs. academic criticism) can determine whether or not, where, and in what quantities an author's work is read. In Charles's case the two factors together favored the translations' early fortunes as a splendid dead-end.

Charles's Poetry in Literary Canons: Critical Reception in France

The English canon-founders of the eighteenth century had an opportunity to do for Charles's poetry what early printers had not done: bring it to public notice and put it on the formative literary lists. The issues just touched upon—biography, nationalism or political history, literary trends, and print availability—will also dominate the eighteenth-century English reception of these poems. These issues remain important for nineteenth-century English critics, but are refocused by romanticism, by the French Revolution, and by Burckhardt's thesis. But first, a brief look at the French reception of the French poems will provide contrastive background for the English reception. Perhaps the nations' separate reception histories can explain what first appears to be a clear demonstration of a canon's power to marginalize a poet. The reception histories may also illustrate what is required in a new culture for translations merely to survive, what it takes for them to gain acceptance, and what it would take for them to flourish as canonical centerpieces and agents of literary change.

In the reception history of Charles d'Orléans, there is, quite naturally, a distinct division at the English Channel. Charles never disappeared from the French literary canon. A bibliophile, musician, and patron of poetry, young Charles was probably influenced by Eustache Deschamps,[48] Alain

---

48. Maître d'hôtel at the court of Charles's parents, Louis d'Orléans and Valentine (Visconti) de Milan.

Chartier, Christine de Pisan, and Jean de Garencières. After his release in 1440, Charles conducted *puys* at Blois, gave young poets like François Villon an encouraging forum, and generally marched along in the unbroken parade of late-medieval–early-Renaissance French poetry. In fact he was imitated and plagiarized well into the sixteenth century. A favorable factor in the French reception—in clear contrast with the English reception—is his early print debut. Seven of his poems appear anonymously in Antoine Vérard's enormously popular 1501 *Jardin de Plaisance,* and seven in Lemaire de Belges's 1531 *Le Triomphe de l'amant vert.* Two hundred sixty-three poems by Charles appear in Vérard's 1509 *La Chasse et le départ d'amours.*[49] Almost a century after its composition, the poetry was sufficiently fashionable not to require the enhancement of titling under the Valois name. These early printings assured the poems' continued availability, and they show us that for the early French readership the poems stood on their own merits even independent of attribution to Charles d'Orléans.

But by the time literary tastes had swung to neoclassicism and the French literary-critical industry had organized itself in the eighteenth century, the poems' position in the new French canon seemed to require the support of politics and biography. The titles of several key works reveal the scholars' conscious attempts to write French literary history, to construct the French canon—and the founding lists include Charles d'Orléans.[50] But he is not included for his popularity. By the time poems have made it to such canon-lists, people are not reading them much any more, or so the truism goes. In this case it seems so: by 1740, large collections of anonymous poems like those so popular in the sixteenth century were not enough to assure a publication. These eighteenth-century literary histori-

---

49. Wrongly attributed to Octavien de St.-Gelais. The earliest critical notice of this was Goujet's in 1745 (*Bibliothèque françoise ou histoire de la littérature françoise,* 9:314–28); for later discussions see Arthur Piaget, "Une Édition gothique de Charles d'Orléans," *Romania* 21(1892): 581–96; and Pierre Champion, "Du Succès de l'oeuvre de Charles d'Orléans et de ses imitateurs jusqu'au XVIè siècle," in *Mélanges offerts à M. Emile Picot,* 2 vols. (Geneva: Slatkine, 1969), 1:409–20. Each century's critical comment has been to denounce the 1509 *Chasse* as plagiarism and to note Charles's sixteenth-century popularity.

50. L'Abbé Sallier praises Charles's poetry in his 1740 *Mémoires de l'Académie Royale des inscriptions et belles lettres* (13:580–92), and l'Abbé Goujet follows suit in his 1745 *Bibliothèque.* Twenty-five poems of Charles d'Orléans appear in Barthélémy Imbert's 1778 *Annales Poétiques ou Almanach des Muses.* Mlle de Keralio includes eight French and two English poems in her *Collection des meilleurs ouvrages françois . . .* (Paris: Lagrange, 1787); 3:139–78. Recent bibliographies of Charles d'Orléans mention Keralio: Nelson, *Charles d'Orléans;* Yenal, *Charles d'Orléans.*

ans noted Charles as much for his lineage as for his poetry. And it is a lineage worth note: grandson of Charles V, nephew of Charles VI, father of Louis XII, uncle of François I, Charles d'Orléans barely missed wearing the French crown and was a prominent member of a most prominent family. Sallier, Goujet, and Imbert, for example, all place the poems in the context of historical biography.[51] In these accounts his historical stature and lineage are prominent; his birth, not his poetry itself, seemed to guarantee his place in the early French canon. Even despite the eighteenth century's very new literary values, Charles's bloodlines were evidently strong enough to excuse any distaste for his poetic lines. Any real evaluation of Charles's poetry according to eighteenth-century French standards of balance, clarity, neoclassical gravity or a fine-tuned *alexandrin* would likely not be favorable to the poetry itself. However, early French critics grant him a secure, stable place in the new literary canon as a sort of national treasure, effectively diverting discussion away from literary values.

Beyond a steady historical interest in matters Orléaniste,[52] nineteenth-century France saw a specific revival of interest in the poetry of Charles. Four major editions in France kept the poetry in front of the reading public and also stimulated critical discussion of it.[53] In fact, the editions of 1842 led to quite a critical skirmish, a "bitter dispute between two scholars."[54] Evidently by this time the poetry of Charles d'Orléans was critical territory worth seizing and worth defending. Yet the nineteenth century's praise of Charles would prove no less consistently connected with his lineage than the preceding century's had been, and in fact seems to have produced an even more focused interest in biographical detail. Chalvet's edi-

---

51. Keralio is the most interested in the literary, saying that Charles, as much as Villon, should be seen as France's first great poet (although she also emphasizes the biography).

52. The secure if not always stable place of the Orléans family in French political history no doubt contributed to the continuous interest in Charles's poetry. From Charles's association with Jeanne d'Arc, to the 1560 États-Généraux meeting at Orléans, to the duc d'Orléans's part in the French Revolution, to the Orléans party's involvement in the 1830 upheavals, a sustained interest in writing French history kept the d'Orléans name and its bearers in public discussion.

53. Vincent Chalvet, ed., *Poésies de Charles d'Orléans, père de Louis XII et oncle de François Ier, rois de France* (Grenoble: Giroud, 1803); Champollion-Figeac, ed., *Poésies du duc Charles d'Orléans;* J-Marie Guichard, ed., *Poésies de Charles d'Orléans . . .* (Paris: Gosselin, 1842); and Charles d'Héricault, ed., *Poésies complètes de Charles d'Orléans. . . ,* 2 vols. (Paris, 1874, rpt. Paris: Gosselin, 1896).

54. See Nelson, *Charles d'Orléans,* 19–20, for citations of and a note on these disputes, which concerned critical standards, fame, and one-upmanship. Most everyone praises Charles's lineage and poetry; Constant Beaufils, *Étude sur la vie et les poésies de Charles d'Orléans* (Paris 1861), is the exception.

tion foregrounds this interest in its very title: *Poésies de Charles d'Orléans, . . . père de Louis XII et oncle de François Ier, rois de France.* An important biography (Deschères's) and no fewer than twenty-four critical articles appear, most of which include a strong biographical slant.[55] Perhaps as an early manifestation of cults of personality, but certainly for historical reasons and because of the growing literary-history industry, Charles d'Orléans's place in the French canon was secure.

In the twentieth century in France this was no less true. With the explosion of literary studies came numerous editions, articles, anthologies, and selections treating Charles. One scholar, Pierre Champion, led French publications on Charles in the century. His 1923 edition of Charles's French poetry is still generally thought to be "definitive."[56] Champion studies the manuscripts, the handwriting, the metaphors, the life, the household documents, the rhyme schemes, and more, in at least a dozen articles, books, and monographs published between 1906 and 1927. The metacritical response to Champion's authoritative work has been steady and respectful, with few disputes.[57] But although Champion towers over the twentieth century's landscape of Charles-reception, two other points of editorial interest deserve mention. In 1944 in German-occupied France, one of Charles's poems found renewed political relevance with the samizdat wartime publication of his famous, patriotic "Complainte de France."[58] And in 1950 an astonishing lithograph edition of poems handwritten and illustrated by Henri Matisse appeared. Nelson notes that each

---

55. See Nelson, *Charles d'Orléans,* 17–26 for annotated citations; Théodore Deschères, "Charles d'Orléans," in *Le Plutarque français* (Paris: Crapelet, 1838), 2:1–12.

56. Not everyone agrees; Gerard Defaux writes at some length of the problems in Champion's addition of punctuation, for example; "Charles d'Orléans ou le poétique du secret: À propos du rondeau XXXIII de l'édition Champion," *Romania* 93 (1972): 194–243. I object to Champion's reordering of the main French manuscript and think we need a good critical facsimile of it; the Medieval and Renaissance Text Society promises a bilingual edition early in the twenty-first century, to be edited jointly by John Fox and Mary-Jo Arn. Arn is at this writing completing a study, "The Order of Composition in Charles d'Orléans's Personal Manuscript (BN f. fr. 25458)." But Champion's work is foundational, and like any Charles scholar I am greatly indebted to it.

57. Daniel Poirion, *Le Poète et le prince* (Paris: Presses Universitaires de France, 1965), in his chapter on Charles (271–310) and also 133–40, 348–60, 391–98, 422–26 passim, and Alice Planche, in her *Charles d'Orléans,* are two other important twentieth-century scholars in France, as is Gilbert Ouy, whose many works on primary materials place him with Champion as a central figure.

58. Paris: Sézille, 1944; La Haye: Stols, 1944. One hundred copies were "published secretly during German occupation," according to Nelson, *Charles d'Orléans,* 37. This poem's original contexts are treated in chapter 5 here.

of the 1,230 copies was signed by the artist.[59] Charles is so frequently anthologized and collected in France that it would be nearly impossible to list all the editions; the most recent collection I have found at the time of this writing is Mühlethaler's 1992 *Livre de Poche* edition of the *Ballades et Rondeaux*. Even this brief look at French reception history indicates that for political, biographical, and also aesthetic reasons, the poetry of Charles d'Orléans has always retained a secure place in the French canon.

Charles's Poetry in Literary Canons: Critical Reception in England

At first glance, the general patterns of reception across the centuries look fairly similar on both sides of the channel: a strong manuscript presence and anthology popularity into the sixteenth century, a period of decline in the seventeenth century, a literary-historical revival in the eighteenth, an antiquarian and biographical frenzy in the nineteenth, and the concomitant seizure of Charles d'Orléans as literary turf worth a battle or two. But any graph of such patterns would show the English lines to have been fainter and lesser. In England his poetry was never as well known as it was in France; critics and historians have been reluctant to award him the place in the English canon that this poetry would merit on its own, were the poet, say, anonymous. There are notable exceptions, of course, but the early English scholar-critics' selections, their comments about the poems and the poet, and even their arranging of critical material in various canon-building works help us understand better why England has not duly welcomed such a skillful, prolific poet, and further, may help us subtilize our current views of canon formation.

Critical Reception in England: Eighteenth Century

Eighteenth-century English criticism seems to have lagged a few decades behind that of the French. I can find no English critical mention of Charles d'Orléans before 1790, a full half-century after Sallier's 1740 *Mémoires;* Nelson's bibliography mentions none before 1823 (Yenal's, none before 1827). Poetic tastes had of course changed dramatically in both countries, but unlike France, England seems to have had no historical reasons to

---

59. *Poèmes de Charles d'Orléans, manuscrits et illustrés par Henri Matisse* (Paris: Tériade, 1950).

keep Charles d'Orléans in critical favor (and good historical reasons to dismiss him).

Yet at least four major eighteenth-century critics who are not noted in the bibliographies on Charles d'Orléans do discuss him: Joseph Ritson, George Ellis, Horace Walpole, and Thomas Park.[60] All four discuss to varying degrees the unusual problems of reception that Charles d'Orléans poses: the problem of his nationality, the problem of viewing his historical era, the problem of his bilingualism (or the fact that we have both French and English poems), and the problem of his royal lineage. A web of critical-editorial problems thus forms itself across the cruxes of Charles's dual (national) and liminal (literary period) status.

First, his lineage makes him both a leader of the evil empire of France and a borderline English royal: the Other is Us. Next, he wrote both French and English poems, and critics sometimes reconfigure the nationality-lineage problem as a language issue. Like Charles's dual-status lineage, the poems' existence in two languages irritates the critical organ that wants to create neat categories (an active organ in any age but perhaps especially important to the eighteenth century). And his era itself was foreign to the sensibilities of the eighteenth century, although one early critic, as we shall see, does in fact try to account for what Barbara Herrnstein Smith calls "contingencies of value."[61] Furthermore, the few eighteenth-century critics who approach Charles as an English poet do so "pre-Roxburghe," that is, with no printed edition and with extremely limited access to manuscripts. To be included in the formative eighteenth-century canon, then, involved more than just writing poetry, even a great deal of very accomplished poetry, in English. Ritson, Ellis, Walpole, and Park respond to the problems of language, nation, and history differently (but generally without the additional barrier of periodicity between "medieval" and "Renaissance" literature that the post-Burckhardtians would erect).

Joseph Ritson is the one among these critics who does not take his initial cue regarding Charles from contemporaneous French criticism. Ritson goes straight to Charles's English-only manuscript, Harley 682, and perhaps for that reason has less trouble dealing with Charles's Frenchness than with his antiquity. Ritson attempts a literary historian's usual schol-

---

60. I place Park in the eighteenth century despite his early-nineteenth-century date, because he edits Walpole, is pre-Roxburghe, and represents, I believe, a latest-eighteenth-century moment or even a turning point of sorts between the critical sensibilities of the two centuries.

61. *Contingencies of Value* (Cambridge: Harvard University Press, 1988).

arly interventions: he lists manuscripts, divides texts by dates, adds punctuation, and so on, but he also evaluates. In 1790, he prints "Lende me yowre praty mouth madame" straight from Harley 682, with commentary. Like any critical judgment, Ritson's commentary necessarily reflects his own century's poetic preferences:

> Among the Harleian manuscripts in the British Museum (no. 682) is a collection of love poems, roundels, and songs, made by Charles duke of Orleans while a prisoner in England, in Henry the fifths time. It is not to be expected that the poetry of a foreigner (and a prince of the blood too) should have much merit in an age in which that of the natives had so little.[62]

His main quibble is with fifteenth-century English poetry's lack of native merit. Charles is seen, worse for him, as representative of his devalued era; Ritson excuses Charles's foreigner status by our native poetry's (de)fault. Unlike the earliest critics across the channel, Goujet and Sallier, Ritson gives little or no weight to Charles's lineage, placing his discussion of Charles in the prefatory section of the *Ancient Songs and Ballads* in order to illustrate "the progress of Song-writing during the fifteenth century."[63] He thus transmits the connection with music Charles's poems have always enjoyed.[64] Although Ritson did not deem Charles an English poet worthy of inclusion in his 1793 *English Anthology*,[65] his *Ancient Songs and Ballads*, with its prefatory remarks including Charles, came out in at least three subsequent editions—1792, 1829, and 1877—this last with W. Carew Hazlitt as editor. Hazlitt adds a note (xlvii) citing the 1827 Roxburghe Club edition of Harley 682, but otherwise lets stand Ritson's implied judgment of Charles as a typically weak ancient songster and Ritson's exclusion of Charles from the English literary lists.

---

62. *Ancient Songs and Ballads from the Time of King Henry the Third to the Revolution* (London, 1790; 1792; 1829; ed. W. Carew Hazlitt, London: Reeves and Turner, 1877). This quote is attributed by George Ellis, *Specimens of the Early English Poets,* 3d ed. (London: G. and W. Nicol, 1803) to Ritson's 1792 ed., lxvii. I have not seen the 1792 ed., nor the editions of 1790 and 1829; I found Ritson's discussion of Charles in Hazlitt's 1877 edition, lviii–lix.
  63. 1877 ed., lvii–lviii.
  64. Charles's verse in both languages seems to exemplify Eustache Deschamps's 1412 dictum that poetry should be "musique naturele" and "paroules metrifiez"; five centuries later, musical settings of Charles's poetry abound. For a concise review and further references, see Jean-Claude Mühlethaler, ed., *Charles d'Orléans: Ballades et Rondeaux* (Paris: Livre de Poche, 1992), 21–22.
  65. London: C. Clarke.

Ritson's contemporary, George Ellis, on the other hand, reveals a concern for larger issues of literary change. Ellis seems aware of the index of difference in which his own opinions inscribe themselves and actually includes Charles's poetry in his narrative of changing literary value. In fact Ellis himself undergoes a change of heart regarding Charles between his initial 1790 publication of *Specimens of the Early English Poets*[66] and its 1803 reappearance, in which he adds specific discussion of our poet. In the edition of 1790, Ellis takes a longer view and tries to explain opinions like Ritson's in terms of style, method, and even typography:

> The regularity and harmony of style, and the minute attention to the artifice of composition which were introduced by the authors of Queen Anne's reign, produced in the public such a delicacy and even fastidiousness of taste, as could not be gratified by the irregular compositions of our early poets, who therefore soon fell into disrepute, and were in a little time consigned to oblivion. The disuse of the black letter contributed, perhaps, to this revolution in taste. (iii)

Ellis has both seen through the "institutions of evaluative authority"[67] and is one himself. Unlike Ritson, Ellis views Charles's era not as a problem but as an explainable phenomenon. He goes on to say that rare remaining copies of such "irregular compositions" are now in private cabinets, "secure . . . but inaccessible" (iii), anticipating by two hundred years the rare-book librarian's dilemma and the editorial critic's power to bring poems to public notice (or not). Ellis wants to understand why "our early poets" are ignored and is at least willing to discuss the possibility that the eye of the beholder and the material facts of possession, printing, and use can contribute to perceived literary value. Furthermore, the phrase "our early poets" does not yet distinguish between medieval and Renaissance poets; the canon-builders may have poured as their foundations the barriers of language and of nationalism, but they had not yet seen the plans for the post-Burckhardtian wall of periodization. Ellis also tries to redress what he considers Samuel Johnson's misuse (in slighting ancient writers) of a critic's canonizing power.

---

66. Ellis's first edition of *Specimens of the Early English Poets* (London: Edwards, Pall Mall, 1790), contains no discussion of Charles, but the 1803 (3d) edition does, on pp. 311–13, as does the (2d) edition of 1801, 1:308–9. The presentation copy of the 1801 edition that Ellis gave to Thomas Park, another critic who prints and discusses Charles's poetry, is discussed in greater detail below.

67. Barbara Herrnstein Smith's term (*Contingencies of Value,* 40).

> It has been lamented by many lovers of poetry, that, when a general and uniform edition of our poets was published under the auspices of Dr. Johnson, no effort was made in favor of these antiquated writers. It should seem, that the director of that literary apotheosis might have recommended to public notice the works of Surrey, Wyat, Raleigh, and the several contributors to our earlier miscellanies, as justly and as successfully as those of Blackmore, Sprat, and Yalden. (ii–iii)

Inclusive Ellis in 1790 laments Johnson's canon's exclusion of poets we make central today; by 1803 Ellis has done what much of our current canon-expanding theory tries to do—perceive the unexamined lenses of taste through which we read and the unexamined assumptions about language and nation by which we shape our canon—and he extends his inclusive impulse back in time and across the channel to Charles d'Orléans.

Ellis's second and third editions of *Specimens* devote several pages to Charles and print three English poems, "Go forth myn hert," "My hertly love," and "Ne ware my trewe and innocent hert." He links the poems critically not to music, as Ritson had done, but to the prison-poems of James I of Scotland.[68] The nationalized purity of the English canon was evidently not as much an issue for Ellis as were the historical circumstances of poetic composition. On the other hand there is a certain subliminal nationalism implied here: to stress the imprisonment is perhaps to stress English power over the composition of the poems rather than the non-Englishness of the poets. The choice of poems printed here would also reinforce an emphasis on English national power over these foreign-engendered texts, since they appear in BL ms. Royal F 16.ii, the luxurious vellum manuscript given in 1501 to Prince Arthur and retained in the Tudor dynastic library at Richmond.

Subliminal English nationalism may lurk beneath Ellis's very odd treatment of the language issue as well. Charles's English poetry, says Ellis, is "proof that our language had at this time acquired some estimation in the eyes of foreigners" (313). That is an unusual claim; in the eyes of one foreign prince, a bilingual poet with a penchant for macaronic and experimental verse, imprisoned in England and thus surrounded by everyday English, perhaps so. But while English was becoming a more widespread and standard language in fifteenth-century England, French was still the

---

68. *Specimens*, 3d. ed., 311–12. Critics of the English poems still do this: see Diane Marks, "Poems from Prison: James I of Scotland and Charles of Orleans," *Fifteenth Century Studies* 15 (1989): 245–58.

higher-status language, probably second only to Latin in terms of pan-European prestige. Yet we know that the fifteenth century was a great cauldron of linguistic change. It would be useful to document how much and what kinds of poetry foreigners wrote in English during this period; without such a record, Charles's poetry, given its unusual genesis, does not seem to me sufficient grounds for Ellis's claim of an international esteem for English in the fifteenth century. However, Ellis's interpretation shows to what lengths one can go when trying to place translated or foreign-born works in a canon.

Other than Ellis's, the most important (and amusing) eighteenth-century critical mention of Charles d'Orléans I can find shows a much more open concern for the English nation and language, but also shows, from early to later editions, a substantive progress of opinion toward inclusiveness. Horace Walpole's 1759 edition of *Catalogue of Royal and Noble Authors of England* does not include Charles d'Orléans, nor does the edition of 1796.[69] Charles does, however, gain backdoor admittance to Walpole's *Works* in 1798 in an appendix to the section that reprints the *Catalogue of Royal and Noble Authors*.[70] Walpole calls Charles "a little eccentric addition" to his appendix of aristocrats, says he is "a curiosity" and a "long-neglected prince," but then claims to include him "on the merit of [his] poetry" (562). Walpole reveals his French connection when he points out Keralio's printings of some English poems in her *Meilleurs Ouvrages* (1787), and lifts two of them, with prose back-translations into French, straight from Keralio's text. Protestant, Whiggish Walpole would seem to have had strong political reasons to disdain the poems of Catholic, royal Charles d'Orléans. In fact Walpole does fret that "the Prince in question, I confess, was not of English blood royal; yet as he paid us the singular compliment of attempting to versify in our language, such a *pursuivant* [*sic*] of poetic royal personages as I am, feels a sort of duty to enroll him in the college of arms of our mount Parnassus" (562). Walpole's dutiful struggles to balance the competing claims of lineage and nationalism, poetry and language, do not abate. Walpole calls Charles the "first purifier of French poetry" (562) but as for English, "if the duke of Orleans

---

69. I have not seen a first (1758) edition, nor editions between 1759 and 1796. Discussion of Charles does not appear in a 1759 (2d) edition (London: R. and J. Dodsley and J. Graham) nor in the Edinburgh 1796 edition. But other, earlier editions may also include discussion of Charles, for Walpole's postscript on p. 1:567 of the *Works* (cited below) states that he wrote this "little addition" to his book before 1789.

70. *The Works of Horatio Walpole, Earl of Orford,* 5 vols. (London: G. G. and J. Robinson and J. Edwards, 1798), 1:562–67.

improved the poetry of his own country, he certainly contributed no graces to ours" (564). Furthermore, bilingualism is a character issue for Walpole: "nor was Charles so far exasperated by involuntary confinement among us, as to disdain to cultivate the language of his jailors—a symptom itself of liberal and noble sentiments" (563). Writing in two languages proves Charles's personal virtue, not a growing foreign esteem for the English language (as Ellis had said).

Walpole, hardly a francophile, cannot resist this: "It grieves me a little to mention, that the fair editor [Keralio] is of opinion that the duke's English poetry is not inferior to his French, which does not inspire a very advantageous opinion of the latter—though indeed such is the poverty and want of harmony of the French tongue, that one knows how very meagre thousands of couplets are that pass for poetry in France" (566). He goes on to note "the unmusical nature of their language" (not an opinion one often hears), to denounce French poetry ("as errant prose as ever walked abroad without stepping in cadence"), and to veer off into a discussion of current French drama (566). But his penchant for biography overtakes even his francophobia in a long, fairly sympathetic though inaccurate historical narrative about Charles's family (563–64). All this appears without any Ellis-like acknowledgment of changing literary tastes. Walpole's conflicted views remain in check until the very end of the passage, when the thought of the recent French Revolution sparks this outburst:

> N.B. This addition was written before the revolution in France in 1789; since when the follies of that nation have soured and plunged into the most execrable barbarity, immorality, injustice, usurpation, and tyranny; have rejected God himself and deified human monsters, and have dared to call this mass of unheard of crimes "giving liberty to mankind"—by atheism and massacres![71]

Walpole suddenly wants to disavow any French taint an inclusion of Charles d'Orléans (however reluctant the praise, however marginally placed) may have given his book. English goodness was so important to Walpole that it is remarkable Charles is in the *Works* at all.

Amazingly enough, considering Walpole's anti-French retraction, Charles's odd, liminal position is fully elevated—given English-royal status—in Sir Thomas Park's 1803 revised edition of the *Works*.[72] (Fully ele-

---

71. Again, note the date problem: he says the material on Charles was written before 1789 but still continues to include it as late as the edition of 1798.

72. (London: John Scott, 1803, 1806), 1:174–78.

vated, but never fully centralized.) Park is an audacious editor who takes great liberties with Walpole's *Works* and whose strong aristocratic and aesthetic preferences conquer most traces of the nationalist impulse. Park moves Charles from the appendix to the first and most important section of the book, "Royal Authors," which is a chronological series of critical essays about seventeen poetizing monarchs. This prime section boasts Richard II, Henry VIII, Elizabeth I, and others, yet at its very end, out of chronological order, just barely making it onto the list of royal English poets, is a discussion of Charles d'Orléans. It is true that Charles, whom Henry V called "cousin," belongs on an outer branch of the English royal family tree, but Park's inclusion of him in this particular list is a remarkable stretch that awards Charles and his poetry a status that he generally only enjoys in France. Poetry and lineage beat nationality and language here, even after the French Revolution. Park, in an editorial coup that itself indicates the critical differences between him and Walpole, pulls Charles d'Orléans across daunting canonical boundaries into the "Royal Authors" section of this influential volume.

Park also considerably expands Walpole's original material on Charles, as we shall soon see; but it is useful to note that he is an important link in this editorial and critical chain, or at least an important member of this English social and editorial circle circa 1800. Park and Ellis were in long correspondence about literary and editorial matters, and Park borrowed books, and perhaps opinions, from Ellis during the years leading up to his edition of Walpole's *Works*. Ellis in fact presented Park with a copy of his *Specimens of the Early English Poets;* this presentation copy is now held at the Folger Shakespeare Library, as is part of their correspondence.[73] In this book are leaves pasted in at Ellis's discussion of Charles. On these leaves, in Park's hand, are copied two of Charles's poems and a few critical notes. One of these notes in particular points obliquely to problems of period, nation, and value in the early modern canon, and, more directly, offers a glimpse of the thinking that informed a set of editorial decisions Park took between 1801 and his revision of Walpole's *Works* in 1803. The first fragment copies lines 2716–29 of Charles's English sequence, the com-

---

73. 2d ed. (London: G. and W. Nicol, 1801); Folger shelf numbers PR1205/E385/As. Col. Other editions—1790, 1803—are held at the University of Virginia's Alderman Library. Thanks to Laetitia Yeandle of the Folger and to the librarians at Alderman's Rare Book Room for their generous help. Professor Yeandle points out that "Park gave the three-volume work to John Bliss . . . it has two different bookplates of William Henry Bliss (1835–1909). In 1871 it belonged to [Sir] J[ohn] D[uke] Coleridge, soon to become Baron Coleridge" (private correspondence, January 1997). The handwritten notes are at 1:308–9, with Ellis's discussion of Charles.

plicated opening stanza of the legal "request" section that helps frame the lyric sequence.[74] The second fragment copies lines 5876–91, stanzas 2 and 3 of Ballade 100. Park's choice of these two fragments and his brief, even cryptic comments reveal his early notice of some of the critical issues to which few editors have attended but which are key to positioning this work in a canon. Park's note above the first fragment reads "ascertains the *author*" (emphasis Park's) and the second links the elaborately rhetorical stanzas to George Puttenham, English Renaissance literary critic. Park thus engages with two problems of canonicity—authorship attribution and periodization—as he is in the process of revising and augmenting Walpole's selections of the poetry, and in repositioning Charles in the English canon by physically repositioning him in the *Works*.[75]

About Park's expansion of Walpole's original material on Charles: Park's stated editorial intentions are consonant with nineteenth-century criticism's incipient moral, biographical, and aesthetic leanings. He explains that the new edition is intended "to accompany a series of portraits suitably engraven" of the royal and noble figures.[76] Park's inclusive spirit is like Ellis's, but with a shade more aestheticism and a shade less nationalism. Park has "added specimens of [Charles's] work," presumably to correct Walpole's negative judgments and his reliance on Keralio. The literary-critical slant of his 1803 edition is clear: Park adds both primary and secondary material to Walpole's essays. Some additions are scholarly; he cites the Ellis and Ritson printings and a reference to Charles in the Paston letters.[77] He also adds historical and biographical background and reminds us that "the duke of Orleans is still very imperfectly known to the public" (175), echoing Ellis's concern that the security of the manuscripts restricts their availability.

Park mentions two manuscripts, Royal F 16.ii and Harley 682, "which

---

74. In Arn's edition, *Fortunes Stabilnes,* 223–24 and 356–57; in Harley ms. 682, fols. 52v and 135r respectively.

75. For full discussion of these notes and their implications, see my "Charles d'Orléans and Thomas Park's Copy of the *Specimens of the Early English Poets.*" *Notes and Queries,* n.s. 44 (December 1997): 465–69.

76. *Works,* v; the portrait is after p. 174. I have been unable to establish the source of this portrait of a youthful, ermine-clad Charles. Engraved just below it are words hard to read but resembling "Gerimia se" or "Genimia je." Another of Park's major editorial interventions is irrelevant to Charles except that it indicates Park's spirit of inclusiveness: he has mixed "Peers" with "Peeresses" in one gender-neutral section, he says, because "this seemed to promise a more agreeable diversity in the lives and in the portraits" (vii).

77. *Works,* 174–75, citing a letter from Robert Repps to John Paston; see *Paston Letters and Papers of the Fifteenth Century* (Oxford: Clarendon, 1971), 1:4.

contains a copious mass of love poems, composed in the language acquired from England, but in measures more suitable to the poesy of France" (175). This is some distance from Walpole's "attempted to versify in our language" and "added no graces to [our language]," but nevertheless indicates that Park, despite his placement of Charles with the royal authors, still thinks of the work as distinct from the rest of the English canon. The comment is metrically inaccurate, of course: Charles writes the French ballades in *octosyllabes* and *décasyllabes,* the English ones mostly in pentameters. A pentameter is not a *décasyllabe,* which is one of the things reading these French and English poems together illustrates very well. Even if such a metrically inaccurate comment were impressionistically acceptable, it would simply mark another segment on the index of critical difference. Park, in the dawning age of Wordsworthian blank verse and Tennysonian tetrameter, perceived the Middle English ballades as more French than English in character. Not until pre-Raphaelite appropriations of French medievalism would the English canon be comfortable absorbing such verse; Park in 1803 was still in the earlier phase, metrically speaking, though his thematic work with Charles looks ahead to critics like Coleridge.

Park offers the opening of Charles's English sequence, lines 1–8 (p. 176), plus two other poems under titles I have not seen them given elsewhere.[78] These are not what twentieth-century critics might think of as the best of Charles's work; maybe the selection, based on Park's romanticizing early-nineteenth-century imagination, is part of the reason we in our century have discounted Charles—what tasted sweet now seems saccharine, what felt sublime now seems ridiculous (as Ellis might have thought). If we only get to read Park's sort of selections, we never see, and thus may never know to seek, the poetry's full range, which is of course the insoluble problem of any canonical set or selection. Park's selections show a side of Charles's work distinct from what Walpole showed: here we have not the princely lover but the singer of reverdies, of a Cupid-letter, of the simplest dimeter couplets imaginable. The selections indicate the values in Charles's work that Park perceived and chose to transmit, and by extension, the values in fifteenth-century poetry more generally perceived and transmitted. Early-nineteenth-century perceptions of "quaint" medieval literature were all about spring songs, simple lyrics, patent letters to

---

78. "To longe, for shame, and all to longe trewely," Ballade 48, under the title "On May Morning;" and "When that ye goo," Steele and Day, eds., *English Poems,* ll. 4505–20, under the title "The Lover's Lament."

Cupid. What Gaston Paris dubbed "courtly" poetry, what Rossetti and Morris would revive at midcentury, is anticipated in this canon-building edition. Limited in this way, the nostalgic selections seem a little patronizing, given that Harley 682 contains (from our contemporary view at least) some really splendid and complex poems. If Park wanted to print laments, why not display the rhetorical interest of Ballade 60, the wistful, understated resonance of Ballade 31, or the emotional power of Ballade 59? Why not the genre-play evident in antireverdies like Ballades 17 and 53? Why not the unusual depiction of Fortune (ll. 4964–5050)? Park's selections evidence the sensibility that shaped and reflected nineteenth-century thinking about medieval culture and may have understandably led twentieth-century readers who preferred more strength, complexity, and wit in their poetry to dismiss Charles before reading further.

Park also wrote, and cites in the 1803 edition of the *Works,* an idealizing sonnet in which Charles figures prominently.

Sonnet XIX. Written near a ruinous Mansion at Groombridge, where Charles Duke of Orleans was many years a Prisoner of War.

Heroic chiefs of this once-boasted hall,
   If e'er your spectred forms at midnight float
   O'er the fall'n battlement or half-sill'd moat,
   Like dubious vapors near some charnel wall
Which the belated way-farer appal;—
   Mourn ye those antique times of proud approof,
   When captur'd banners wave'd beneath your roof,
   To taunt the royal Troubadour of Gaul?
Yet, let your modern sons revere the day,
   Howe'er in some degenerate changes sunk
   When hostile arms to civil arts gave way.
And moats to rills, and towers to hovels shrunk:
   While the fierce clarion to the sheep-bell yields,
   And tented moors to cultivated fields.[79]

The sonnet marks fallenness, diminution, a georgic domestication of the heroic. It makes Charles the object of his implied romanticizing *ubi sunt.*

---

79. The note indicates that the poem was printed 1797 for G. Sael, London. Charles was not at Groombridge, although the Orléans arms appear over the door. His brother Jean may have been a prisoner there briefly; see Steele and Day, eds., *English Poems,* xiii n. 1. Facts aside, the "Troubadour of Gaul" merited a sonnet.

Its gothic landscape captures the imaginative medievalism that would characterize Park's century. Although Park gets some of the historical facts wrong (Charles's birthdate and his presence at Groombridge), is not strict about literary-historical definitions (Charles was born some centuries too late to have been a troubadour), and seems nearly cloyingly nostalgic, his sonnet and his expanded essay on Charles, not to mention his placing Charles with the English royal authors, are remarkably imaginative and sympathetic (if inherently distorting) responses that make their way into a prominent critical vehicle, Walpole's 1803 *Works.*

These English canon-founders—Ritson, Ellis, Walpole, and Park—did worry at the critical problems of nationality, lineage, language, and historicity such a dual-status poet presents, but none was fully able to clarify Charles's and his translated poetry's status and position in the young canon.

Critical Reception in England: Nineteenth Century and After

By the 1820s, just as in France, editions sprang up and critical discussion ensued. Yet Dr. Johnson's silence echoes long, it seems, for Charles d'Orléans does not appear in the main antiquarian repositories: not in Percy's *Reliques,* not in Cibber's *Lives,* not in Palgrave. Although Charles is included in several nineteenth-century literary lists,[80] critical interest tilts during this period toward the question of the English poems' authorship— which in this case is really also a question about language and nationality. This deflection of interest away from the poems themselves, paradoxically enough, begins almost immediately after the appearance of the first printed edition of the complete English poems.

In 1827 George Watson Taylor edited for the Roxburghe Club the *Poems Written in English by Charles, Duke of Orleans during his captivity in England after the battle of Azincourt.*[81] In the introduction, Watson Tay-

---

80. Thomas Warton's *History of English Poetry from the Twelfth to the close of the Sixteenth Century,* ed. W. Carew Hazlitt, 4 vols. (1871; rpt. Hildesheim: Georg Olms Verlagsbuchhandlung, 1968) does include the English poetry of Charles, duke of Orleans at 1440 in a chronological list of early manuscripts, and notes the Roxburghe Club printing of them (1:32). W. J. Courthope's *History of English Poetry* (3 vols., T. Tegg, 1840; 6 vols., London: Macmillan, 1895–1910), places Charles in a table of English and European authors under, and only under, France. Courthope also calls Hoccleve "the only other considerable English poet in the first half of the fifteenth century" (1:133)—other than Lydgate, he means.

81. London: Nicol, 1827. Note the perhaps deliberately inclusive orthography. It is always *d'Orléans* in France, of course, but some editors and critics in England partially or fully anglicize the name, to *Charles of Orléans* or *Charles of Orleans.* My own effort to recover Charles for the English canon is reflected in this book's title, but in his French contexts I sill call him "Charles d'Orléans."

lor begins by mentioning Charles's lineage and history (i–iii) and declares that "the English version has all the spirit of originality, and evinces a masterly knowledge of that language, which would do credit to the native writers cotemporary [sic] with [Charles] . . . the merit of many other passages will not escape notice, such as these [quotes Ballade 9 and parts of Ballade 21, Ballade 17, and fragments of others]" (iv–vii). Almost immediately, in the *Retrospective Review,* Thomas Croft denies that the translated English poems are by Charles at all, although he concedes that some of the roundels without French analogues may be by Charles.[82] The critical dispute in England, unlike that simmering among his editors in France at the time, focused on vehement assertions and denials of Charles's authorship of the English poems. The English-authorship disputes went more or less unchecked until John Fox's arguments in "Charles d'Orléans, poète anglais?" and even until 1993 with Mary-Jo Arn's convincing review of evidence in *English Studies.*[83] The long discussion of this point and related matters—whether or not there was a mysterious English translator, which poems came first, and so on—has gnarled critical responses to Charles d'Orléans since the nineteenth century. In an age of "unprecedented literary interlingualism," as Barzun calls the nineteenth century, there is a strangely persistent desire on both sides of the channel to keep the poet as French-only, or at least, to deny that the poetry belongs or could belong to both canons. Literary nationalism is, in this case at least, a powerful force for marginalizing bicultural texts.

---

82. *The Retrospective Review, and Historical and Antiquarian Magazine* (London), 2d ser., 1 (1827): 147–56. He also accuses the publisher of "literary avarice" for printing so few copies (see Nelson, *Charles d'Orléans,* 18). In France Aimé Champollion-Figeac takes it for granted that Charles wrote the English poems, but treats it as a minor endnote point: "Leur vrai mérite pour nous est d'être en anglais du XVème siècle, et de donner la preuve que ce prince étudia cette langue pendant sa prison" (*Poésies du duc Charles d'Orléans,* 444–45n). One French critic, Francisque Michel, in a literary dog-in-manger act, does assert (without support) that the English poems were done not by Charles but by an anonymous contemporary. *Rapports à M. le Ministre de l'instruction publique sur les anciens monuments de l'histoire et de la littérature de la France qui se trouvent dans les bibliothèques de l'Angleterre et de l'Écosse* (Paris: Comité Historique des Arts et Monuments, 1838), 267–78. The Germans tend to hold similar opinions: Georg Bullrich in *Über Charles d'Orléans und die ihm zugeschriebene englische Übersetzung seiner Gedichte* (Berlin, 1893), and Paul Sauerstein, *Charles d'Orléans und die englische Übersetzung seiner Dichtungen* (Halle, 1899), echo Michel. One later scholar posited as mysterious "translator" Charles's friend Suffolk: Henry MacCracken, "An English Friend of Charles of Orleans," *PMLA* 26 (1911): 142–80. See Yenal, *Charles d'Orléans,* 32–37.

83. Fox, *Romania* 86 (1865): 433–62; Arn, "Charles of Orleans." William Calin took up the question again in "Will the Real Charles," but Arn's evidence and her edition of 1995 will likely have finished this dispute.

Nationalism is not the only force at work here, of course. One influential nineteenth-century critic's pronouncement moves beyond the English-authorship dispute into a discussion of poetic values, and it goes badly for Charles. Robert Louis Stevenson's response to Charles in *Familiar Studies of Men and Books* shows the particular qualities his age sought in vain in Charles's poetry.[84] Stevenson's long essay, the second longest of his book, doubts that Charles wrote the English poems (249 n. 1) yet devotes much space to his curious defects as an English poet. The essay may help explain why, beyond Charles's Frenchness, an antiquarian age chose not to embrace these antique poems. The poems derive, complains Stevenson, "from the very idleness of the man's mind and not from intensity of feeling" (270); Charles is not Shelley, in other words. The poems are "autobiographical," but they are "uneventful" (270), and they so lack "definite experience" that we do not even know who the woman is (271)—not Tennyson's *Maud,* Rossetti's Lizzie Siddal, or even Wordsworth's Lucy—nothing here, that is, to satisfy the biographical demands of Stevenson's Romantic-Victorian imagination. Nor will Charles's work feed a nineteenth-century hunger for truth or edificatory opinion. "Great writers," notes Stevenson,

> are struck with something in nature or society, with which they become pregnant and longing; they are possessed with an idea, and cannot be at peace until they have put it outside of them. . . . But instead of communicating Truth, [Charles] observes the laws of a game. (270)

And "these forms [ballades and roundels] are suitable rather for those who wish to make verses, than for those who wish to express opinions" (246–47). In bourgeois Stevenson we also find a certain resentful classism. Charles "was born a great vassal but conducted himself like a private gentleman" (268), and "his birth . . . was above his merit" (230). Stevenson's thinly veiled antiaristocratic prejudices[85] blend with an unwillingness to take the poetry on its own terms, outside the evaluative criteria of Stevenson's literary moment. Stevenson is no self-aware, open-minded Ellis.

Where eighteenth-century critics discussed the problems of Charles's language and nationalism, nineteenth-century critics solved both problems by tightening the canonical boundaries. Part of their continuing

---

84. Of which there are a dozen or more editions; I cite here *Familiar Studies of Men and Books* (New York: Dodd, Mead, 1887), 229–74.

85. Evident also on pp. 232–34, 248, 251–52, 265–66, 268.

reluctance to admit Charles's work to the English canon seems to have been related to an equal reluctance to think of translators as poets or to think of poetic translation as poetry. It should be no surprise that this belief about the relation between source and translated poem—really a belief about poetic originality—is asserted in the early nineteenth century, the age of Romantic poetry in which spontaneity, emotion, and an individual's responses to sublime nature were prized. Romantic standards for poetic originality attach themselves, in Charles's case, to English nationalism: since the poems are "only" translations, not original in the Coleridgean sense, and maybe not even written by the prince in question, who was French anyway, nineteenth-century critics could justifiably exclude them. Add Burckhardt's foundational definitions of "Renaissance," influential "medievalist" notions about the courtly and the chivalrous from writers like Gaston Paris, and the sum is an end-of-century periodization that places Charles d'Orléans as a medieval poet because of his birthdate; a nationalism that places him as a French poet because of his birthplace; and a literary aesthetic and theory that dismiss even self-translations as nonoriginal poems. Three strikes, and Charles is out of the English canon. This trebly liminal figure fared badly, falling outside the threshold on each count, despite the increased attention he received after coming into print in 1827. It is a measure of the nineteenth century's enduring influence on today's literary canons (as if we needed more evidence of it) that each of these positions—that Charles is a medieval poet only, a French-only poet, that he did not write the English poems, that there was a mysterious translator, that for whatever reasons his 6,531 lines of English poetry are not fully part of our canon—still is sometimes assumed, and each still had occasional adherents in twentieth-century criticism.[86]

In the twentieth century, most leaders in the movement to reconsider the English poems were medievalist editors, critics, and anthology-gatherers. Before Robert Steele and Mabel Day's landmark Early English Text Society edition of 1941–46, most critics, typified by Chambers and Hammond, relied on extensions of nineteenth-century approaches to this

---

86. Theo Stemmler, "Zur Verfasserfrage der Charles d'Orléans zugeschreibenen englischen Gedichte," *Anglia* 82 (1964): 458–73; Eleanor Prescott Hammond includes Charles in her list but also questions that English authorship (*English Verse between Chaucer and Surrey* [Durham, N.C.: Duke University Press, 1927]); Calin, "Will the Real Charles."

poetry.[87] Since Steele and Day there has been increasing tendency to consider Charles an English poet, a tendency evidenced in the criticism of Cecily Clark, John Fox, Diane Marks, A. C. Spearing, and Mary-Jo Arn, editor of the comprehensive critical edition of Harley 682. The Steele and Day edition did more to broaden English critical response to this corpus than did two hundred years of sporadic critical mentions, illustrating again that the real canon-shaping power, the long-term power, is in the hands of editors. One hopes that the considerable extensions of our knowledge about the poetry and poet in Arn's edition will have still further effects.

Also since Steele and Day, the poems have been somewhat more frequently anthologized, generally with qualifications. Selections are still few, considering the relatively large manuscript presence, and are not fully representative of the poetry's range. Davies, Stevick, and Robbins, typical of midcentury anthologizers, still keep Charles outside the center where Langland and Chaucer bide.[88] Burrow's Longman anthology is better proportioned: one lyric each by Lydgate and Hoccleve, five poems from the Sloane manuscript, five Chaucer lyrics, and four Charles lyrics, a sample much more closely in line with the relative numbers of surviving works (though a bit heavy on the Sloane).[89] Such a proportion evidently attempts to reflect the state of what we currently know about the poetry, forming itself less on how we currently regard the poet (less, in other words, like Walpole's or Stevenson's opinions or Park's sonnet). Epistemologically

---

87. Consider the remarks in E. K. Chambers and Frank Sidgwick, *Early English Lyrics* . . . (London: Sidgwick and Jackson, 1911; rpt. 1937), which anthologizes two poems (Ballade 67 and Roundel 174): "Modern scholars are disposed to regard the English poems . . . as being translations . . . made by a fifteenth century writer other than Charles himself" and cites Bullrich, Stevenson, and Champollion-Figeac, who, they say, "prints as his some English poems from sources other than Harley 682, *which may be genuine*" (emphasis added)—as if the BN f. fr. 25458 poems and Royal F 16.ii poems are not "genuine." They mean by that, I think, "genuinely by an English author," demanding a biographical certitude that may become less relevant in future criticism as a criterion for canon formation.

88. R. H. Robbins, *Secular Lyrics of the XIVth and XVth Centuries* (Oxford: Clarendon, 1952): five poems to which he adds silly titles and a long discussion of authorship in which a number of facts are wrong (282–83). Robert Stevick's *One Hundred Middle English Lyrics* (Indianapolis: Bobbs-Merrill, 1964), prints one poem and gets the dates wrong (120). R. T. Davies, *Medieval English Lyrics* (Evanston, Ill.: Northwestern University Press, 1964), prints four poems and equivocates on the authorship question (341). Arn's edition should improve future anthologizers' credibility.

89. *English Verse, 1300–1500* (London: Longman, 1977), 289–95. Ballade 6, Roundel 48, Roundel 57, and the ever-reprinted Ballade 97 ("O sely ankir").

speaking, such an anthology implies a canon formation that follows the material rather than the critical, attempting to ground itself in current bibliographical evidence rather than current fashion. Even Burrow, though, still hesitates: "the question of the authorship of the Harley poems has been much debated, and is still unresolved" (289). On the other hand he reads the poems as parallel texts: "the English poems generally derive from the French, but they are not translations. They are more varied in mood and style. . . . Echoes of Chaucer . . . and of Lydgate . . . alternate with slangy expressions . . . and violent outbursts" (289). But Charles's poems still are not on American readers' high-canon short-list: none appears in the sixth edition of *The Norton Anthology of English Literature,* despite the desperate paucity and poverty of fifteenth-century lyric there represented.[90] The 1999 *Longman Anthology of British Literature,* an anthology that makes one of its chief goals "a new literary geography" (xxix–xxx), expands the "British" to include Marie de France, for example, but does not contain a single poem by Charles of Orleans.[91]

It seems entirely understandable that the boundaries of our canon, and the epistemological basis for those boundaries, should change over time, especially where ambiguously bicultural texts like these are concerned. Perhaps such a corpus presents an ideal opportunity to a critical era that announces its desire to "globalize":[92] I for one am trying to use Charles and his curious reception history as a stimulus to a more globalized way of thinking of early modern poetics. Cross-cultural histories, (inter)nationalisms, changing poetic values, and the actions of editors and critics have affected the reception of Charles's poems in England and in France more, I would argue, than have the usual canon-forming categories of class, gender, and race. Editors, in conversation with one another across temporal and cultural distances, shape the availability and reception of literature more powerfully than most contemporary critics (especially those who are not themselves editors)[93] might grant. Particularly for manuscript material

---

90. M. H. Abrams, gen. ed. (New York: W. W. Norton, 1993).
91. David Damrosch, gen. ed. (New York: Addison Wesley Longman, 1999).
92. Witness the call for papers in late 1998 for a special issue of *PMLA* on the topic "globalizing literary study."
93. Bourdieu, for instance, sees canonical exclusions as class-based sociological phenomena, what he calls the "sense of distinction" (*Les Règles de l'art,* 142) and the social ability to generalize that sense of distinction to aesthetic works, recognizing them as legitimate or not. Guillory, *Cultural Capital,* reads for institutional factors; Deleuze and Guattari, *Kafka,* focus on the oppression and colonization of the Other. Each approach offers valid but limited explanations for the complexities of literary history.

and old or out-of-print books, editions are perhaps the prime locus of canon struggle. Other factors—fashions in genre and changing aesthetic sensibilities, accidents of friendship, editors' choices to modernize certain texts and not others, and probably even modern readers' difficulty with Middle English orthography—may have directed the long course of reception in this case. Charles is also a casualty of a strong post-Enlightenment drive to periodize our canons: as chapter 6 discusses in other terms, Charles's English poetry falls through the chasm that opens up in the nineteenth century between "medieval" and "Renaissance"; or rather, the critics and editors who discuss him do not agree about where to place him, so he remains unplaced, lost in translation, or either slotted less perfectly in the English canon as the medieval poet he more clearly is in French. This case, in other words, underscores a few additional factors in literary canon formation and reminds us, I hope, that such factors are inevitably multiple and interactive and fluctuating.

The most canonically marginalized part of Charles's work (his several hundred parallel Latin poems) is effectively invisible to modern readers. It is the side of his oeuvre that has most been lost, and, paradoxically, it is that for which, at the end of his life, he took the greatest care to translate so as to seek permanent fame. This work, found in Grenoble ms. 873, is treated in the following chapter.

5

Creating World Lyric: Translation, *Ordinatio,* and the Politics of Selection in Grenoble Ms. 873

After years of frustrating political negotiations and after tens of thousands of écus in ransom, Charles's twenty-five years in England came to an end. Upon arriving in Calais in 1440 he fell and kissed the ground, spoke to the duchess of Burgundy, who had helped arrange his release, returned to his home at Blois. But despite his middle age and whatever justifiable weariness he felt, he did not retire: he conducted literary *puys,* rebuilt his holdings, married Marie de Clèves, and had more children (one of whom would become Louis XII of France). He entertained the duke of Suffolk and other foreign visitors and remained fairly active in French politics and court life. Charles also traveled a good bit; relevant here are his trips to reestablish his claim to the province of Asti (a claim he inherited from his mother, Valentina Visconti). During this time he encountered Antonio Astesano, a professor of letters who had corresponded with Charles during his captivity. This relationship lasted until the end of Charles's life, it appears, and yielded another intriguing lyric sequence, a 159-folio book held in the Bibliothèque Municipale de Grenoble (Rés. U.1091). Grenoble manuscript 873, unedited since 1842 and only rarely discussed since then, is a large, illuminated vellum production that contains selections from Charles's French poetry, with Latin translations by Antonio Astesano in facing-column format.[1]

It will have become clear that Charles's considerable body of lyric poetry crosses boundaries of language, of nation, of literary tradition in its

---

1. The only editions of this manuscript are Champollion-Figeac, *Poésies du duc Charles d'Orléans;* and Chalvet, *Poésies de Charles d'Orléans.* BN f. fr. 9224 is a copy of it. On Astesano, Charles's secretary and translator, see Balzaretti, "Antonio Astesano traduttore," and the *Dizionario biografico degli italiani,* ed. A. Ghisalberto, vol. 4 (Rome: Istituto della Enciclopedia italiana, 1960–), s.v. "Astesano."

TABLE 1. General Contents of Grenoble Ms. 873

Section	Folios	Kinds of Material	General Theme, Subject(s), Comments
A	1r–9r	Latin verse and prose	Prefatory and dedicatory materials
I	9v–22r	French and Latin facing columns begin here; narrative verse; nine ballades, one per page	Introductory appeal to Cupid, *lettre de retenue,* and conventional love-lyric settings
II	22v–37v	Fr. and Lat.; fifty-seven short poems (chansons and rondeaux), two per page except the final poem	Brief expressions of the situations and problems of romantic love; no particular narrative chronology but with thematic subgroups
III	38r–52v	Fr. and Lat.; Complainte; twenty-seven ballades, generally one per page	Series about absence, presence, listening, and telling
IV	53r–67v	Fr. and Lat.; Complainte; twenty-two ballades, roughly one per page; eight chansons, two per page	Wishes, encounters, and actions of the lover and the lady
V	68r–82v	Fr. and Lat.; "death" ballade; fifteen ballades; two chansons; four ballades; twenty short poems (chansons and rondeaux)	An anti–*in morte* performance: poems after the death of the lady include those about chess playing, games, various diversions, and the taking of a new lady
VI	83r–97r	Fr. and Lat.; Songe en complainte; La requeste; Départie ballades 1–7; six ballades; ten short poems (chansons and rondeaux), two or three per page	Renunciation of love and departure from love's service
VII	97v–112v	Fr. and Lat.; Complainte de France; twenty ballades; four chansons; final ballade; three blank pages	Political section treating the morality of kingship, warfare, and empire; French-nationalism; includes correspondence (epistolary ballades) between Orleans and others
B	113r–134	Latin verse and prose	Epistolary and narrative; considerable historic interest here; references to current events and important personages

multiple copies in French and English. Clearly, too, the poetry appears in various selections and arrangements at a crucial period in the national and literary histories of England and France. In Grenoble ms. 873, Charles's last lyric book, his oeuvre also spans the gap between vernacular and Latinate traditions, or rather, tries to hedge its bets in both traditions. Table 1 briefly lists the manuscript's sections and their general contents, and the appendix is a description of the manuscript and its contents.[2]

These contents hold many potential fascinations for scholars of the period: the manuscript's provenance and material bibliography, its place in the history of facing-column translations, its place in neo-Latin literature, and the historical and topical interest of the Latin back matter and its associations with Charles VII of France and Joan of Arc. However, the modest focus of this chapter is on the significance of its *ordinatio,* in the senses of that term used by M. B. Parkes, Roberts Adams, George Keiser, and Shearle Furnish, among others.[3] Parkes, for example, shows how the twelfth- and thirteenth-century movements to reorganize and recompile texts selectively influenced the disposition and arrangements of secular and vernacular materials for nonacademic readers, and even affected liter-

---

2. Champollion-Figeac's edition, *Poésies du duc Charles d'Orléans,* includes a first-line index to the French poems only and adds poems from other manuscripts. He assumes that all poems not in Grenoble but in other manuscripts were written later and that Grenoble 873 was finished in 1453 because its last poem can be reasonably dated near that time. The material evidence for composition of any of these poems is sketchy, but Arn's detailed tracking of the various "campaigns of copying" in BN f. fr. 25458 ("Order of Composition") will likely revise Champollion-Figeac's (and Pierre Champion's) notions of how and in what order the poems were composed, as opposed to how they were arranged in that manuscript. Regardless of what is yet to be discovered about that manuscript, this one does not follow the order of poems in 25458 except locally, in clusters; rather, Grenoble 873 forms its sections from poems found in various quires of 25458, selecting and ordering them not by copying directly from the order that appears in the main manuscript. Champion, ed., *Poésies,* 1:xii–xv, describes some features of Grenoble 873; full codicological description and material analysis are outside the purview of this preliminary survey, although the appendix presents new observations.

3. Adams, "Langland's *Ordinatio,*" especially 51, 54, 55–57. Keiser, "*Ordinatio* in the Manuscripts of John Lydgate's *Lyf of Our Lady:* Its Value for the Reader, Its Challenge for the Modern Editor," in *Medieval Literature: Texts and Interpretation* (Binghamton, N.Y.: Medieval and Renaissance Text Society, 1991), 139–57; especially relevant here are pp. 141, 144, and the contemporary examples on pp. 141–46. Furnish, "The *Ordinatio* of Huntington Library MS HM 149: An East Anglian Manuscript of Nicholas Love's *Mirror,*" *Manuscripta* 34, no. 1 (1990): 50–65. On the history of the concept and meanings of *ordinatio* in scholastic and monastic traditions, see Parkes, "The Influence of the Concepts of *Ordinatio* and *Compilatio* on the Development of the Book," in *Medieval Learning and Literature,* ed. J. J. G. Alexander and M. T. Gibson (Oxford: Clarendon, 1976), 115–41.

ary forms.[4] Grenoble 873 would have been an instance, though admittedly a highly refined, literary, and subtle instance, perhaps even an extreme case, of what Parkes calls the "much greater sophistication in the production of books" after the fourteenth century (133). It is useful here to make distinctions among some various critical uses of the word *ordinatio:* it can translate the Greek idea of ταχις, with its martial as well as rhetorical connotations,[5] but differs from the sometimes nearly technical medieval notion of *ordinatio,* which as Keiser points out, can mean the overt announcement or tabulation of the parts of the book.[6] My use of the word *ordinatio* here differs also from a word sometimes interchanged with it, the more general and far-reaching notion of *ordo* or order that Jesse Gellrich has explained. Gellrich analyzes the divine *ordo* as "a structural principle of far-reaching potential" and the medieval book as a signifying manifestation of that principle;[7] here I use *ordinatio* to describe the text's disposition and arrangement, as distinguished from *ordo,* the higher (and non-Foucauldian) order of things. Charles's conception of the order of the book, at least in this manuscript, seems to have been less grandly theological or numerological, and not nearly as overt as medieval *accessus* or *tabulae auctoritates* would have provided. *Ordinatio* here seems closer to that architectural conception discussed by Vitruvius Pollio, a matter of how parts and wholes relate to one another: "Architectura constat ex ordinatione quae Graece 'taxis' dicitur, et ex dispositione. . . . Ordinatio est modica membrorum operis commoditas separatim universaque proportionis ad symmetriam comparatio" (I.ii.1–2).[8] Grenoble 873 more resembles a product of a Renaissance poet seeking architectural decorum, proportion, and coherence than a product of Gellrich's authors actualizing a theological principle or of Parkes's medieval compilers seeking to enumerate, organize, or cross-reference their contents.[9]

Furthermore, one ought not miss the significance of this translation as a poetic action that is fairly unusual in the fifteenth century. Before the

---

4. See especially pp. 120–21, 127, 130, 133.

5. As discussed in Aristotle, *Rhetoric* 1414a29 and 1366a2.

6. Including tabulae, accessus, marginal glosses and pointings, rubrics, and even incipits and explicits; see pp. 139–42.

7. *Idea of the Book in the Middle Ages* (Ithaca: Cornell University Press, 1985), 20.

8. Vitruvius, *De Architectura,* ed. and trans. Frank Granger (Cambridge, Mass.: Harvard University Press, 1995), 1:24–25.

9. On Renaissance habits of lyric order, see Doranne Fenoaltea and David Rubin, eds., *The Ladder of High Designs: Structure and Interpretation of the French Lyric Sequence* (Charlottesville: University Press of Virginia, 1991).

print age, writing one's collected secular "Lyric Works"—and especially selecting several hundred of one's secular poems and having them translated into Latin—must have seemed an unlikely and an unusually self-assertive poetic act.[10] As such, its aim at a Latinate audience surpasses even the extensive copying of the poems into French and English manuscripts. This French-Latin manuscript is designed to assure a worldwide and permanent readership; its implicit *exegi monumentum,* a seeking after posthumous fame by means of eternal poetry, is more typically a maneuver of classical and Renaissance writers. More writers before the sixteenth century seem to take as their implicit mottoes *contemptus mundi* or *omnia vanitas* rather than the *exegi monumentum* that would come to prominence during and after the sixteenth century. Charles, however, uses all means at his disposal to achieve a cosmopolitan and permanent fame for his secular lyrics: the Latin language alongside the French vernacular, a professional translator and a professional scribe to render it, a beautiful and expensive format featuring one or two poems per page, and elaborate illuminations placed so as to give hierarchy and a visual structure to the book more subtle than, say, a table or index apparatus.

More to the point than its extraordinarily fine production is its *ordinatio,* the particular selections and arrangement of the poems. The selections and arrangement of Grenoble 873 represent this poet's remarkable end-of-life effort not only to fix, preserve, and extend the reach of his lyric works, but to reshape the whole idea of a lyric book. That effort involves reconfiguring some of the most important contextual and signifying features of early modern lyric poetry, since Charles evidently selects and arranges the lyrics according to principles different from those that had governed the other manuscripts. For one thing, the vernacular copies of Charles's poetry have all the marks of a coterie process: personal names, several hands, poems by several authors, poems copied into spaces previously left, poems copied over a period of time, for example. Again, that does not mean that the vernacular copies are strictly private productions, for the copies are relatively widespread in Europe, as we have seen. These are quite sociable and socially grounded productions: a dozen or more

---

10. In the words of André Vernet, "Peu de poètes français ont eu les honneurs d'une traduction latine" ("Les Traductions latines d'oeuvres en langues vernaculaires au Moyen Âge," in *Traduction et Traducteurs au Moyen Âge* [Paris: Éditions du CNRS, 1989], 239). Amid scores of other medieval examples of serious vernacular material translated into Latin, the two poetic examples he finds are the *Codicille* of the Pseudo Jean de Meun (fourteenth century), and the poetry of Charles d'Orléans in the Grenoble manuscript.

poems in the autograph manuscript, BN f. fr. 25458, are part of a *liber amicorum,* in which the poems of guests and friends are included and in which the results of some of Charles's famous *puys* appear.[11] An interplay of public and private dimensions in early modern lyric books is common enough, even well into the Renaissance, as Arthur Marotti and others have demonstrated.[12] Grenoble 873, however, unlike Charles's other lyric books, bursts out of coterie mode, presenting these selected "sociable" and personal poems so as to direct the attention of an implied, distant-future readership away from the lyrics' immediate social contexts and toward long-term historical considerations (especially, as we shall see, in the final section of the manuscript). The *ordinatio* of the manuscript—its explicit selection and rearrangement—implicitly reshapes coterie poems into a lyric book that emphasizes political and historical retrospective. Gellrich reminds us to consider "the extent to which the idea of the Book in the middle ages consists not simply of a definitive content, but rather of specific ways of signifying, organizing, and remembering."[13] Grenoble 873 reveals, I believe, an identifiable shift in the poet's ways of signifying, organizing, and remembering—really, a shift in this lyric oeuvre's potential to operate well beyond its original courtly contexts and to act much like a printed *Selected Works* (a radically different and individuated yet public Idea of the Book). This book aims to be public "world lyric" for all time.

Charles's translator, Antonio Astesano, admits as much in the polished Latin verses with which he prefaces the book. First, amid the usual prefatory praises, he claims for the poetry a worldwide audience:

> . . . Aegre cum ferrem quod solum gallia tanti
> ingenii tantum nosceret esse ducem
> namque ut se totus terrarum noverit orbis
> exigit hoc mirum principis ingenium
>
> (Fol. 9v; ll. 30–33)

> [. . . since I was feeling vexed that only France knew that so great a prince has so great a talent. For surely this wonderful talent of the prince demands that the whole wide earth know it.][14]

---

11. For example the poems written by several of Charles's acquaintances that begin with the line, "je meurs de soif auprès de la fontaine."

12. Marotti, *Manuscript, Print.* See also May, "Manuscript Circulation."

13. *Idea of the Book,* 248.

14. Many thanks to Lia Rushton, who transcribed Astesano's preface from a difficult microfilm copy, and whose translation and interpretive knowledge guide my understanding of it.

He also positions Charles's lyrics in an illustrious line:

> Admiratus eram Nasonis saepe libellos:
> quos in Pontana scripserat exul humo;
> at tantum vatem mirari desino: quando
> carmina captivi principis ista lego;
> in versus igitur librum hunc transferre latinos
> institui.
>
> (ll. 19–24)

[Often I had admired Ovid's books of verse that he had written as an exile in Pontus. But I cease to marvel at so great a poet when I read those songs of the imprisoned prince. I have taken it upon myself, therefore, to translate this book into Latin verses.]

Astesano glances at a Horatian truism, suggesting that Charles's poems not only delight but instruct: "non solum flores liber ille jocosos: / Sed fructus etiam" [that book (seemed to me to have) not only amusing flowers but fruit as well] (9–10). Clearly one part of the work of this translation is to stress the serious side of Charles's love-lyric and to elevate the poetry from the status of *libellus* to *liber*. Astesano's verb *transferre* is significant: it means "to translate," of course, but it also reminds us that Astesano aligns his translation with the old paradigm of *translatio studii*.[15] In fact he overtly links his work here in lyric to the lofty aims of venerated classical translations of epic, philosophy, and historiography:

>   tantum grande michi reputo decus esse latina
> efficere istius gallica scripta ducis
> quantum illi qui de graecis fecere latinos
> libros quos magnus scripsit aristotiles
> quosve poetarum princeps cantavit homerus
> seu quos plutarci condidit ingenium
> seu reliquos quorum de graeco copia magna
> a multis quondam facta latina fuit . . .
>
> (ll. 40–47)

---

15. On Charles's rejection of the paradigm of *translatio studii* in his own vernacular translations, see chapter 2 above, or my "*Translatio,* Translation, and Charles d'Orléans's *Paroled* Poetics," *Exemplaria* 8, no. 1 (1996): 169–92.

[I reckon it to be for me as great an honor to execute in Latin the French writings of that prince as it was for (the translator) who made Latin books from the Greek books that the great Aristotle wrote or that the first of poets, Homer, sung, or that the genius of Plutarch produced or all the rest (of the Greek texts) of which a great abundance were once translated into Latin from the Greek by many men.]

In equating Charles's French lyrics with the Greek works of such venerable and venerated *auctores* as Homer, Aristotle, and Plutarch, Astesano elevates the former considerably above fifteenth-century generic norms for lyric book (the *liber amicorum;* the pleasant secular songs; the gathered flowers generally expected in a *libellus*). Astesano's preface makes it abundantly clear that by translating the poems into Latin, Charles's lyric book aims at a worldwide, public, and permanently elevated status.

Had the poems in Grenoble 873 been copied in order from the autograph manuscript, BN f. fr. 25458, or even from BL Harley 682, the main English manuscript, and then translated into Latin, one could proceed directly to editing it for publication; the chapter could end right here with a statement about the importance of Latin in early modern Europe as a preservative force, as a force for cultural continuity, global cohesiveness, and literary fame. These poems, however, are not all the same ones, nor are they in the same order, as the poems in Charles's other manuscripts. What we have here is not only an end-of-life effort to establish a permanent world-lyric oeuvre, though that is significant enough. The selection and arrangement of the poems carry further significance, for they indicate what final shape and emphasis the poet wanted his work to take.[16] This

---

16. Or at very least, what shape and emphasis he agreed with Astesano the work should take. Robert Adams points out that *ordinatio* in fourteenth- and fifteenth-century manuscripts is "likelier to derive from the publication process, with its aims of facilitating access to an author's work or suiting the tastes of an individual purchaser, than from the author himself" ("Langland's *Ordinatio*," 54) but also that "the general presumption that *ordinatio* derives from the publication process by no means excludes the possibility that some features of textual segmentation or display in a given work may come from the author himself" (55). In this case, since we know that Charles was intimately connected with the creation of the manuscript, we might assume a certain involvement or direction on Charles's part, or at least a different balance of authorial interest than might be the case in Adams's other examples (in some cases involving an author deceased at the time of manuscript production, or involving widely lateral transmission). Minnis's discussion of the several functions of *auctor, scriptor, translator,* and *compilator* (*Medieval Theory of Authorship*, 73–74, 94–95) is relevant here: Charles and Astesano probably did not divide authorial functions in any schematic way, Charles having handled his own manuscripts and translations as well as hiring out scribal

shape and emphasis alter our view of Charles's place in the history of early modern lyric, and show him privileging epideixis of place over the epideixis of person that more generally characterizes his work.[17]

In general, this shift of epideixis and the reshaping of the lyric book reveal themselves first in the work's politics of selection, and second, particularly, in the presentation and arrangement of the manuscript—its *ordinatio*. First, by "politics of selection" I mean the poet's tactfulness about or sensitivity to the political and personal concerns of audiences envisioned for the work—his politic sense—but I also mean the poet's emphasis on political content in the selection—his political sense. The selection of certain lyrics for inclusion in Grenoble 873, when compared with selections in Charles's other manuscripts, represents a decidedly patriotic, even a nationalistic revision of his oeuvre. His omission of certain poems in the English manuscript is politic; his placements of them here reveal his political positions. Second, furthermore, the larger arrangement of Grenoble 873 represents a rethinking of the lyric sequence as book. The order of this

---

work and having friends write poems in his books. It is unwise, as Minnis shows, to apply modern notions of authorial function and responsibility to medieval texts; in this case it is also impossible to do more than guess which textual actions were the particular decisions of Charles, of Antonio Astesano, or of his brother Nicholas Astesano, who is thought to have been the scribe of Grenoble 873. Whether Charles or Astesano originated the plan, selected and omitted particular poems, and arranged the poems, the work of the brothers Astesani would have been consonant with Charles's wishes. Antonio Astesano worked for more than a decade as Charles's secretary and administrative assistant, and they corresponded even when apart. Astesano, who was in 1435 known to be professor of "belles-lettres" at Asti (Champollion-Figeac, ed., *Poésies du duc Charles d'Orléans,* xxiii), had written verse to the captive Charles; Champollion-Figeac speculates that they corresponded circa 1435, met in 1449, and were in France together 1450–53 (xxiv). More research needs to be done on Astesano and on the relationship between Charles and Astesano; see Balzaretti, "Antonio Astesano traduttore"; L. A. Muratori, *Rerum Italicarum Scriptores* (Mediolani: Typographia societatis palatinae, 1738–42; rpt. Bologna: A. Forni, 1965), vol. 14. In speaking of the distinctions among producer-initiated, consumer-initiated, and author-initiated books in his introduction to the Griffiths and Pearsall collection, *Book Production and Publishing in Britain, 1375–1475,* Derek Pearsall makes the point that "France was perhaps more old-fashioned, in that here still it would more often be the great patrons who initiated production. . . . Here too, however, authors would often intitiate production" (Pearsall illustrates the point with Machaut and Christine de Pisan; 5–6 but 2–6 passim). I would say that in this case Charles is in the multiple position of being able to initiate this book as both its author and patron, in cooperation with Astesano who is both its author-translator of the Latin section and the brother of its physical producer, scribe Nicolas Astesano.

17. Thanks to an anonymous reader for pointing this out; for more on early modern lyric epideixis, see A. Leigh DeNeef, "Epideictic Rhetoric and the Renaissance Lyric," *Journal of Medieval and Renaissance Studies* 3 (1973): 203–31; Paula H. Payne, "The Poet Orator's Praise: Epideictic Discourse in Sidney's *Astrophel and Stella*," *Sidney Newsletter* 9, no. 1 (1988): 11–21; or Hardison, *The Enduring Monument.*

lyric book provides a set of responses to the experience of romantic love that are not the idealizing, spiritually transcendent ones Petrarch established in the *Rime*. Charles's ultimate answers are political, historical: his final "Lyric Works" answers the private concerns of individual experience so intensively explored in the English work with a retrospective turn toward public and political issues. In this sense the manuscript proposes an early modern alternative to spiritual or personally confessional Petrarchist sequences that nevertheless argues for the permanent value of secular lyric.

Visual Divisions, Introductory and Closural Procedures, and Lyric *Ordinatio*

Grenoble 873 has a more planned, architectural character than have the other main manuscripts of Charles's French and English poetry (BN f. fr. 25458 and BL Harley 682). Unlike the others, this manuscript features striking illuminations that mark different sections, and different levels of organization, in the book. The organization is based on literary principles, not physical ones: the book's physical construction reveals that the quires of poetry were most likely planned, ruled, copied, decorated, and bound as one literary project (see appendix for more details). The general contents of each section are summarized in table 1 and described briefly below. While all of the individual poems can be found in the French and/or English manuscripts, they are selected and reordered in this manuscript according to discernibly different principles. The *compilator* or *compilatores* took care to distribute the poems evenly into sections of thirty pages each (literary sections, that is, for the quires are in eights, and these literary sections are unrelated to the material divisions of quires). Great care has also been taken to divide these literary sections visually and, furthermore, to rearrange the poems within sections for clear introductory and closural impact. The new *ordinatio* also relies on thematic and formal groupings of poems within sections and showcases political themes in the final section.

The visual dividers between these literary sections are of two kinds. Full-border illuminations—borders crossing top, bottom, sides, and center of the page—separate the Latin front matter (section A) and back matter (section B) from the seven central sections containing the poetry itself (sections I–VII). These full-border illuminations appear on folios 9r, 9v, and 113r. Figure 2, an image of folio 113r, exemplifies full-border illumination. The inner seven sections, those containing the poetry itself, are also divided, but at a lower order of division, by partial-border illuminations (borders at top, bottom, and center but not along the sides of pages). These partial-border illuminations appear on folios 22v, 38r, 53r, 68r, 83r, and 97v. Figure 3, a reduced photocopy of folio 53r, exemplifies partial-border illumination. (For more detail about the deliberate hierarchy of decoration, see the appendix.)

Each of these seven visually divided sections of poetry is made up of thirty pages, or fourteen to fifteen folios, except for the twenty-five-page introductory section I (fols. 9v–22r). These seven interior sections of poetry, of even length and divided visually as equal parts, seem also to have a certain thematic and formal coherence, or at very least an arrangement that differs from that of the main English and French manuscripts. The introductory section, containing the *retenue d'amours,* the *lettre de retenue,* and the initial set of ballades, describes a conventional context for late-medieval love poetry, that of the lover entering Cupid's service (fols. 9v–17r). This section also accomplishes certain introductory rhetorical functions, for in it the sixty-five-year-old author presents his self-naming speaker, Charles, duc d'Orléans, represents that speaker as a young lover and as a writer, and places the speaker's experience within some familiar parameters of medieval love literature. This first section retains almost perfectly the order of the vernacular manuscripts[18] and is the most traditional of all the sections. The other six sections of poetry present various problems and joys of the experience of love in a series of snapshots. Briefly, these are as follows: section II, which describes various settings, delights, and problems traditional in love; section III, which treats the problem of absence and the consolation of writing; section IV, the central section of the manuscript, treating the speaker's need to act and various actions of loving; section V, which opens with the lady's death and proceeds through the speaker's decision to take a new love; section VI, emphasizing the speaker's renunciation of love; and finally, section VII, which turns sharply to political and moral poems treating war, peace, politics, and patriotism. The larger general motion of the sequence, then, is from the lover's initiation through various experiences of loving, past the renunciation of those experiences, and finally to a consideration of more serious issues, issues perhaps less personal but no less deeply felt.

---

18. Folio 21, "Mon cueur m'a fait commaundement," is a ballade inserted out of the vernacular order: in BN f. fr. 25458, it appears on fols. 121–22; there is no English analogue.

Some of the specific changes concomitant with this new general arrangement are discussed further below, but for the moment it is important to note the ways in which the larger general arrangement differs from that of either main vernacular manuscript. The English lyrics in Harley 682 are set in extensive, witty, revisionist narrative-verse frames. There, the lyric snapshots of the lover's experience are set in self-consciously fictional contexts: dream-visions, dialogues, prosopopoeias of Venus and Fortune, and a love banquet.[19] These contexts would have been familiar to an English coterie readership such as the Suffolk circle, and Charles's particular innovations and revisions of them (some of which are very ingenious indeed) would likely have been received appreciatively by such an audience or audiences. Harley 682 follows the speaker through the joys and disappointments of successive love affairs—again, Charles is no one-woman Petrarch. The English lyric book ends with a powerful valedictory poem that is, as I have argued at the end of chapter 3, as much the poet's farewell to the reader as it is the speaker's farewell to the lover. The English sequence concerns itself as much with the writing "I" as the loving "I," and political moments are fleeting, are expressed indirectly and figuratively, and are scattered. Harley 682 offers a loosely structured literary framework for the lyrics, but it focuses on the writerly concerns of presence, absence, voice, and silence.

The English sequence affords no final transcendent vision, and such *in morte* consolation as it offers is brief and occurs relatively early. The arrangement of the poems about the lady's death in the English work is as follows: news of the lady's sickness (Ballade 55); news of her recovery (Ballade 56); news of her death (Ballade 57, "Allas Deth who made thee so hardy"); his suffering at this news (Ballades 58–60), his deliberations about taking a new lady (Ballades 61, 62, 65), his "God rest her soul" poem (Ballade 63) and a nearly Boethian or Ecclesiast ballade with the refrain, "That this world nys but even a thyng in vayne" (Ballade 64). The English speaker, that is, takes a new lady a mere seven poems after the *in morte* announcement; in Grenoble 873 this anti-Petrarchan effect is exaggerated, for the poems that are clustered with these describe divertissements that verge on the unseemly. If the speed with which the speaker recovers from his grief is in this manuscript especially disconcerting, it does suit the new emphasis (implied in the larger order of sections) on responding to the problems of love with a return to more pragmatic concerns. With section

---

19. For discussion, see Arn, "Charles of Orleans" and "English Poems."

VII and a return to the concern for political history, the sequence does offer strong, complex closure.

The main French manuscript, BN f. fr. 25458, on the other hand, offers very little in the way of closure—its final poems are a set of rondeaux—and while one does get a sporadic sense of thematic concern from certain groupings of poems, the overall feel is not that of a planned sequence. Instead, BN f. fr. 25458 reads something like a record kept over time of certain lyrics, Charles's own and those by others, that he felt were worth preserving and from which other copies might be made.[20] One reason for this impression is that on a number of folios, spaces were left at the tops of pages above chansons, and other short poems were copied into those spaces at some later point. Some scholars have speculated that these spaces had originally been intended for musical settings of the chansons or for further illuminations, but others think this unlikely.[21] Either way, the poems written in later imply an *ordinatio* resulting from order of composition,[22] in Arn's words campaigns of copying layered upon one another. It seems a production not deliberately planned as a complete lyric book, certainly not executed by one scribe at one time without afterthoughts. In other words, the main French manuscript, BN f. fr. 25458, was not wholly conceived in advance, and it has an overall effect that is additive, almost organic, rather than preformed or architectural.

On the contrary, deliberate planning and execution of a careful order is precisely the impression Grenoble 873 gives. Physically, it shows evidence of careful conception: uniform ruling, spacing, quire construction, paleography, and decoration, as explained in the appendix. Moreover, the evenly divided, visually separated, thematically cohesive sections of Grenoble 873 move from a young lover's initiation through his experiences of loving,

---

20. Pierre Champion studies BN f. fr. 25458 in *Manuscrit autographe*. On the difficulties of dating the composition of any of these poems, see Arn's introduction to the English poetry, *Fortunes Stabilnes*, 37–38, 109–13, 119–23. Arn's unpublished work "The Order of Composition in Charles d'Orléans's Personal Manuscript (BN f. fr. 25458)" should solve many of the difficult problems of the order in BN f. fr. 25458.

21. These spaces are also left in Harley 682. For a summary of the complex arguments of Champion, Sarah Spence, Alice Planche, Nigel Wilkins, Nancy Regalado, and Arn as to whether these spaces were originally intended for illuminations, musical settings, or for some other purpose, see Arn's introduction to *Fortunes Stabilnes*, 106–9 and notes 303–11. For our purposes here it seems sufficient to remark that poems copied later might have been thought in some sense to "go together" with the poems copied earlier, since earlier and later poems do in some cases reappear together in Grenoble 873. Questions of composition, copying, and arrangement need much further investigation.

22. It is, however, a mistake to assume the reverse, that order of composition necessarily or perfectly dictates order of appearance in this or any manuscript.

past his renunciation of those experiences, and finally to a consideration of higher issues: kingship, war, peace, and patriotism. When compared with the French and English sides of Charles's oeuvre, then, Grenoble 873 comes across, because of its distinct *ordinatio,* as a purposeful sequence, a lyric book with motives. The overall coherence and motion of Grenoble ms. 873 represent a new principle of lyric construction and self-representation, and a new and broader appeal to new and broader audiences.

In addition to serving as thematically cohesive parts of a larger, coherent order, each individual section is visually separated as such with partial-border illuminations of the sort exemplified in figure 3. The whole holds together, but the evenly sized parts are clearly defined, just as Vitruvius advises. Most sections also begin with a "big" poem, a poem either that is formally distinct from the others in the section and/or that introduces the section's theme and ideas.[23] Sections III, IV, VI, and VII, for example, begin with *complaintes.* These *complaintes* are complex, highly stylized poems that convey a lofty formality and serious tone. The *complaintes,* furthermore, are not presented in the order in which they appear in the other manuscripts of Charles's works.[24] Here, Complainte III is lifted out of its position in BN f. fr. 25458 to open section III, and Complainte II likewise to open section IV; the "Songe en Complainte" now opens Section VI; and Complainte I, the "Complainte de France," is now relegated, or rather elevated, to folios 97v–99r, where it opens the final section of poetry, section VII. In other words, the *complaintes* are specially selected, removed from prior contexts in Charles's oeuvre to open each section here—selected, it seems, for their formal complexity and annunciatory power to help create these new contexts. (Figures 3 and 4 demonstrate the visual emphasis given such poems by means of decoration in the manuscript.)

Complainte III, for example, announces that the lover must be absent

---

23. Section I, as mentioned above, begins with the traditional introductory appeal to Cupid and *retenue d'amours.*

24. Here are the poems in question in order of their appearance in Grenoble 873; the BN f. fr. 25458 folios where they appear are in brackets for ease of comparison.

Fols. 38r–39r [302–5]: Complainte III
Fols. 53r–54r [299–302]: Complainte II
Fols. 83r–85v [100–105]: "Songe en Complainte"
Fols. 97v–99r [192–93]: Complainte I (the famous "Complainte de France")

An English version of the "Songe en Complainte" appears on folios 48v–52v of Harley 682, copied in, not so as to begin a new page, but simply placed without fanfare among other surrounding lyrics.

126   *Canon, Period, and the Poetry of Charles of Orleans*

("Quant il me faillu partir," l. 16), rehearses in twelve stanzas his adoration of and service to the lady, and seeks her remembrance ("Or, veuillez donc avoir pensee / ... Maintenant que, contre mon vueil, / Me faut etre de vous loingtains," ll. 73–78 and "Si vous suppli, tresbonne et belle, / Qu'ayez souvenance de moy"). This *complainte* opens a section in which the poems return again and again to the themes of absence, presence, listening, telling, and remembering. Likewise, Complainte II (fig. 3) is selected here to begin section IV. "Amour ne vous veuille desplaire" seems conventional enough, but its insistent tone spurs the whole section: it is a "now or never" section, and this poem begins it by imploring Cupid for immediate help: "Je vous empry a jointes mains / *Car il en est temps, ou jamais*" (ll. 7–8; emphasis added). Later, the "Songe en Complainte" is appropriately delayed in this manuscript; it proclaims the renunciatory theme of section VI with its dream-vision in which the lover makes a formal request to be released from Love's service. And finally, Complainte I, the "Complainte de France," very appropriately announces the political theme of the poems in the final section of poems, section VII (fig. 4).[25]

In addition to these annunciatory *complaintes,* rearranged so as to open various sections of the manuscript, we find groups of poems reordered within the sections. Certain regroupings of poems indicate a deliberate creation of thematic emphasis. For example, poems on folios 29v through 32v are rearranged out of the autograph manuscript's order to form a "kiss" group here.[26] Likewise, there is a group of "eye poems" on folios 33v, 34r,

---

25. One of the "big" annunciatory poems is not a *complainte.* Section V opens with the very serious ballade, "Las mort qui t'as fait si hardi," a poem announcing the death of the beloved and the poems in the following section that record the speaker's various attempts to deal with it. Section II, filled with fifty-seven rondeaux and chansons, simply opens with a May poem, perhaps annunciatory in marking the beginning of the season of love.

26. I list the poems in question here in order of their Grenoble folios; the BN f. fr. 25458 folios are in brackets for ease of comparison.

Fol. 29v [273]: Chanson XXXIII, "Dedans mon sein, pres de mon cueur"
Fol. 30r [271]: Chanson XXXV, "Prenez tost ce baiser mon cueur"
Fol. 30v [276]: Chanson XXXVII, "Je ne prise point telz baisers"
Fol. 31r [279]: Chanson XLI, "Sil vous plait vendre vos baisers"
Fol. 32v [276]: Chanson XLVIII, "Votre bouche dit baisez moi"

Chanson XLIII, fol. 31v, [281], "Logiez moi entre vos bras," and Chanson XLV, fol. 32r [277], "Va tost mon amoureux desir," do not use the word *kiss* ("baiser") but are erotic poems in keeping with the thematic group. It is interesting to note that this section closely follows the order of the English manuscript—corresponding poems appear in the same order (Roundels 33 through 48), and only three poems there, Roundels 38, 40, and 42, are skipped here. This in itself does not mean that the English volume was the copy text for Grenoble 873—I think that is unlikely; further studies are needed.

and 34v gathered out of order from folios 287, 283, 284, and 286 (of which there are no English analogues). There is also a group of poems about exploring the lover's inner landscapes (fols. 51r–52r) in which the initial poem in the group is inserted here to introduce the others: it begins by "opening the gate of thought" inward ("Mon cueur ouvrez l'uis de pensee"). There is also a loose grouping of calendrical or seasonal poems on folios 70r–78r, marking the passage of time and the theme of the speaker's long experience of love, but not spread through the sequence as if to create a calendrical order. The seven *départie* poems all appear together here, as they do in the French and English manuscripts, but there they are followed by further love chansons, roundels, and ballades. In other words, the ordering of the vernacular manuscripts tends to dilute the thematic potency of the *départie* group. Here, though, this group of poems is much more convincing because it is recontextualized: right after them comes an immediate turn toward the serious, nonromantic material in section VII that more than makes good on the renunciatory promise of the *départie* group. That final section of poems, section VII, contains the most strongly reordered thematic group, that of the political poems, brought together in folios 97v–111r to close the sequence. To summarize: the reordering of individual poems tends to result in thematic groups or sets within sections, introduced by major, illuminated poems that clearly mark *ouverture* and in some ways predict the direction of the lyrics placed in each section.

Likewise, the last poems in each section mark the sections' conclusions and in some ways predict the turns toward a subsequent section. These last poems are generally not "big" poems[27] but instead appear to have been chosen for their particular closural tactics. An emphasis on closure—a sort of deliberate poetic punctuation, if you will—is an important distinguishing feature of Grenoble 873: neither vernacular manuscript has anything like the heavy closures created here between sections. For instance, section V ends with a pair of inverted rondeaux, "Bien defendu bien assailly" and "Bien assailly bien defendu" (fol. 82v). The love-games are tied at this point, and this self-sealing pair of poems puts a full stop to it.[28] Other closural poems seem to predict or lead into the subsequent section; in several cases these are question-poems. For instance, "Que faut il plus a un cueur

---

27. Though the elaborate two-page ballade that closes Section I, "Fresche beaute tresriche de jeunesse" (fols. 21v–22r), certainly is.

28. The first poem is by René d'Anjou, dear friend and frequent companion of Charles; the answer poem is by Charles. See Champion, ed., *Poésies,* 2:628.

amoureux?" (fol. 37v) ends section II. What more, the question implies, does a lover's heart need than all this that has come before?—a question that section III then attempts to answer. In turn, section III, which explores the problem of absence and the consolations of writing and which contains a thematic group about listening, telling and writing, ends with Ballade XXXVI. In this curious and emotionally oscillatory poem, "Je ne vous puis ne scay aimer," the speaker at once despairs of and hopes for the presence of the lady, says her letter has caused him pain, and both bitterly and tenderly quotes words from one of her letters as his refrain lines ("en esperant que bref vous voye"). The ballade culminates the section's polyvocal treatments of writing, absence, and mutuality. Next, section IV closes with this woefully questioning chanson:

> Me fauldrez vous a mon besoing
> Mon reconfort et ma fiance?
> M'avez vous mis en oubliance
> Pour tant se de vous je suis loing
> Navez vous pitie de mon soing?
> Sans vous savez que n'ay puissance.
> Me fauldrez vous . . .
> On feroit des larmes un baing,
> Qu'ay pleures de desplaisance
> Et crie par desesperance
> Ferant ma poitrine du poing:
> Me fauldrez vous . . .

Section V then opens with the lady's death; the speaker will indeed have lost his confidence, comfort, and "puissance," and will come (at least in the section's initial poem) to be bathed in tears. Section VI, in which the speaker receives his "quittance" from love and in which are the seven *départie* poems, is a nearly valedictory section in thematic intent. The section ends appropriately with a rondeau that asks a leading question: "what more is there to say?"

> Que voulez vous que plus vous die
> Jeunes assotez amoureux?
> Par Dieu, jay este l'un de ceulx
> Qui ont eu vostre maladie!
> Prenez exemple, je vous prie

> A moy qui m'en complains et deulx;
> Que voulez vous . . .
>
> Et pour ce, de vostre partie,
> Se voulez croire mes conseulx,
> D'abregier conseiller vous veulx
> Voz faiz, en sense ou en folie:
> Que voulez vous . . .
>
> Plusieurs y treuvent chiere lie
> Maintesfoiz et plaisans acueulx:
> Que voulez vous . . .
>
> Mais au derrain, Merencolie
> De ses huis fait passer les ceulx
> En deuil et soussi, Dieu scet quieulx!
> Lors ne chault de mort ou de vie.
> Que voulez vous que plus vous dies,
> Jeunes assotez amoureux?

Strongly closing the penultimate section of poetry in this way leaves the reader less with a self-deconstructing inexpressibility topos than with a nonrhetorical question that cries out for a real answer: What more *could* there be to say to besotted young lovers about the "exemple" of the range of miseries displayed in the preceding 180 pages?

Political Closure, Selection, and Repatriation

The answer comes in the final section of poetry, section VII: what more there is to say is all about war, morality, diplomacy, kingship, and nationhood. The section's series of political reflections opens with the famous "Complainte de France," a poem that is Complainte I in the main French manuscript (fols. 191–93 in BN f. fr. 25458; here, see fig. 4, a reduced image of fol. 97v).

> France jadis on te soulait nommer
> En tous pays, le tresor de noblesse,
> Car un chascun pouvoit en toy trouver
> Bonté, honneur, loyauté, gentillesse,
> Clergie, sens coutoisie, proesse.

> Tous estrangiers amoient te suir.
> Et maintenant voy, dont jay desplaisance
> Qu'il te couvient maint grief mal soustenir,
> Trescretien, franc royaume de France!
>
> Scez tu dont vient ton mal a vray parler?
> Cogniois tu point pourquoy es en tristesse?
> Conter le veuil, pour vers toy m'acquiter,
> Escoutes moy et tu feras sagesse.
> Ton grant orgeuil, glotonnie, peresse,
> Couvoitise, sans justice tenir,
> Et luxure dont as eu abondance,
> Ont pourchacié vers Dieu de te punir,
> Trescretien franc royaume de France!

The next seven stanzas of this very stylized, formal poem exhort the French to repent; the poem recalls the names of heroic French Christians past and evokes a series of sacred and semisacred images (dove, fleur-de-lis, the singing of masses, the Virgin Mary). In the final stanza the poet names himself again and explains that he wrote his poetry in captivity.

> Et je, Charles duc d'Orlians, rimer
> Voulu ces vers en temps de ma jeunesse,
> Devant chacun les vueil bien advouer,
> Car prisonnier les fis, je le confesse.[29]

The poem is a powerful, serious, complex statement about the national destiny and the moral problems of warfare and empire in the fifteenth century.[30] Its refrain bitterly reproaches the nation but (in later stanzas) also promises the solution to the nation's problems: to return to God and goodness. Complainte I can be usefully read as Charles's poetic application of the then widely accepted idea of *translatio imperii*. In chapter 2 we

---

29. This stanza could be read as a retraction of sorts.
30. Champion dates the poem 1433; the poem must be post-Agincourt, but is probably pre–Jeanne d'Arc, so Champion's date is likely close. On the other hand, the final stanza makes the poem seem a retrospective, written, as this manuscript was, long after his return to his homeland. The poem appears in ten other Charles manuscripts, including the BL Royal F 16.ii manuscript, owned by Henry VII and VIII. The manuscript placement and provenance of the political poems are fascinating but outside the scope of this study. See Champion, ed., *Poésies,* 2:57.

saw that Charles Christianizes Sallust's classic statement of that idea ("Ita imperium semper ad optumum quemque a minus bono transfertur" [thus empire is always transferred from the less good to the best], *Bellum Catilinae* 2.6)[31] in order to interpret the battle of Agincourt and the latter years of a century of warfare between France and England. For France's moral failures, God has withheld glory and victory. Stanzas 6 and 7 write of the great history of his nation and of the epic national heroes Roland, Olivier, and Charlemagne and rouse his nation to a once and future glory. The "Complainte de France," like Petrarch's "Italia mia,"[32] reproaches a nation in military and moral crisis and exhorts it to return to moral and thus political greatness. It is no wonder that during World War II, this intensely patriotic lament was secretly printed and distributed by the French underground resistance forces during German occupation.

In fact, for such a singularly unambiguous statement, the poem's responsiveness to its historical and material contexts is remarkable. Its reappearances across several centuries illustrate the effects of such contexts on interpretation: in BN f. fr. 25458 the poem seems personal, occasional, one among several personal reflections on various situations; here in Grenoble 873, opening the political finale section in heavy illumination, the poem seems splendidly annunciatory and historiographic, with the English as the enemy (an enemy that finds itself in defeat in the last poem of the section, "Comment voys je ces Anglais esbahis"). In BL Royal F 16.ii, the Tudor manuscript held at Richmond Castle, the poem (illuminated with a woeful crucifixion image, fol. 89, and without "Comment voys je ces Anglais esbahis") seems to reinforce English victory and, in that worldview, moral superiority. Five centuries later in a small (18 × 12 cm) plain-paper booklet, the "Complainte de France" is a single poem printed in World War II samizdat, the enemy is Nazi, the allies are English, and the moral reproach is against collaborators.[33]

Back to Grenoble 873, where the "Complainte de France" introduces a section of poems exploring war, peace, and the struggles for power that took place in the closing decades of the Hundred Years' Wars. Some of the

---

31. Charles's bibliophile parents, Louis d'Orléans and Valentina Visconti, owned several copies of Sallust, one of which was probably used in educating Charles and his brother Jean d'Angoulême; for details, see note 36 in chapter 2 above.

32. Petrarch, "Italia mia," in *Petrarch's Lyric Poems: The Rime Sparse and Other Lyrics*, trans. and ed. Robert M. Durling (Cambridge: Harvard University Press, 1976), 256–57.

33. Paris: Sézille, 1944; La Haye: Stols, 1944. One hundred copies were "published secretly during German occupation," according to Nelson, *Charles d'Orléans*, 37.

poems in this final section of the manuscript are sweeping statements about war and peace ("Priez pour paix," fols. 99v–100r, is an especially moving example). Others are versions of some of Charles's diplomatic correspondence while in captivity. There is a set between Charles and his cousin, the duc de Bourbon, a set between Charles and the man who helped free him, the duc de Bourgogne, and a witty poem saying that the news of his death has been greatly exaggerated, for he's still, as ever, in captivity in England.[34] Section VII, in other words, seems to attempt a poetic record of the final decades of the war, which Charles spent in a diplomatically and politically active captivity, negotiating not only his own release but several treaties and agreements. The section refocuses attention on this political activity and redefines, with the support of Astesano's Latin translations, what had been in the rest of the sequence a set of amorous terms: the "virgo" and "sola magistra mea" are now not the courtly lady but the Virgin Mary to whom Charles prays for peace and deliverance. The "electa puella" (in Astesano's Latin historiographies that form the final contexts for this poetry) is Joan of Arc, not a chosen love-interest. This recoding of key terms is not just a function of Astesano's scholarly and historiographical impulses. Even in French in the "Complainte de France," the comforting breasts of the virgin become those of the Virgin Mary who may intercede on behalf of the nation, not of the erotic mistress who may grant personal favors:

> Requier pardon, bien te vendre aidier
> Nostre Dame, la trespuissant [sic] princesse
> Qui est ton cry et que tiens pour maistresse
> Les seins aussi te vendront secourir.
>
> (ll. 75–78)

And instead of the "trésor de ma pensée" or the "treasure of thoughtfull fantase" as a place the lover holds his memories of encounters with the lady, as it has been in the English and French sequences, in this section, "Paix est le trésor qu'on ne peut trop louer" or, as Astesano's succinct

---

34. Folio 101v, "Nouvelles ont couru en France." Folio 102r and 102v contain poems to his cousin Bourbon; folios 103r through 105r contain poems to Bourgogne; these poems mainly treat peace and deliverance. There are a few coterie-style poems in this group, one in particular thanking a host and hostess (perhaps Suffolk, one of his favorite host-captors; fol. 109v) and another indicating travel to Blois (fol. 108v) and the calling of a council of friends (fol. 109r).

Latin has it, "Pax est thesaurus" (fol. 99v). Instead of the absent lady that the lover longs to see during the French and English sequences, the significant absence in this final section of Charles's work is his nation: a refrain-line repeats that his whole desire is "De voir France que mon coeur aimer doit." Small-scale details like this support the revised large-scale order and emphasis: the section closes the sequence by turning from the lover's woes to the nation's woes; from love to war; from a beloved lady to a beloved homeland.

Section VII itself closes—and the entire poetic oeuvre closes—with what must have felt, to a Frenchman who had been held captive in enemy territory for twenty-five years, a very consoling poem about the battles that returned territories of Guyenne (Aquitaine) and Normandy to French control. This final poem exults in French victory less than it celebrates English defeat:

> Comment voys je ses Anglois esbays!
> Rejoys toi, franc royaume de France.
> On apparçoit que de Dieu sont hays,
> Puis qu'ilz n'ont plus couraige ne puissance.
> Bien pensoient, par leur oultrecuidance,
> Toy surmonter et tenir en serviage,
> Et ont tenu a tort ton heritaige.
> Mais a present Dieu pour toy se combat
> Et se montre du tout de ta partie;
> Leur grant orgueil entierment abat,
> Et t'a Rendu guyenne et normandie.

The ballade's third stanza notes the treacheries that place the English monarchy in jeopardy:

> N'ont pas Anglois souvent leurs rois trays?
> Certes . . .
> Et encore le roy de leur pays
> Est maintenant en doubteuse balance:
> D'en parler mal chascun Anglois s'avance;
> Assez montrant, par leur mauvais langaige
> Que voulontiers lui feraoient oultraige.
> Qui sera Roy entr'eux est grant desbat;
> Pour ce, Fraunce, que veulx tu que te dye?

De sa verge Dieu les pugnist et bat
Et t'a Rendu guienne et normandie.

Charles was not far off the mark here: in 1453 after these battles, Henry VI was losing control, the regency was of growing concern, and in 1454 civil war, the Wars of the Roses, began in earnest. The English monarchy was indeed "en doubteuse balance" and would not stabilize again until the final years of the century under Henry VII. In this important political section, Charles holds onto the paradigm of *translatio imperii* (as he does not visibly do in the vernacular manuscripts), but this final poem reverses the positions of England and France in that paradigm.

By writing England's return to turpitude and France's victory, the section's closing poem reverses its opening poem, and again accounts for the fortunes of war in terms of the national moral character (or lack of it) on both sides. The moral fortunes of war, it seems, form a slightly more stable category than those of love—at least in this manuscript. Yet Charles acknowledges the provisional nature of his nation's victories: "mais *a present* Dieu pour toy [France] combat" (emphasis added). This anti-English poem inverts, at least *à présent,* for now, the positions set forth in the "Complainte de France," which opened the section; in some measure, "Comment voys je ses Anglais esbahis" records the fulfillment of the "Complainte"'s promise of recovering the national glory. At the same time, the poet acknowledges the provisional nature of such glory. Thus does Charles close his culminating section of political lyric, and the sequence, and, in retrospect, his whole oeuvre.[35]

The Politics of Translation?

It is not surprising that he did not translate "Comment voys je ces anglais esbahis" into English.[36] In fact, this is not the only political poem Charles tactfully omitted from the English corpus and deliberately placed in this final section of his lyric works. The politics of selection and context here

---

35. Charles died in 1465; this manuscript was the last one he made or had made.

36. The question of composition dates intervenes again: this poem had to be composed after the battles it celebrates (that is, after 1453). We cannot assume, however, that other poems in this section were composed after Charles's return to France: in fact, several of the correspondence poems were composed during his captivity. This important poem appears also in Bibliothèque de Carpentras ms. 375, BN f. fr. 1104 (probably owned by Catherine de Medici), and BL Harley 6916, a paper copy of some of the poems, probably made in the late fifteenth century; and of course in BN f. fr. 25458.

contrast usefully with that of BL ms. Harley 682, the main English manuscript. He does not translate into English, for example, one of the verse letters to Burgundy,

> Pource que je suis a present
> Avec la gent vostre ennemi
> Il fault que je face semblant
> Faignant que ne vous aime mye,

a poem that exposes his necessary duplicities while captive (fol. 106v). Nor does he translate into English "Cueur trop est plein de folie," a poem that complains bitterly about his imprisonment (fol. 101r). Fortune, he says, has kept him "moult longuement / Au royame d'Angleterre," and "l'estat de prisonnier / Est que souvent lui ennuye / et endure maint dangier / dont il ne se peut vengier." The English poems never speak of his imprisonment in this way, nor certainly of any desire to avenge himself. In fact the English poems disguise all references to prison as prisoner-of-love metaphors. In the political context of this section of the Grenoble manuscript, however, he strips away the figuration and speaks more plainly. Likewise, in "Je fu en fleur au trespasse denfance," another poem not translated into English, he complains openly that he longs to return and find himself "tost refreschi au souleil de France" (fol. 100v).

His politic sense of the political contexts for translation is perhaps most evident in two of the poems that he does render in English in Harley 682 as well as in Latin and French here. These poems, like several other such pairs, were sent between Charles and the duke of Burgundy, Philippe le Bon, some time during Charles's captivity.[37] "Pour le haste de mon passage," from Charles, has as its refrain a line that pledges loyalty: "De cueur de corps et de puissance" (fol. 104r–104v). Following convention, Philippe returns a poem that uses the sender's refrain for its first line; in it he promises help and support in trying to free Charles. Both poems are quite specific about the two writers' efforts to negotiate the end of the war, and as a key part of that, to arrange Charles's release.

---

37. See Ann Tukey Harrison, "Orleans and Burgundy: The Literary Relationship," *Stanford French Review* 4 (1980): 475–84, who sees three phases in their long friendship and summarizes the content of their correspondence. Philippe's father, Jean Sans Peur, had Charles's father Louis assassinated in 1407; it is a curious alliance against the English that the two form later in life.

B LXXXVIII [Orlians a Bourgogne][38]

Pour le haste de mon passage
Qu'il me couvient faire oultre mer,
Tout ce que j'ay en mon courage
A present ne vous puis mander.
Mais non pour tant, a brief parler,
De la balade que m'avés
Envoyee, comme savés,
Touchant paix et ma delivrance,
Je vous mercie chierement,
Comme tout vostre entierement
De cueur, de corps et de puissance.

Ie vous envoyeray message,
Se Dieu plaist, briefment sans tarder,
Loyal, secret et assez sage,
Pour bien a plein vous infourmer
De tout ce que pourray trouver
Sur ce que savoir desirés;
Pareillement, faut que mettés
Et faictes, vers la part de France,
Diligence soigneusement;
Je vous en requier humblement,
De cueur, de corps et de puissance.

Et sans plus despendre langage,
A cours mots, plaise vous penser
Que vous laisse mon cueur en gage
Pour tousjours, sans jamais faulser.
Si me vueilliez recommander
A ma cousine; car croyés
Que en vous deux, tant que vivrés
J'ay mise toute ma fiance
Et vostre party loyaument
Tendray, sans faire changement
De cueur, de corps et de puissance!

38. Material in brackets appears in the manuscript in Charles's hand, underneath the numbers. See Champion, ed., *Poésies,* 2:558.

Or y parra que vous ferés
Et se point ne m'oublierés
Ainsi que g'y ay esperance.
Adieu vous dy presentement.
Tout Bourgognon sui vrayement
De cueur, de corps et de puissance!

Clearly Charles's veiled language implies political secrecy: he cannot at this time say everything he wishes in a hasty verse letter to his ally (stanza 1), but promises more informative messages later and issues a covert warning about affairs in France (stanza 2). Charles expresses confidence in their family connections (stanza 3) and pledges his loyalty to the Burgundian faction (envoi), an alliance that would indeed eventually win his release, since Charles helped arrange the marriage between Henry VI and Marguerite d'Anjou (a relative of Philippe). Philippe's respectful and sympathetic reply to Charles, although somewhat less skillful poetically, is similarly political in nature:

Ballade LXXXVIIIa [Responce de Bourgogne a Orlians]

De cueur, de corps et de puissance,
Vous mercie tres humblement
De vostre bonne souvenance
Qu'avez de moi soingneusement;
Or povez faire entierement
De moy, en tout bien et honneur,
Comme vostre cueur le propose,
Et de mon vouloir soyez seur,
Quoy que nul die ne deppose.

Ne mectes point en oubliance
L'estat et le gouvernement
De la noble nation de France,
Qui se maintient piteusement.
Vous saurés tout, quoy et comment;
Je n'en dy plus pour le meilleur.
Mais on en dit tant et expose
Que c'est a oïr grant orreur,
Quoy que nul dye ne depose.

Pensez a vostre delivrance,
Je vous en prie chierement;
Car, sans ce, je n'ay esperance
Que nous ayons paix nullement.
On la hait tant mortellement
Que trop peu treuve de faveur!
Ne sera, comme je suppose,
Se ce n'est par vostre labeur,
Quoyque nul dye ne deppose.

Or prions Dieu, par sa doulceur,
Qu'a vous delivrer se dispose,
Car trop avez souffert douleur,
Quoy que nul dye ne deppose.

Although Philippe pays Charles the compliments of reusing his rhyme-words and beginning his reply with the refrain-line of the letter received, he is not up to Charles's more complex rhyme scheme and eleven-line stanzas. Still, it is clear that poetically, and perhaps politically, Philippe is willing to play along. Rumors about the sorry state of France and about Charles and his release are of concern to both of them, and they seem to agree that Charles's release is essential to peace. Philippe's refrains reassure Charles of his political loyalty "no matter what people say."

However, the English translations of this pair (Ballades 111 and 113) are sharply revised: no mention of alliances, Charles's release, peace negotiations, or government affairs. The duke and duchess of Burgundy have vanished. In the process of translation, Charles adapts the poems to their English literary context (a sequence of love ballades ostensibly addressed to a beloved by a lover-speaker) and to his own historical context, an English imprisonment.

Ballade 111

Honure, ioy, helthe, and plesaunce
Vertu, ricches habundaunt with good vre
The Lord graunt yow (which hath most puysshaunce),
And many a gladsom yere forto endure,
With loue and prays of euery creature,
And for my loue (all prevayle it small)

I gyve hit yow, as be ye verry sewre,
With hert, body, my litill good, and all.

And so youw not displese with my desire,
This wolde y yow biseche: that of yowre grace
Hit like yow to graunt me all þis yere
As in yowre hert to haue a dwellyng place,
Al be hit neuyr of so lite a space,
For which as this the rente resceyue ye shall:
Mi loue and seruice as in euery case,
With hert, body, my litill good, and all.

And syn hit is to yow no preiudice
Sum litill, prati corner sekis me
Within yowre hert for, parde, lo, iustice
If y offende, hit must yowre selven be
To punysshe liche as ye þe offensis se,
For y as name nor haue no thing at all
But it is sovl yowre owen in eche degre,
With hert, body, my litill good, and all.

What so ye will, y wil hit to obey,
For payne and smert, how so þat me bifall,
So am y yowre and shal to that y dey
With hert, body, my litill good, and all.

Octosyllabes expand here into English pentameters, roughly, with the liberal use of cheville, as is Charles's habit. The political secrecy of the French parallels the sexual secrecy of the English, but this is hardly the same poem: only the refrain is the same, its traditional "my litill good, and all" implying a traditional pledge ("with all my worldly goods I thee endow") including the traditional modesty of the lover's unworthiness. The speaker rather conventionally wishes the lady well and pledges loyalty, but nothing prepares us for the remarkable economic conceit. The "cueur en gage" may have suggested it, but that old topos did not allow for the topical specificity in the English poem. The poem amplifies its main statement of complete loyalty with an extended metaphor of the speaker's renting and occupying "sum litill, prati corner" of the lady's heart and submitting himself to her justice. The speaker's proposal is unusual, specifying as it does a contractual-term tenancy in the beloved's heart ("all þis yere") but labor service there ("For which as this the rente resceyue ye shall: / Mi loue and seruice as in euery case") instead of the usual fixed-rent payments that tended to accompany contractual tenures.[39] The speaker throws in an odd element of seigneurial ownership ("for y as name nor haue no thing at all / But is sovl yowre owen in eche degre"), more often a feature of servile, not contractual, tenancies. Most oddly the speaker proposes a servile-at-law tenure in the beloved's heart (iustice / If y offende, hit must yowre selven be / To punisshe liche as ye þe offensis se"). This pledge may offer an erotic thrill, but it recalls the predominantly Catalan and French practice of the *ius maletractandi* and the required submission to siegneurial justice, which did not generally accompany an English contractual or fixed-term tenancy; in England the *districtus* meant that the lord had a general local judicial authority. In short, the speaker presents the lady an unusual deal for the time, a bicultural hodgepodge of a deal, including some elements of old continental feudalism and some elements of the English postdepression practices Charles could have seen around him in the 1430s. In literary terms, too, his is an especially contingent, freewheeling, temporizing proposal: not an eternal pledge of troth—just occupancy for a year—but an intense, unusual surrender of power.

Similarly, in translation Philippe's political reply-ballade becomes a love poem to a lady. Ballade 113 reconventionalizes the refrain's concern with rumor in terms familiar from the *Roman de la Rose* traditions (stanza 3) but also introduces a good bit of Charles's trademark erotic wishfulness (stanzas 2 and 3):

Ballade 113

With hert, body, and my hool puysshaunce,
I thanke yow, swete—or more, if more may be—
Of yowre goodly remembraunce

---

39. On the complex and ever-changing land tenure situation in late-medieval England and France see E. B. Fryde, *Peasants and Landlords in Later Medieval England* (New York: St. Martin's, 1996), 9–11, 13, 62, 63, 145–68, 227–41; Robert DuPlessis, *Transitions to Capitalism in Early Modern Europe* (Cambridge: Cambridge University Press, 1997), 20–22; Pierre Bonnassie, *From Slavery to Feudalism in South-western Europe,* trans. Jean Birrell (Cambridge: Cambridge University Press, 1991), 322, 332, 338–39; M. M. Postan, ed., *Cambridge Economic History of Europe,* 2d ed. (Cambridge University Press, 1966–87), 322, 325, 730–33; M. A. Visceglia, "Rente féodale et agriculture dans les Pouilles à l'époque moderne, XVIè–XVIIIè siecles," in *Prestations paysannes, dîmes, rente foncière, et mouvement de la production agricole à l'époque pré-industrielle,* ed. Joseph Goy and E. L. R. Ladurie, 2 vols. (Paris: Mouton Editeur, 1982), 1:237–58, 240–42.

The which ye oft han shewid me.
So doon with me in eche degre
What yow good lust in any thing at all,
For in no poynt excepte y nought
Nor to my deth y neuyr shall,
Whatsoeuyr be seid or thought.

Forgete ye not now, in substaunce:
Ye wot what þat y myght se
Vnto my blisse and most plesaunce,
For thynke ye hit that y am he
Not all out of adversite
Nor shall to that yowre myddil smal
Be onys within myn armys brou[gh]t,
Nor to my deth y nevir shal,
Whatsoevir be seid or thought.

So shape me of hit deliueraunce
When ther are noon but y and ye
In lessyng of þe gret penaunce
I haue had thorugh þe crewelte
Of daungere and of ielowsy
That yvil thrift on þer chekis falle,
For nygh my deth as han þei wrought,
But now y trust they nevir shal,
Whatsoevir be seid or thought.

Sett tyme or that þe wynd apalle
And clowdid be þe mone aloft
No more but yowre y [am] and shall,
Whatsoeuyr be seid or thought.

Here again we see how translation can depoliticize poems with a shift of metaphor and context: the "delivrance" sought is orgasmic rather than political release. The main thing for the addressee to remember in stanza 2 is not the dreadful state of the French nation as it was in the French and Latin analogues, but the speaker's particular sexual wishes. The addressee knows what these are and can "shape" them into his "deliverance." The English version imagines an erotic scene, the lovers' embrace: the speaker hopes to have her "myddil smal . . . within [his] armys" again when they are intimate, or as he puts it, "when ther are noon but y and ye." Secrecy is now required not against political rumor but because of gossip about the lovers—conventional obstacles to love, "jealousy" or "dangier." The speaker reassures the beloved of his personal, not political, loyalty. The envoi, with its mild pun on "sett tyme" (hurry, or fix a time), stresses the need to meet soon, while trysting conditions are favorable and the night is young (and cloudless). The only meeting possible in the French version is a deferred one; here the possibility seems real, imminent. Depending on which version was written first—and we have no codicological evidence either way—translation effects either a "safe" recoding of the political into the sexual or vice versa, a kind of sublimation of sexual desires into political desires. In either case, translation, or rather, strong rewriting in another language, suits poems to contexts. Likewise, one could argue that even without verbal alterations, the presentation of "Des Nouvelles d'Albion" in BL Royal F 16.ii, with its illustration (fig. 1) emphasizing isolation, deracination, and English power, is "translated" differently for that Royal manuscript than it is here, where it is not foregrounded so but merely appears in a series of political-captivity poems leading up to an English defeat. Context and presentation are essential to translation, in other words, and Charles shows every sensitivity to this aspect of poetic decorum.

However, when Charles creates his world lyric in the political section of Grenoble 873, these poems, and others like them, are restored to function in a repoliticized context. All of these epistolary poems, in fact, resonate quite differently in Grenoble 873. In the vernacular manuscripts, they vanish into a vast tapestry of hundreds of love lyrics: translated into seamlessness with the English poems, and threaded late in BN f. fr. 25458 as incidental, occasional verses to fellow expatriates or allies at home. In Grenoble 873, however, the new contexts, with the Latin translation alongside, place these poems as part of Charles's serious sustained commentary on war, peace, kingship, and nationhood.

This final manuscript represents a reselection, a reshaping, a reconfiguring and re-presentation of Charles's lyric "works" in a public book that ends with a deeply patriotic section. The "message" (if we must state such a thing) is that the vagaries of love are many, but one's homeland is what really matters. The political poems are given last, best place—the final word—for a kind of transcendence that may include a Petrarchan renunciation of love but is not Petrarchan in structure or content[40]—is rather, sui generis, Orléaniste. Petrarch, for all his political emphasis elsewhere, chooses a spiritual rather than a political turn to answer the renunciation of love: the oppositions he uses to ground his *ordinatio* are *in vita/in morte,* earthly versus heavenly love. The "Italia mia" does not head a thematic section, richly illuminated, nor does it introduce a political finale to his *Rime* nor to his personally selected poetry.[41] (With respect to problematic period categories in the history of lyric poetry, this can be seen as one way in which Petrarch is more "medieval" than Charles.) In the Grenoble manuscript, the personal is answered by the political, or at least by a set of concerns alternative to the universal concerns of lovers: the concern for the character and future success of the nation. Astesano dedicates the work in part to Charles VII, and four quires of Latin epistolary back matter are addressed to various important people, from dukes to chancellors to doctors to functionaries. The historical material that physically surrounds the lyric poetry in the front and back matter is a significant shaping context that should be of considerable interest to historians and literary scholars alike. This material has not been edited or translated, as far as I can discover, but is outside the scope of this study. For now, it must suffice to say that Grenoble ms. 873 fully repatriates Charles and his lyric poetry into the long history of the "treschretien franc royaume de France," yet does so for a Latinate world audience.

One detects, in fact, a subliminal tension between the assertive French patriotism of the final section and the claims to cosmopolitanism implicit and explicit in the production of the manuscript as a whole. However, Astesano's preface claims that this poetry is not *libellus* but *liber,* that it should stand alongside the works of the exiled Ovid and the most serious Greek writers as a public book—and it is by means of this last political section and the contextualizing Latin front and back matter that the oeuvre is most fully reshaped to integrate those two larger aims, the French-national and the Latinate-cosmopolitan. The poetry preserves the national

---

40. Mia Cocco, "The Italian Inspiration in the Poetry of Charles d'Orléans," *Mid-Hudson Language Studies* 2 (1979): 46–60, disagrees, finding stilnovist imagery and themes in the sequence.

41. On the differing order of Petrarch's Vat. Lat. 3195 and Chigi L. V. 176 manuscripts, see Ruth Phelps, *The Earlier and Later Forms of Petrarch's Canzoniere* (Chicago: University of Chicago Press, 1925), especially 5, 166, and 189–91; on "Italia mia," 106–32. William Kennedy's *Authorizing Petrarch* (Ithaca: Cornell University Press, 1994) analyzes the various printed versions of Petrarch's poetry.

glory internationally, or at least that seems to be the attempt. The poems in Grenoble 873 are selected, translated, arranged, and presented so as to revise considerably the poetics of the lyric book. Instead of an overt organizing device like a table, *ordinatio* here means something implicit, something that structures and presents the work for the reader, something now fully absorbed into the act of creating a poetic book. This manuscript represents an extraordinary assertion of authorial self re-presentation: it is effort at the end of Charles's life to reshape the poetry he had been writing all his life, to place it in a new, specifically political, moral, and patriotic context, and to make that new shape and context permanent for a cosmopolitan readership.

6

Translation and Periodization; or, Charles d'Orléans, Renaissance Poet?

This chapter has two main purposes: first, to demonstrate that Charles's English poetry differs from other fifteenth-century poetry and resembles some sixteenth-century poetry in unexpected and significant ways;[1] second, to explore the implications of this with respect to translation and periodization. Like the rest of the book, this chapter finds Charles a writer rather unlike the one presented in most critical opinion, and the differences change several larger pictures in the periodization of English lyric. Any discussion of literary periodization has to use (but should also question) the terms and categories that mark perceived periods—in this case, *medieval* and *Renaissance* or *early modern*. I do not use these terms innocently here but defer questioning of them until the latter part of the chapter, asking the reader instead to focus on specific attributes of the literature usually categorized as medieval or Renaissance. In particular the chapter examines the poems' bicultural literary contexts, and then (1) Charles's dramatic and experiential revisions of old love topics, and (2) the English work's focus on the surfaces of words (particularly on the erotic possibilities in puns and wordplay), as well as (3) the poet's rhetorical and formal choices and the speaker's tone, voice, and *sprezzatura*. Next, the chapter revisits the "subjectivity" expressed in the sequence, its "inwardness," and what is curious, given the historical contexts, its apparent lack of an effort to respond to Petrarch in any but selective and partial ways. Reading across the accepted but amorphous medieval-Renaissance gap, the chapter then explores some of the specific historical, biographical, and literary continuities between the two periods in Charles's life and work. The chap-

---

1. Limitations of space have made it impossible to treat fully this extremely large body of poems, so, as has been the case throughout this book, poems chosen are representative of the rest of the work.

ter closes with a discussion of the wider implications of the case and translation's challenges to literary periodization.

Literary History and Bicultural Contexts

Some of the most interesting features of literary works, after all, are their departures from their moment—their backward-looking, archaic, or nostalgic aspects, and their forward-looking or proleptic aspects. Fifteenth-century writers thus hold special appeal, for they stand Janus-like in what is often called a transitional age.[2] In a transitional age, authors and poems may not be as easy to classify, but their nostalgic and proleptic characteristics show to great advantage. And in this regard, Charles d'Orléans is doubly fascinating—a four-faced Janus, if you will—because his works stand poised between nostalgia and prolepsis not in one but in two major literary traditions. In France, he is most often seen as a "latest medieval" figure whose poetry looks back on, culminates, or even exhausts centuries of fine Provençal and French lyric poetry. Paul Zumthor, for instance, takes this view: "L'oeuvre de Charles d'Orléans marque . . . un aboutissement: moins une fin qu'une convergence, à très long terme, de toutes les traditions issues des formes les plus anciennes du chant. . . . La sève de son oeuvre provient de ses profondes racines médiévales."[3] And yet I would argue that even in France he is not exclusively backward-looking—we have seen in chapter 5 his forward-looking authorial self-presentation, and after midcentury at Blois he helps launch the lyric future with his patronage of *puys* poets like Guillaume Fredet and François Villon.

In England, however, Charles's literary position is quite different. His English poems look forward at least as much as back, and Zumthor's assessment of the French poetics, that "Charles d'Orléans est entièrement et seulement de son temps. Il n'innove pas, il n'anticipe en rien," is not true for the English work. The first, most obvious ways Harley 682 stands out from its English moment are in genre and production. Most lyric in England during Charles's captivity (1415–40) and during the centuries pre-

---

2. Mapped well by A. C. Spearing, *Medieval to Renaissance in English Poetry* (Cambridge: Cambridge University Press, 1985). Parts of the section below were given in a talk at the International Medieval Congress, Kalamazoo, Mich., May 1995.

3. *Essai de poétique médiévale* (Paris: Éditions du Seuil, 1972), 279. On the other hand, from a twentieth-century view, the French poems may seem "modern"; Huizinga places them with Villon's work as examples of a productive anticlassicism. *Autumn of the Middle Ages*, trans. Rodney J. Payton and Ulrich Mammitzsch (Chicago: University of Chicago Press, 1996), 389.

ceding it was haphazardly collected and arranged. The "lyric book" was not yet an important form of presentation for English lyrics, which tended to be fleeting or scattered, as Julia Boffey has conclusively demonstrated.[4] In France of course this was not the case; the lyric book had thrived since Machaut.[5] Deschamps, Froissart, Pisan, Chartier, and a number of less well known practitioners wrote lyric books in addition to other dominant forms—allegory; romance; treatise; stanzaic philosophical, moral, and religious verse; and so on. In England, however, these other forms dominated to such a degree that fifteenth-century poets devoted relatively little effort to lyric and virtually none to the lyric sequence. Perhaps Charles mainly looks back in French but in English mainly looks forward simply because in 1440 there was not much grand English lyric tradition on which his poetry *could* look back—no *trouvères,* not as much court patronage of lyric, no lyric theorists like Deschamps or Machaut to articulate patterns and conventions for lyric. Not that England was unlettered, of course, but lyric did not enjoy in England the self-consciously textual status it did in France at that time: most lyric available in England was in French until the sixteenth century.[6] But Charles's English lyric book is something new to England, and there is no love-lyric sequence as large or with as much literary self-consciousness until Watson's 1582 *Hekatompathia.*

Charles, Medieval English Poet?

In many ways, of course, this poetry does fit in with its fifteenth-century field. Its orthography, its courtly metaphors, its reliance on ballade and roundel forms, its flower-and-leaf poems, its personifications, its dream-vision incidents, and especially its opening narrative verses that introduce a young lover to the service of Cupid—all these features must have made it familiar to its original English audiences (and have been the features most often discussed by medievalists).[7] Some scholars have pointed out that

    4. *English Courtly Love Lyrics.*
    5. See especially J. Cerquiglini, *"Un engin si soutil": Guillaume de Machaut et l'écriture au XIVème siècle* (Geneva: Slatkine, 1985); S. Huot, *From Song to Book* (Ithaca: Cornell University Press, 1987); and K. Brownlee, *Poetic Identity in Guillaume de Machaut* (Madison: University of Wisconsin Press, 1984).
    6. Boffey, *English Courtly Love Lyrics.* See also, for example, "Literary Culture," Scattergood's essay on the courts of Richard II. Even in the late fifteenth and early sixteenth centuries our lyric was more heavily reliant on French than we have tended to discuss.
    7. For lists of articles and books on such topics, see Galderisi, *Charles d'Orléans;* Nelson, *Charles d'Orléans;* Yenal, *Charles d'Orléans;* and the extensive bibliography to Arn's edition, *Fortunes Stabilnes.*

Charles's English work does often glance back at Chaucer's in diction and descriptive technique.[8] Arn, for instance, expands Steele and Day's introduction considerably on this point, especially in her notes on Chaucerian echoes throughout the poetry. We know that Charles's brother Jean d'Angoulême read Chaucer, for his copy of *Canterbury Tales* is extant.[9] Charles also spent time captive in the household of Chaucer's granddaughter Alice, the duchess of Suffolk, and developed an enduring friendship with her husband, William de la Pole, duke of Suffolk.

In light of these connections, it seems remarkable that Charles's English work is not more "Chaucerian" than it is. The Chaucerian Charles is found mostly in the narrative framework of Harley 682, and the several hundred English lyrics are not primarily Chaucerian in technique or tone. By that I mean not primarily narrative, not primarily focused on the creation of character and the mimesis of social actualities, not primarily attempting a "Chaucerian" authorship in the way that, for example, Seth Lerer in *Chaucer and His Readers* shows other post-Chaucerian inheritors to do. Derek Pearsall does point out that traces of the Chaucerian court spirit—"elegant, witty, carelessly sophisticated, alert to every allusion and flash of irony"—remain in Charles's poetry and that of the Suffolk circle; nevertheless he admits that "their elegance is neo-French rather than Chaucerian."[10]

Likewise, although they do share vocabulary and certain underlying ideas with Charles, most other fifteenth-century English poets write in nonlyric modes. The *Kingis Quair,* despite its Boethianism and its similar origins from the pen of a foreign prince-prisoner (James I), is a stanzaic narrative that does not emphasize the same singularity and immediacy of experience. Nor do Langland and the *Gawain*-poet devote their energies to lyric expression. Clanvowe's *Boke of Cupid* is a love-narrative that does not emphasize a singularity of experience. Hoccleve does, in his *Complaint,* acknowledge the fragmentation of the singular inner self in an experiential rather than an allegorical way; though he seems especially Charles-like in penning his own interiority, Hoccleve does not use an extended set of lyric forms as the vehicle of his expression, and he operates in a clerkly-literary context unlike that in which Charles wrote and maintains a more confessional or autobiographical narrative. Hoccleve's chief work is the

---

8. Arn, ed., *Fortunes Stabilnes,* 39–43.

9. BN f. ang. 39, studied by M. M. Crow, "John of Angoulême and His Chaucer Manuscript," *Speculum* 17 (1942): 86–99.

10. *John Lydgate,* 70.

Regement of Princes, and his other work is largely stanzaic and moral-narrative in form and theme.[11]

Lydgate writes a fair number of ballades, but most are occasional pieces and/or moral-religious pieces—a sheriff's dinner and a mutable Boethian "midsomer rose." Pearsall points out that Lydgate's courtly poetry comes early in his life[12] and discusses a poem relevant to our consideration of the essential separateness of Charles's poetics from the main fifteenth-century trends. "A Reproof to Lydgate" was written probably by Suffolk or someone in the Suffolk circle (recall that Charles resided with Suffolk for several years and the two remained in contact even after 1440). The "Reproof" appears in the Fairfax 16 manuscript. After a stanza of sincere praise of Chaucer's poetry comes this fainter address to Lydgate:

And to the monke of bury now speke I
ffor thy connyng ys syche and eke thy grace
After Chaucer to occupy his place
Besychyng the my penne to enlumyne . . .
Yit god defende that euery thyng were trew
That clerkes wryte for then myght thys be preuyd
That ye haue sayd which wyll not be byleuyd
I late yow wyt for trysteth verely
In your conseyt yt is an eresy.[13]

The rest of the poem takes Lydgate to task for his misogynist views, and like Skelton ("Philip Sparowe," ll. 804–12), for instance, this author seems to find Lydgate a pompous gasbag. "There is a suggestion of parody . . . of Lydgate's invocatory style" in the poem, which, as Pearsall says, "is a neat literary spoof, and the tone of condescension is what we might expect of an aristocratic poet who was also a friend (and gaoler) of that most aristocratic and sophisticated of poet-exiles, Charles d'Orléans."[14] Members of this circle evidently perceived themselves as separate, and cultivated poetic

---

11. On Hoccleve's contexts as distinct from Charles's, see Ethan Knapp, "Bureaucratic Identity and the Construction of the Self in Hoccleve's *Formulary* and *La male regle,*" *Speculum* 74 (1999): 357–76. On the *Regement of Princes,* see Derek Pearsall, "Hoccleve's *Regement of Princes:* The Poetics of Royal Self-Representation," *Speculum* 69 (1994): 386–410.

12. *John Lydgate,* chap. 4.

13. Transcribed from Eleanor Prescott Hammond, *English Verse between Chaucer and Surrey* (New York: Octagon Books, 1965), 200; the full poem with discussion is on 198–201.

14. Pearsall, *John Lydgate,* 163, 184. Lydgate's *Fall of Princes* includes Louis d'Orléans, Charles's father. How Charles may have responded to that is unknown.

habits distinct enough that they could parody the poetry of the Monk of Bury. Pearsall, too, perceives the distinctiveness of their sensibility: "They [Charles, Suffolk, and Sir Richard Roos] are the exceptions to the record we have" of fifteenth-century poetry (70).

Outside of Charles's small, distinctive literary circle, the only other poet roughly contemporary with Charles who works in lyric and lyric sequences—and the resemblance is, finally, very slight—is Gower. Like Charles, Gower supervises the copying and material presentation of his work, something R. F. Yaeger reminds us is "most unusual."[15] Gower, in the generation before Charles, also does write two lyric sequences, the *Cinkante Ballades* and the *Traitié pour essampler dez amantz maries.* That these sequences are in French reminds us that the lyric book/lyric sequence was still, in fifteenth-century England, a French-affiliated form.[16] Gower's *Cinkante Ballades* resembles Charles's French work more than it resembles his English work—courtly, abstract, polished in the Machaut-Deschamps tradition—but Gower's other poetry is narrative (*Confessio amantis,* e.g.) and is thus better aligned with other late-medieval English poets than is Charles's lyric book. Gower's other lyric sequence, the *Traitié,* is didactic, intended to instruct married people on how to stay faithful to each other. Robert Quixley in fact translated the *Traitié* into English in 1402, but it is an occasional translation made for his daughter's marriage.[17] Formally a ballade sequence, the *Traitié* of "moral Gower" is after all a treatise, not a secular and highly literary lyric book like Harley 682.

In form, production, purpose, context, and content, then, Charles's poetry stands out quite distinctly from other late-medieval English poetry. Some recent scholarship, however, has called into question certain assumptions about writerly subjectivity and the status of authorship in this period, and it bears on the case at hand. For instance, some scholars have modified, for example, Boffey's and Yaeger's sense of how rare it was for late-medieval authors to intervene in the copying and revision of their work.[18] A. C. Spearing sees this attention to the codicological existence of the writing as one aspect of a gradually growing sense, beginning in the fourteenth century, of what it is to be a vernacular poet:

---

15. *John Gower's Poetic* (Cambridge: D. S. Brewer, 1990), 2.

16. On the matter of the choice of languages, see Yaeger, "'Oure Englishe' and Everyone's Latin," *South Atlantic Review* 46 (1981): 41–53, or *John Gower's Poetic,* 9–10 and 85–88.

17. MacCracken, *Quixley's Ballades Royal.*

18. Boffey, *English Courtly Love Lyrics,* says of Charles that "no other fifteenth century poet prepared and polished his work in this way" (63).

> The emerging figure of the vernacular poet expresses a consciousness of poetic vocation: he presents himself as a writer, for whom poetic composition is a goal in itself. . . . And this consciousness frequently extends beyond individual compositions and individual genres to include a sense of the poetic oeuvre as a unified achievement attached to a name that will last.[19]

Spearing's examples of this poetic self-consciousness, however, are not primarily English: Chaucer and Langland, yes, but also Machaut, Froissart, Petrarch, Christine de Pisan, and of course Charles d'Orléans. Placing the bicultural Charles in this particular cross-cultural line of self-assertive vernacular poets helps us clarify both his unusual position and its English literary context: he is part of something admittedly new and important in medieval poetics, but he is nevertheless an extreme representative and early avatar in England of a fundamentally continental (and mainly French) sense of what it means to be a poet. In other words, while Charles's writerly identity and efforts at creating a lyric book are indeed extraordinary in fifteenth-century England, they do not come out of nowhere, but rather stand out as a significant development (against a less well developed English context) of "poetic identity" and authorial agency. Spearing has pointed out other ways in which Charles's poems look both forward and back;[20] he explores some remarkable similarities in the self-presentations of authors such as Chaucer, Hoccleve, Margery Kempe, James I, Skelton, Charles, and Spenser, who are writing in English during the "transitional" time. Burrow's *Thomas Hoccleve* also suggests that the attempt at singular authorial positioning is fundamentally a French phenomenon: in the *Series* Hoccleve follows the French tradition "in which a sequence of what might otherwise be freestanding pieces is held together by the author's presence in the text as the 'I' who composes them."[21]

In general, then, where Charles's poetry is like that of other fifteenth-century English poets, it is due to some Frenchness or French-rootedness of Middle English poetry, not to Charles's adaptation to his English milieu. Burrow and Spearing remind us that there is cross-cultural conti-

---

19. "Poetic Subject," 36.
20. *Medieval to Renaissance in English Poetry,* especially 279–80.
21. (Newcastle-upon-Tyne: Athenaeum Press, 1994), 25–26 n. 102. For other connections between Hoccleve and France, see Burrow's "Hoccleve and the Middle French Poets," in *The Long Fifteenth Century: Essays for Douglas Gray,* ed. H. Cooper and S. Mapstone (Oxford: Clarendon, 1997), 35–49.

nuity, not only division, between the late-medieval and Renaissance periods in this respect. Nevertheless, "continuity" and "similarity" do not necessarily mean "transition": *transition* implies a linear progress in literary change, a moving between one thing and another. "Transitional" thus may not be the best word for this case, since Charles's singular sort of expression of authorial agency, subjectivity, and self-consciousness, not to mention this sort of production and assembly of the lyric book, is not widespread in English lyric until the sonnets of the sixteenth century. In that sense Charles works proleptically as much as transitionally in his chosen genre; his unusual English lyric "I" occupies an early, extreme position in what scholars like Spearing, Burrow, Middleton, and Brownlee have identified as a gradual continuum of increasingly self- and text-conscious medieval writers. Until Charles and Harley 682 (and after him, not until the 1580s and 1590s), we simply did not have in English this conception of the secular lyric book as high and serious literature nor of the high lyric poet. Our main modes for literary high seriousness were hagiographic, allegorical, philosophical, religious, and even romance forms, while our short forms were largely religious, georgic, or occasional. When regarded across national and period boundaries, then, Charles's work in English represents a significant innovation in and reshaping of the work venue of the serious poet—a considerable extension of the fifteenth-century literary field.

Charles's Departures from Medieval Modes: Representative Examples

When Charles turns away from fifteenth-century modes of allegory and narrative to create what is in English a new sort of literary production, he forges new treatments of old themes. As Helen Vendler once remarked, there are really only three topics, themes, or content areas in love lyric: I love you, please love me back, and I'm sorry you're dead.[22] Charles handles all three, and given this rather limited topical range in a relatively "contentless" genre, we might expect a limited number of similar or standard themes in books of love poetry even across periods. The "lover's hope," for example, is a standard early modern love-theme, but Charles handles it more in the manner of a sixteenth- than of a fifteenth-century poet. His English treatment of the lover's hope shares as much with Wyatt

---

22. In a presentation at the University of Virginia, April 1993.

or even Sidney as it shares with his own French poems or with the English poems of his contemporaries. A Chaucerian poet might have opened with something along the lines of this *Romaunt de la Rose* fragment (an English version attributed to Chaucer):

> Blessed be Hope with which desire
> Advances lovers in such manner
> Good Hope is courteous to please
> To keep all lovers from dis-ease
> Hope kepith his bond, and wil abide
> For any peril that may betide . . .
> (Sweet thought) makes lovers have remembrance
> Of Comfort and of high Pleasaunce
> That Hope hath called them for to win . . .
>
> If Hope fails me then am I
> Ungracious and unworthy
> In Hope wil I comforted be
> For Love, when he taught to me,
> Sais that Hope whereso I go,
> Should be release to my wo.
>
> (Fragment B, 2775–2803)

The lines are descriptive, conventional, and heavily proverbial; they personify and elevate the abstraction in the fairly typical allegorical method of a foundational medieval love poem. As Daniel Poirion has explored, Charles keeps his use of Esperaunce in the French poetry in an allegorical line.[23] In English, however, Charles alters the allegorical, beginning his Ballade 52, for example, with a vivid, questioning apostrophe: "What meanest thou, hope? dost thou me skoffe and scorne? / For wordis moche thou hast and flattering." This straw-man personification does not serve a larger allegory. It is closer to the treatment of hope in, say, Sidney's *Astrophel and Stella* 67, which begins by asking, "Hope, art thou true, or dost thou flatter me?" moving straight past Hope to other matter. Consider the resemblances between their opening lines: the direct address, not allegorical description; the nearly identical, skeptical questions, not a plaintive iconography that adheres to the conventional hierarchies. The persona

---

23. Daniel Poirion, "La Nef d'Espérance," in *Mélanges de langue et de littérature de Moyen Âge et de la Renaissance offerts à Jean Frappier* (Geneva: Droz, 1970), 2:913–28.

suspects he is being manipulated and is not afraid to speak up. Charles shares with Sidney a notable lack of reverence toward what had been, at least since the thirteenth century, a rather powerful allegorical figure, Esperaunce or Hope. Hope is a rhetorical pretext for Sidney and Charles.

If Charles can reduce Hope to a brief rhetorical tool, could he also scorn Despair? Despair was the worst of Love's five "bad" or deadly arrows (*Roman de la Rose,* 957–84), really a sin changed to secular icon. Desespoir (or Desesperaunce) appears allegorically to thwart the lover in Charles's French lyrics (e.g., in Rondeau XII; in the highly stylized allegory of Chanson XXIII; in Rondeau CCLXVIII, a request that Fortune keep him safe from conquest by Despair; in Complainte VIb 310). But in Charles's English, Despair becomes despair. Of his six English uses of forms of the word *despair,* only one is allegorical (1018); in the other five cases the speaker expresses his particular, individualized experience of despair. Ballade 108, for example, begins: "Half in dispeyre—not half, but clene dispeyrid, / I take my leve of loue for onys and ay" (ll. 6101–2; see also ll. 1934, 2750, 5634, and 5844). Charles's speaker seems, in fact, closer to despairing, angry Wyatt than to a conventional medieval poet—despite the considerable variety of "conventional" medieval poetry—even when he is not using the actual word *despair.*[24] Wyatt-like, Charles in English explores aspects of the experience of love darker than frustrated desire and does so in ways much less conventionally courtly or medieval. In this roundel, for example, the speaker expresses resentment and anger toward the beloved in apostrophe.

> Ye schal be payd after your whylfulnes
> And blame nothyng but your mysgouernaunce
> For when good loue would fayn had you auans
> Then went ye back wth wyly frauhyednes
>
> I knew anon your sutyl wylenes . . .
> Ye schal be payd after your wylfulnes
>   . . . Ye might have been my lady and maistres
> For evermor withouten variance
> But now my hert in ynglond or in fraunce
> Ys go to seke other new besynes
> Ye schal be payd . . .
>
>   (BN f. fr. 25458; BL Royal F 16.ii)

---

24. Another medieval English poet who expresses a similar personal desperation is Hoccleve, as he looks in his mirror and explores his own mental illness (*Complaint* ll. 155–68).

This dark, postbreakup vengefulness does not, for instance, personify "Willfulness" or "Misgovernance," nor does it set them in any intricate web of allegorical action ("Willfulness rose from her thorny bed and joined hands with Misgovernance in attacking Love" or some such). Rather, Charles's poem anticipates, for example, Wyatt's voice in this "Song,"

> But since to change thou dost delight
> And that thy faith hath taen his flight
> As thou deservest I shall thee quit
> I promise thee, I promise thee,[25]

or even the tone of "They flee from me":

> But all is turned thorough my gentleness
> Into a strange fashion of forsaking
> And I have leave to go of her goodness
> And she also to use newfangleness
> But since that I so kindly am served
> I would fain know what she hath deserved.

The poems share more than tone and theme, however. The apostrophe and the wrangling with an unsatisfying "ex" create a kind of direct emotional agon that results not in a series of static pictures, not a "story" of love handled allegorically or narratively, but in something else: a shifting kaleidoscope that imitates the changeable experience of love (and meanwhile displays the lyric speaker's versatility). Sometimes the confident voice praises, is witty, is awestruck; sometimes it doubts, accuses, is despairing and vengeful. This variability, this restlessness, is a significant departure from the more level and abstract courtly conventions that had troped the medieval experience of love. We are a long way from the flower and the leaf, "la chiere lie," and Pleasant Bewte in the Garden of Deduiz. (We are also, notably, rather far from the usual Petrarchan dynamic of frustrated yet continually idealizing desire.) Like many sixteenth-century English sonneteers, Charles in the English poetry adds to the old allegori-

---

25. Wyatt, Song 214, *The Complete Poems*, 271–72. One scholar connects Wyatt and Charles because they both use the phrase "They Flee From Me": Leonard Nathan, "Tradition and Newfangledness in Wyatt's 'They Fle From Me,'" *Journal of English Literary History* 32 (1965): 1–16, discusses Charles's Ballade 38, in which the phrase appears, and Rondeau 69. To my mind the phrase appears in very different contexts and its use is less important than the tone and self-struggling persona that connect these two poets.

cal treatments of standard themes of love these direct, rhetorically playful, and experiential treatments. Daunger, Esperaunce, Disport: while these do appear, personified and not, in Charles's lyrics, and while the length of the sequence would permit full allegories, he does not in the English poems set such figures in the consistently analogical relationships he does in the French poetry. Although his French lyrics are allegorical in that they sustain personifications and analogies in a consistent and extended double network of meanings, Charles in the English lyrics is not aiming primarily at allegorical representation.[26]

Now we are in the gray area of the individual reader's apprehensions: Arn's edition adds capitalization that in my opinion tends to overemphasize personifications; reading that edition might let one more easily perceive an allegorical Charles (which is to say a "medieval" Charles). But editorial choices of course influence and are influenced by interpretive choices; Arn adds the capitalization because, feeling that medieval readers may have assumed more allegorizing than we do,[27] she prefers to emphasize the allegory: and it works. George Watson Taylor's edition, though not scholarly, gives a very different impression, as it does not capitalize in this way. William Calin wisely suggests that some of Charles's lyrics are condensed allegories.[28] I would add that many Renaissance conceits or extended metaphors could be "unpacked" as miniaturized allegories, and that one identifiable feature of literary change during these centuries is an increasing compression and condensation in figurative language, not unrelated perhaps to what Alastair Fowler sees as a Renaissance "epigrammatic shift."[29] If we were to add capitalization to any number of Renais-

---

26. For expanded discussion of this point, and some disagreements, see Ann Tukey Harrison's *Charles d'Orléans*. For a look at the more allegorical Charles, or at least at his use of personifications, see Ballade 29, Ballade 41 (in which Hope could be either a personified or an introjected agent), Ballade 80, or Ballade 44 ("A daunger here y cast to thee my gloue," challenging the old personification to an updated courtly contest). For readings that discuss allegorical motives in Charles's poetry (and that emphasize the French, of course) see Susan Stakel, "Allegory and Artistic Production in the Poetry of Charles d'Orléans," *Fifteenth Century Studies* 14 (1988): 161–78; and Paul Zumthor, "Charles d'Orléans et le langage de l'allégorie," in *Mélanges offerts à Rita Lejeune*, ed. J. Ducolot-Gembloux (n.p., 1969), 2:1481–1502. Zumthor, for instance, treats only the French poetry yet provides a working definition of allegory that allows one to see Charles's work in a continuum of figurative method: allegory is "une métaphore, plus ou moins développée, comportant une ou plusieurs personifications" (1481).
27. *Fortunes Stabilnes*, 126.
28. "The Density of the Text: Charles d'Orleans," in *Mélanges de langue et de littératures offerts à Alice Planche*, 2 vols. (Paris: Les Belles Lettres, 1984), 1:97–104.
29. *Kinds of Literature* (Cambridge: Harvard University Press, 1982), 195–202.

sance lyrics, in other words, we might read into them a more "medieval" effect, but still not find allegory. Think of Sidney's "A strife is grown between Virtue and Love" (*Astrophel and Stella* 52), "Queen Virtue's court, which some call Stella's face / Prepared by Nature's chiefest furniture" (9), "Virtue, alas, now let me take some rest / Thou sett'st a bate between my Will and Wit" (4): repeated personifications, even capitalized, do not necessarily add up to allegory. Sidney's condensed figurative method, like Charles's, uses repeated apostrophes to various entities (personified and not), but allegory involves a more consistent use of the personifications in a sustained connective ideation. In any case, relative to Charles's own French poetry and relative to the English poetry of his day, Charles's English lyric mode, with or without the added capitalization, is less allegorical than it is densely figured, experiential, dramatic, direct.

Instead of allegory, or, in addition to condensed allegories, there are also Charles's dramatic openings, his puns, and his inclusion of the erotic. Specific examples of all three will be treated here as part of what distinguishes Charles's poetry from its milieu, but, in general, the three features work together and tend to involve a play of tone and voice and a ludic sensibility. Puns in the English poems (the several noted in chapter 2 above and any number of others) indicate a playfulness with words and a hyperconsciousness of the surfaces and depths in any given line of poetry. In one sense, allegory and pun are opposite methods. Allegory directs the reader's attention to deepening and consistently connected layers of meaning, to a network of meaning that spreads as the poetry proceeds. Allegory asks the reader to take the word as a sign and to learn gradually, over the course of a work, what is indicated behind and unfolded beneath it. Puns, on the contrary, demand a reader's quick apprehension and immediate attentiveness to the surface of the word, to its multiple and simultaneous possibilities, and to the connections among these possibilities. Puns point to the immanent lexical potential residing in a word and to the immediate contexts of the word—the line, the stanza, the poem. Where allegory asks the reader to go deep and to go long (aerobic), puns ask for quick anaerobic bursts of flexibility and an apprehension of polyvalence in multiple semantic contexts.[30] Puns are also intensely social, like in-jokes; they create instant community of shared (fleeting) experience. Either you get it or you

---

30. As Susannah Brietz Monta points out, Spenser would be a notable exception, since he manages to weave the surface textures of puns into the deepening allegorical ideation of his epic (private correspondence, May 1999). But in general, puns and allegories demand different things of readers and authors.

don't; Charles relies on his audience's immediate phonetic and lexical apprehension and on their sense of (literary) humor as well. Critics and theorists of polysemy and paranomasia have called this serious intellectual play, a defining characteristic of Renaissance literature, "wit."

Often Charles's puns have sexual connotations. A favorite pun in the English sequence, for example, the "kercher of plesaunce," plays on the phrase's literal meaning, a veil of fine linen, and on the other meaning of *pleasaunce,* romantic or sexual pleasure. Charles repeats the pun in both lyric and narrative sections of the English work. In the narrative frame, it is Venus who wears a kercher of plesaunce around her middle (4764, 5170, 5183, 5184, 5285). Arn notes that in the English depiction of Venus, "the use of a head-covering for a loincloth is intentionally remarkable" and is special to Charles, although wordplay in French on *plesaunce* was not. "As usual, Charles borrows [from Chaucer's *Parliament of Fowls*] but does not imitate; he replaces *Valence* with *plesaunce,* a word . . . which offers better opportunities for word play" (508). I would add that his is less an allegorical than a concrete and descriptive mode of wordplay, and one with an erotic charge. In the lyrics, *plesaunce* is a bandage, literal and figurative, to the ailing lover ("For of plesaunce his wounde hit hath a tent," l. 404). It is elsewhere part of the English heart's "mortgage" in a list of goods to be traded for a kiss:

If hit plese yow yowre cossis forto selle
I redy am here forto bie hem welle
Which geue yow shall myn hert as in morgage
Hit to dispende as yowre owen heritage
Mi loue and of pleasaunce a thousand elle.

(Roundel 41)

An "ell" is about forty-five inches of cloth; "a thousand elle" promises quite a lengthy pleasaunce by any standards. The pun invites an imagined erotic richness like that found in Marvell's hyperboles of foreplay in "Coy Mistress," though here the promise of extended lovemaking is compressed into a single double-entendre, and love is troped as a sort of pawnshop trade, depreciating the English conceit in the courtly economy. The French version's traditional vocabulary maintains its loftier level:

Mon veuil et mon desir entiers
Sont vostres, maugré tous dangiers,

Faittes, comme loyalle et sage,
Que pour mon guerdon et partage,
Je soye servy des premiers . . .

(Chanson XLI)

The French poem keeps to the usual vocabulary of love-tokens, without the erotic wordplay on *plesaunce* that Charles adds to the English version. Pleasaunce also serves as a safe package for the heart in one of the more conventional heart-exchange poems. The speaker of Ballade 32 tells the lady his heart "wrappid is parde / Hool in a plesaunt kercher of plesaunce / And so is closid for a more sewrete." Charles never forgets the tactile, erotic, and bodily dimensions of love, and he often lets this be known through such puns and tonal play.

French love-allegory's codified extended vocabulary and its euphemized eroticism give way in Charles's English to concrete images, sexy puns, frequent apostrophe, interrogation, implied speech, acknowledgment of physical desire—all accompanying the particular tone or stance we call (in speaking of Renaissance poets) *sprezzatura*. As in Renaissance sequences, Charles's dramatic opening lines keep steady attention on the central speaking position, the persona. They also create a convincing impression of speech and presence, of encounters between the speaker and beloved (as do, for instance, Donne's dramatic first lines: "Stand still, and I will read to thee," "Mark but this flea," or "Busy old fool, unruly Sun"). In fact, about every third or fourth poem in this sequence begins with an exclamatory or interrogative phrase. The poems move among apostrophe, meditation, and deixis in much the way Renaissance sonnet sequences of Sidney, Daniel, or Spenser do. "I yield my self to you! Save you my life!" cries Ballade 102; "Lodge me, dear heart, in your arms twain, / And give me a sweet kiss, two or three" insists Roundel 43. "Madame, ye ought well know," Ballade 16, is one among many that directly address the lady. "Oh Fy! Fortune Fy!" (Ballade 118), "Oh Fy, Love, Fy!" (Roundel 70), "Alak! Y kan now neither love nor may" (Ballade 36), and "Allas, sir, allas, sir, pardon me!" (Ballade 76) are among the many exclamatory openings addressed to others.

Chapter 3 treated Ballade 14 ("Now what tydings my lady and maistres / How farith our love I pray you hertily?") in an extended discussion of textual self-consciousness and the lyric "I." That poem's dramatic opening implies a confident, effortless presence, a *sprezzatura*, but the poem also contains a tension and drama between the lover and lady that has anti-courtly implications. Charles's speaker does make many of the conventional vows of fidelity and service.[31] But he also, as Donne or Wyatt might do, reminds the lady that he needs from her the same kind of promises, and more than promises. The refrain of Ballade 14, "But in like wise let se acquiteth yow," emphasizes the mutuality of this relationship and implies distrust, repeating so often that the lady had better be faithful too. That the lady is assumed not to be a chaste Laura or an ethereally ethical Beatrice also moves Charles's sequence closer to Wyatt than Petrarch. Charles's lady *is* superior, according to several heavily conventional ballades: Ballade 1 begins, "Most goodly fayre aboue alle þo lyuyng," and Ballade 9, for example, praises her particular qualities:

> Fresshe Bewte, riche of yowthe and lustynes,
> The smylyng lookis casten so louely,
> The plesaunt speche gouernyd bi wittynes,
> Body wel shape, of port so womanly,
> The high estat demenyd so swetely,
> The well ensweridnes of word and chere,
> Without disdeyne shewyng to lowe and hye
> (For which all folk hir prayse, and so do y)
> Alle thewis goode this hath my lady dere.

Even her superiority is not completely conventional: he includes the shape of her body and her equal treatment of the lowly. And there is plenty of trouble in paradise. Not only the refrain of Ballade 14, "but lyke wise let se acquiteth yow," implies mistrust; Ballade 110, a poem about gossip, implies the lady and speaker have argued over it and that the speaker is powerless over the situation ("What may y more? Y sory am therfor"). Ballade 46 figures love as a chess game in which the speaker plans his next move. "But al is not as y koude wisshe it were," the refrain of Ballade 114, admits realistically that things aren't going so well. Poems like this throughout the sequence offer socially grounded expressions of the speaker's and lady's experience of the less dreamy sides of desire. In addition to praise of an ideal love-object, Charles includes erotic desire, doubt,

---

31. "But for this tyme, my lijf forth dewring / . . . That wolde y axe withouten wage or fee / In yowre service to spende my lustynes" (Ballade 1); he vows "to serue and nevyr fayne" (Ballade 11) and to remain "in trewe service" (Ballade 12). See also Ballades 13, 15, and 16. The conventional vows of fidelity and service come most frequently early in the sequence.

hesitance, a desire for mutuality, and acknowledgment of the many troubling possibilities in love.

Ballade 115, like so many others, opens by implying a dramatic encounter. "Allas madame what maner strijf / Is ther bitwene yowre mouth and y," the speaker asks. The speaker reads the lady's face as if he were Astrophel explicating Stella's features (cf. *Astrophel and Stella* 3, 9, 43, 52, 66, 67, 71). The first lines contain a flirtatious, bodily pun, too, implying, with the pun on "y" (eye and I), both a struggle within the lady (your mouth and your eye, or your words and your glances, are in strife) and a struggling kiss (your mouth and I, the lover, are in strife). The lyric dialectic of the absent-presence is no idealized, Petrarchan one for Charles, and no abstract allegorized one, either. He is as much a poet of the body and of drama and doubt in love as are Sidney and Donne, imagining as he does a very present contact between their bodies.[32] The speaker's woes are specifically erotic: he'll wail and weep henceforth, "Syn that y may not stroke þe sidis smal / Of yowre swete body, ful of lustynes" (Roundel 60). He regrets no longer being able to rub her slender body ("that y ne may now stroke yowre sidis pleyne," Ballade 11). He imagines her physical being: "As y haue thoughtis on yow where y goo / Of yowre fayre body & streight sidis playne" (Roundel 9). When he actually does see her, he reports that her slender waist and vibrant youthfulness are what give him particular joy ("Myn hert even full is of gladnes / When y biholde the yowthe and lustynes / Of yowre body with long streight sidis tay," Roundel 7). Elsewhere, the speaker recalls having played "footsie" with the lady.

> She was when last we partid compane
> Which plesid hir say (to bring me out of woo,
> Tredyng my foot and that so pratily),
> "Teys yow to whom y loue am and no moo"
>
> (Ballade 47)

There are "kiss" poems, chiefly roundels. There are also a number of poems that venture beyond the conventional euphemisms of desire into the specifics. With a hushed intensity, he writes directly of his desire, "the

---

32. Compare the kiss poems in *Astrophel and Stella* ("Second Song," 73, 74, 79, 80, 81, 82); compare Donne's Elegy XIX or "Dream" or Carew and Lovelace's implied and recounted encounters.

next time, my lady and mastres, / I come to yow to doon my obeyshaunce," to be alone together in intimate darkness: "Hadde y my wisshe, / y were [without] candill light / Even with the verry sorse of womanhed" (Ballade 51). He longs for her body: not only her "smylyng mouth and laughing eyen grey" but "the brestis rounde and long smal armys twayne / The hondis smoþe, þe sidis streight and pleyne / Yowre fetis lite" (Roundel 69). The brief blason leaves the rest to the imagination, as most blasons do, ending with a safe but tantalizing "what shulde y ferþer say?"

One controversial poem, Ballade 116, is built on the possible sexual connotations in the word *occupy*.[33] This racy, punning poem begins with a scene in which the speaker is on his knees before the lady, begging her to "lend" him her mouth. (It is unclear which orifice he means, since throughout the poem both coitus and oral kisses could be implied.) The lady asks why he wishes to "occupy" her mouth—a word with a history of erotic double-entendre. Occupy: to hold or possess lands, offices, or goods (*MED* 1–4), to be busy with (*MED* 9a), to come before a city to propose battle (*MED* 12); but also to employ or to have in one's employ (*MED* 11), to fill a space, to fill up, to take up a space in or on, or to inhabit (*MED* 5, 6, 7), and, from *occupare amplexu,* to have sexual relations with (9b). His answer, that he wishes to occupy the mouth so as to kiss it two or three times before he "dies," recalls the use of *die* to imply orgasm in sixteenth-century songs and poems (though this is not an attributed use in the fifteenth century, according to *MED*). The word *occupy* joins metaphoric and literal possibilities—the metaphoric being in this case the possession, employment, besieging of the mouth, and the literal being the bodily occupation of the space of the orifice.

> [*Amant.*] Lende me yowre praty mouth, Madame
> Se how y knele here at yowre feet?
> [*Lady.*] Whie wolde ye occupy the same?
> Now wherabowt first mot me wite.
> [*A.*] Iwis, dere hert, to basse it swete
> A twyse or thrise or that y die.
> [*L.*] So may ye haue when next we mete
> Toforne or ye it occupie.

---

33. Arn's note to line 6639 reviews the critical mentions and provides further references (*Fortunes Stabilnes,* 537).

[*A.*] Or y it occupy? Wel wel!
Is my reward but such a skorne?
[*L.*] Ye woo is me for yowre seek hele,
But it may heele right wel tomorne.
[*A.*] Then se y wel: though y were lorne
For oon poore cosse, ye sett not by
[*L.*] Seide y yow not ynough toforne:
Ye may haue or it occupy?

[*A.*] Ye, for that cosse y thanke yow that,
Forwhi yet am y nevir þe nere.
[*L.*] Then come agayne, this wot ye what,
Anothir tyme—and not to yere.
[*A.*] A fy! Wel wel! A, swet hert dere
By verry god, ye mot aby!
[*L.*] Nay, bete me not, first take it here
Toforne or ye it occupy.

[*A.*] Ye so so swete! Ye so swete hert!
Good thrift vnto þat praty eye!
[*L.*] Nay, erst lo must ye this avert—
How y seide "or ye it occupy."

Thomas Reed, following Utley, says this is a poem "in which a lover is utterly stymied by his mistress until he threatens to beat her, which apparently so amply demonstrates his virtue and love that she relents"; I find that a serious misreading of the playful, mutual sexual banter in the poem.[34] Even Arn doubts the "risqué overtones" of the poem, and Steele and Day's edition notes only the connection of the word *occupy* with its Latin ancestors. My reading is admittedly more bold than this; since most critics have said that the meaning is obscure or have avoided the poem altogether, and since its features are relevant to the larger poetic issues here, it is worth a closer look. The poem, I believe, is a witty, playfully erotic one that can best be read as a bantering dialogue in which tone of voice carries implications and in which certain repeated lines undergo a change of meaning. This sort of punning or double entendre, as is the case

---

34. Reed, *Middle English Debate Poetry,* 163; Utley, cited in Arn, ed., *Fortunes Stabilnes,* 537 n. 6369.

with many of Charles's poems, relies on and creates a vivid impression of speech.

The male speaker expresses specific desires, and the lady defers but teases him, eventually granting at least some sexual favors. These seem to include or at least allude to oral-genital foreplay as well as intercourse—after all, he is kneeling before the lady and wishes to kiss the mouth before him, the mouth he wants to "occupy," twice or thrice before he "dies" (ll. 6371–72 especially provoke the imagination of oscular oscillations). The female speaker puts him off but in doing so uses provocatively punning language. Read with one tone of voice, a lightly joking, nay-saying tone, lines 6373–74 reject the man firmly: "so may ye *haue* [died] when next we mete / Toforne or ye it occupie" (emphasis added), or in modern speech, "yes, you'll have died indeed before you ever get to kiss me." On another level the words more mockingly hint that he may well "die" before she lets him kiss her—in other words, he will reach orgasm elsewhere, or otherwise not "occupy" successfully. Immediately, the male speaker takes umbrage at this "skorne," this insult. The female speaker's next words hold out the possibility that something yet may happen between them: you're in love-woe now, she says to him, but you may be "healed" of it tomorrow (ll. 6377–78). (There is a hint here of the classic question, "But will you still love me tomorrow?") Seeing an opening, as it were, he presses, begging for just "oon poore cosse." Her changed refrain, "Seide y yow not ynough toforne: / Ye *may* haue *or* ye ocupy?" (emphasis added, but metrically sound) calls him back, especially if said with a smile in the voice (ll. 6379–80). The altered rhythm of the new refrain creates the tonal change that revisits and revises her previous refrain: "Didn't you hear what I said before? not that you may have *died* before you get a kiss"—although that was indeed a natural way to interpret the cadences of her first refrain—"but that you may *have* [a kiss] *before* you 'occupy.'" She asks him here, in other words, to reread between her lines, and in fact rereads the line for him, playfully changing the emphasis of her refrain to accommodate increasing desire. (This is sometimes known as flirting and can be quite pleasurable.)

Next, in the white space between stanzas—just as in poems by Donne, for example—the lovers evidently kiss, for the man begins stanza 3 by thanking the woman for that kiss and regretting his frequent absence from her (ll. 6383–84). She then petulantly says, as if in response to the sudden reminder that he's only a part-time partner, "Then come back again, and not before a year!" At this the male speaker sputters in anger, "Well, stay here then!" and implies that he'll walk out on her now. She, however, detains him: "Nay bete me not, first take it here / Toforne or ye it occupy." This is the controversial line that leads Reed and Utley to assume a physical threat, but "bete" had figurative as well as literal usages, according to the *MED*. Not only to strike or beat, but to punish (1), to overcome, conquer or get the better of (3), and even to discuss extensively, as in "to bete the matere" (8). A related verb, *beten* (v. 2) means to mend, repair, or better; this sort of aural evocation of opposed but similar words reminds one of the plays Charles made on the words *shirten* and *forpeyne,* analyzed in chapter 2. True, there are many more literal than figurative meanings of "bete" recorded in the *MED*. But a literal reading of "bete" makes less sense in this context than the figurative meaning does. The female speaker says, essentially, "Oh, don't be like that, don't punish me, don't get the better of me: and take this kiss first *here* before 'occupying.'" (Again, this kiss is bestowed from an unspecified place, though at this point the male speaker is presumably imagined to be standing, having just become frustrated enough to move to walk out; an oral kiss makes better dramatic sense here.)

More kissing takes place in the gap between stanza 3 and the envoi, at which point the male lover expresses his delight: "Ye so so swete! Ye so swete hert! / Good thrift vnto that praty eye!" The "praty eye" is most likely a literal eye and is the only other line that would remotely work with a literal beating—if he socks her in the eye and then suddenly wishes it luck—but the common "good thrift unto ye" blessing works better with the rest of the poem when it is read as a figurative or colloquial phrase, not an address to a literal eye that just been hit. Our "bless your heart" is not literal, just as "rubbing shoulders" or "butting heads" or any number of other typical English idioms do not mean that physical contact has taken place.[35] The last words in the poem are the female speaker's response to this colloquial blessing. They imply further deferral or an erotic wish to slow things down: she asks him to be advised, to heed how she had asked

---

35. We have seen Charles's penchant for the English colloquial ("ye kast me lo a kayle," etc.). "Eye" is another fascinatingly complex word, however: eyes are orifices, openings, hollows in the body (*MED* 5), as well as organs of vision, watchfulness, understanding, or insight (*MED* 1, 2, 3, 4); the "nether eye" is the anus and the "eye of the yerd" is the male urethral opening (*MED* 5a). To do something "by the eie" is to do it in an unlimited way, without stint; to "fillen by the eye" is to fill something to the brim (*MED* 7).

for kisses "*before* you occupy," essentially asking the lover to heed her desire for foreplay (directed at whichever "praty mouth") before intercourse.

Like so many of Charles's English poems, Ballade 116 is enriched and complicated when read aloud; tone and voice are essential to his effort here. Not only does this male-authored poem imagine female desire and a scene of provocative banter in which, ultimately, the female speaker gets what she wants, but what she wants and gets is essentially to control the pacing and execution of the sexual encounter. The male fantasy here is of an erotic success—itself unusual enough in early modern lyric sequences—and one that includes female desire and control. This is a vivid imaginary dialogue, including mutuality, playfulness, and fluctuations of feelings on the part of both lovers. I propose this reading—admittedly speculative, but much better aligned with the rest of the poetics of the sequence than a "beating"—to point out again how important it is, in this work as in so much other earlier poetry, to attend to tone, voice, and wordplay. Charles's treatments of the sensual and the erotic, like his willingness to treat experientially and not only as allegory the anger, hope, despair, and desire that accompany love, make this sequence considerably less idealizing and medieval-courtly and more anticipatory of later English poets in the line of Wyatt, Sidney, and Donne, poets like Marvell or Carew.

Certain formal choices and rhetorical figures, too, take on a slightly proleptic flavor here. First, generally, is the *dispositio* of the ballade form. Charles's English ballades tend to create some of the same effects as (or at least a poetic motion similar to) Elizabethan sonnets. By "poetic motion" I mean the way a poem's parts move the reader through to its conclusion, or the way a poem's inner "punctuation" and rhythm (pauses, crescendo, internal arrangement) are handled. In the English ballades, first stanzas often begin in apostrophe or exclamation, followed by an explanation of the speaker's situation. Second stanzas sometimes extend or amplify that situation; sometimes they provide history or background. Third stanzas usually contain some kind of result or promise, sometimes an imaginative projection into the future or a *point culminant* of the situation. And the envois generally turn in direct address either to plead, to call for action, to summarize and recapitulate, or, especially, to make textual self-reference (discussed at length in chapter 3). Ballade 20 is an example: the first stanza is particular ("When y last partid from myn hertis swete . . ."), the second generalizes the lover's situation ("Who ist may lyue or longe goon on his feet / Without an hert?"), and the final stanza explains how the lady finally heeded pity and mercy and decided to leave her heart with the speaker. The envoi asks a typically self-referential, "What nede y more my papir spende or enke?" Sometimes the stanzas offer background, then personalization, or they each present separate aspects of one problem, as is the case in Ballades 53, 45, or 97, for example. This general disposition parallels that of the Elizabethan sonnet, with its three equal quatrains (in which, respectively, a situation is often presented, amplified, and projected) followed by a couplet that may contain an appeal or a pithy summative declaration. Three elaborated and equal parts plus a closing part half as long as the preceding parts seems to me to be the poetic motion that both Charles and the sixteenth-century sonneteers sought for their lyrics (the latter in more compressed format).

Certain specific structures Charles uses also remind one of sixteenth-century poetry. Consider the chiasmus and oxymora in Ballade 60:

> For dedy life my livy death y wite
> For ese of payne in payne of ese y dye
> For lengthe of woo, woo lengtith me so lite
> That quyk y dye and yet as dead lyue y
> Thus nygh a fer y fele the fer ys ny
> Of thing certeyne that y vncertayne seche
> . . . .
> O wofull wrecche O wrecche lesse onys thi speche
>
> What is this lijf a lijf or deth y lede
> Nay certes deth in life is liklynes
> For though y fayne me port of lustyhede
> Yet inward lo it sleth me my distres.

This may remind us of, for instance, Spenser's *Amoretti* 25,

> How long shall this like-dying life endure
> And know no end of her owne miserie
> But wast and wear away in termes unsure
> Twixt feare and hope depending doubtfully
> Yet better were at once to let me die,

although Spenser does not choose chiasmus to express his state and alliterates more heavily than Charles does. Not that chiasmus and oxymoron were discovered in the Renaissance, but such a concentrated structural use of antithetical devices is unusual in England circa 1440. Although there are medieval examples of these and other rhetorical devices (Lydgate's antithesis poem, for instance), verbal art of this kind was of constitutive importance to sixteenth-century poets and readers themselves, as treatises like Puttenham's and Scaliger's testify. Renaissance poets, especially in and after the 1590s, did rely more heavily on those devices that create tension and opposition, such as antimetabole, antithesis, and oxymoron, which have been defining characteristics of the so-called metaphysical poetry of the seventeenth century, and many of which were the usual Renaissance vehicles for the torments of love taken from Petrarch (burning ice, freezing fire, and so on). In Ballade 99, for example, the refrain of stanza 1 offers good opportunities for an extended series of playful poetic oppositions in the rest of the ballade.

> With axcesse shake, forsekid, & forfaynt,
> The poore karkes so enfeblisshid is,
> The hert in woo forswelt and so attaynt
> That even a deth it is to lyue as this;
> The gost dispeyrid lo so in me ther nys
> The body hert or gost in any ese,
> But all my wele, so helpe me god as wis,
> In his amverse me turnyth in disease.
>
> For all my joy is turnyd to hevynes,
> Myn ese in harme, my wele in woo,
> Mi hope in drede, in dowt my sikirnes,
> And my delite in sorow loo,
> My hele seeknes, and ovirmoo,
> As euery thing that shulde me plese
> Iturnyd is (god help me soo)
> In his amverse, to my disese.
>
> For who with sorowe list aqueyntid be,
> As come to me and spille no ferthir wye,
> For Sorow is y and y am he
> For euery ioy in me in goon away.
> Allas! What wight as may ther write or say
> That hath of sorowe more then y to lese,

Syn euery wele in me so (welaway!)
In his amverse [is] tornyd to disese.

Now good dere hert, me nedith not say yow how
That ye the langoure mowe in me appese;
If ye good list, ye konne do well enow
In the amverse to turne all my disese.

(5840–67)

Lovesickness indeed, an "enfeebled carcass" elaborated into a full three-stanza conceit. The metrically constructed sequence of oxymora in stanza 2, the pun in stanza 3 ("welaway"), and the *occupatio* and appeal in the envoi that cleverly varies the refrain—these are typical rhetorical maneuvers in Charles's English poetry and are also more typical of the verbal art that we have identified with "Renaissance" than with "medieval" poetics.

Thomas Park, in fact, probably because of such rhetorical maneuvers, links Charles's poetry to Renaissance rhetorician and theorist George Puttenham.[36] In his copy of Ellis's *Specimens of the English Poets,* Park copies two fragments of poetry from Charles d'Orléans, one of which is part of Ballade 100:

Who is the cause herof then? Is hit ye?
Ye? nay, it is my freel hert!
Hert? nay my fonnyd loue, parde!
Loue? nay, my rakill lookis stert!
Lokis? nay, for this y may aduert:
That ther nis noon kan do so wel, ywis,
But false tongis in sugre terme covert
Of wikkid folke therof wol say amys!

But [sic] maugre them—lo this y yow ensure:
Not maugre, but in spite—y shal yow serue.
—Not only serue, but loue while y endewre.
—Not only loue, but drede to that y sterue.
—Not only drede, but alle thre to deserue
Yowre thank. Deserue? My lijf may not in þis,

---

36. For more detailed discussion of this connection, see my "Thomas Park's Copy." The implications of Park's notes for Charles's place in the English canon are explored above in chapter 4.

> But for this dome [sic] to yow y hit reserue
> In spite of alle þat lust to say amys!
>
> (5876–91)

Above his copying of Ballade 100, Park pencils in "[In] Puttenham for another extr.," a note that makes it clear that he has remarked the rhetorical or "Renaissance" aspect of Charles's poetics. The note refers to George Puttenham, author of the *Arte of English Poesie* (1589).[37] Park's note is of course ahistorical or even antihistorical: there is no evidence that Puttenham read Charles's poetry, and Charles (1394–1465) obviously could not have consulted Puttenham. The note concerns reception, not influence or literary cause-and-effect. Park saw fit to link Charles's poetry and Puttenham's criticism, and the link is one of considerable interest to questions of interpretation, period, and canon.

If we accept the period boundary between "medieval" and "Renaissance" poetry, George Puttenham and Charles d'Orléans make an unlikely couple. But the pairing makes unexpectedly good critical sense, once fifteenth-century poet and sixteenth-century theorist are read side by side, as Park's cryptic note invites us to do. Although Park's note does not specify with which part of Puttenham's treatise on poetics he connects Charles's poetry, it seems most reasonable to me that he is thinking of an extended section of book 3, chapter 18, "Of figures sententious, otherwise called Rhetoricall." The two stanzas Park copies from Charles's Ballade 100 employ at least nine of the "figures sententious" Puttenham explains and exemplifies in the chapter.[38]

The question-and-answer sequence guiding lines 5876–80, for example, might be read as either what Puttenham calls "symploche, or the figure of replie" (209–10) or better, as what he calls "antipophora, or the figure of responce" in which "we will seeme to ask a question to th'intent we will aunswere it our selves, and is a figure of argument and also of amplification" (214–16). These opening lines of the excerpt clearly also exemplify what Puttenham calls "anadiplosis or the Redouble . . . another sort of repetition when with the worde by which you finish your verse, ye

---

37. Ed. Edward Arber, facsimile ed. (London: Constable, 1906); ed. Baxter Hathaway, facsimile reprint (Kent, Ohio: Kent State University Press, 1970).

38. That chapter explores sixty-one rhetorical figures using terms in ways rather different from those we generally accept now. Puttenham draws examples from Chaucer, Sidney, Oxford, Queen Elizabeth, and a copious variety of others.

beginne the next verse with the same" (210). Lines 5884–88 more loosely illustrate this figure, and Puttenham might have been happier calling them the "Clymax or the Marching Figure" (297) because of the momentum Charles gives the repeated elements. The opening lines might also be read as a *correctio,* which Puttenham calls "metanoia or the Penitent": "Otherwhiles we speake and be sorry for it, as if we had not wel spoken, so that we seeme to call in our word againe, and to put in another fitter for the purpose" (223). Park also would have readily perceived that "not only serve ... not only loue ... not only drede" is anaphoric, and without thinking necessarily of Puttenham (208). Charles's lines also use "merismus or the Distributer," or as Puttenham puts it later, "merismus in the negative" (231). "Parison, or the figure of even" (222–23) might be thought the figure Charles uses in writing such strong caesuras. Finally, the stanzas Park copies, like all of Charles's lyrics but here to a lesser extent, make use of "epimone or loueburden," the refrain (223). Refrains of course were prominent skeletal features of medieval ballades, rondeaux, and caroles, but Puttenham's examples remind us that the refrain enjoyed a renaissance as well. Unfolding Park's brief reference, we see that no one of Puttenham's "figures sententious ... or Rhetoricall" will do to exhaust the complexity of Charles's lines.

In his other 120 English ballades, Charles relies on many other such devices, to a degree and with a variety that invite reconsideration of the rhetorical efforts in this first English lyric sequence. Since Puttenham heavily exemplifies such figures and devices by quoting and citing classical and Renaissance poets, not medieval ones, Park's note indicates that, at least in jotting this bit to himself, Charles's work brings to mind not Chaucer or Charles's near-contemporaries Gower, Hoccleve, or Lydgate, but rather the work of Puttenham's predominant sample poets, Wyatt, Sidney, the earl of Oxford, Elizabeth I, and the classical authors they imitated. Park, in other words, looked across the early emerging period lines at these rhetorically and formally complex aspects of Charles's lyrics. Unlike other early canon-founding critics, Park considered Charles's work in terms of English critical theory, and found in it an anticipatory affinity with Renaissance rhetorical poetics. Park's connection of a fifteenth-century ballade with a sixteenth-century rhetorical guide shows that at least some English canon founders did not divide the canon in the way it has now come to be divided. His note reminds us that such categories are not fixed or impermeable, but rely on particular constructions of similitude and difference that are worth (re)discovering.

Charles d'Orléans, Renaissance Poet? Or, Un-Petrarchism and Inwardness

The particular constructions of similitude I have introduced throughout the book illustrate a "Renaissance" or Renaissance-defined poetic sensibility in Charles's English work (all skepticism of period labels still sharply in place). Chapter 2 touched on a few aspects of it in a particular example—the wordplay, the rhetorical-dramatic flavor, the turn away from allegory. Chapter 3 discussed at greater length the poems' persona, their textual self-consciousness, and their variable and carefully constructed writerly subjectivity, three of the important anticipations in this poetry of sixteenth-century lyric practice. Chapter 5 studied an act of authorial self-assertion that rivals those of Petrarch or Ben Jonson; late in life Charles establishes an authorial presence with an implicit energy that would align him, were he writing in the print age, with the most assertive of Renaissance self-fashioners. We have seen in this chapter that it is characteristic of him to create dramatic speaking effects that playfully highlight these qualities: emphatic opening lines, enjambments, and repetitions in exclamatory lines achieve this. And the sexy, vividly realized tone, the puns, the rhetorical play, the bodily and erotic implications of some of Charles's poems: all this amounts to a sensibility that is fairly unusual around 1440 in English poetry but is common enough in sixteenth- and early-seventeenth-century poetry. Furthermore, Charles's poetry displays a sustained "inwardness" that has come to be seen as characteristic of Renaissance poetry.

Strong in Charles's work is this quality that Katharine Eisaman Maus (writing on English Renaissance theater) has extensively explored.[39] We saw in chapter 3 how very much Charles creates a speaker who "has that within which passes show." The speaker reports the conflicts between the inner and outer selves variously, and often enough as necessary duplicities:

> When that y ought bere forth a gladsom chere
> In placis straunge or ellis in company
> Not kan y shewe but who seith a manere,
> For though my mouth outshewe a laughtir dry
> Or speke a sportfull word, yet verily

---

39. Maus, *Inwardness and Theatre in the English Renaissance* (Chicago: University of Chicago Press, 1995).

Distres and daunger, with payne in fere,
Abak they thristen my poore pleser.

(Ballade 25)

His "chere," his demeanor, is affected by a sense of the need to be careful what he shows: "And so hath holde (o welaway) to longe / Mi poore hert this cursid trayter face" (Ballade 24). He carefully constructs an exterior attitude and sometimes has trouble deciding just how to construct it, as he admits in the opening line of Ballade 42, "Not wot y now what wise to bere my chere." Often he is so sad, he says, "That y withdrawe from every gladsome feere" (l. 1501). Soon he gives his heart advice to the contrary: "Wherefore the best avise y kan thee lere / Is that thou draw thee to disportis ay / Thi trowbely sorow therwith to aclere" (ll. 1709–11). Beginning at line 1505, the speaker relates an incident in which he kept his feelings entirely to himself in order to silence the gossip of "opinioun." Lines 5912–19 likewise treat "A secret hert . . . disgisid under shame." The problem of inner realities that conflict with external appearances, as we saw more specifically in chapter 5, results from a real-life political situation, but in the poetry it is primarily addressed within himself, as the speaker's own difficulty. Yet at times he does interrogate the conflict of inner and outer realities as a more general problem. He explores Fortune's duplicity ("the douwbill turnys of thi iuparty" that "deseyve by sleight or trechery," ll. 6439, 6437). *Fortunes stabilnes,* after all, lies in its very changeability, an insight Spenser will also explore in the *Cantos of Mutabilitie.* And Charles more personally treats the problem of the lady's inwardness, which seems to conflict with her appearance:

So fresshe bewte, so moche goodlynes,
So skace of grace, so large of crewelte
. . . So lustyy yowthe, so replete of bounte,
So litil mercy and so gret disdayne.

(Ballade 120)

One French poem (Ballade XCIV, without an English version) explains Charles's own personal duplicities in openly political terms.

Pour ce que je suis a present
Avec la gent vostre ennemie,

> Il fault que je face semblant
> Faignant que ne vous ayme mie:
> Non pour tant, je vous certifie
> Et vous prie que veuiller penser
> Que je seray toue ma vie
> Vostre loyaument, sans faulser.

He pretends to speak ill of the duke of Burgundy, to whom this ballade is addressed, "Pour aveugler leur faulse envye," and tells Burgundy also to pretend enmity:

> Faignez envers moy mal talant
> A celle fin que nul n'espye
> Nostre amour . . .
> Il ne fault pas, ne tant ne quant,
> Quilz sauchent nostre compagnie. . . .
> Tant quil soit tamps qu'on me publie.

This is "loving in truth, and [feigning] in verse" indeed (*Astrophel and Stella* 1). Burgundy did in fact help negotiate Charles's eventual release, and this poem's envoi states that Charles is sending it with a loyal courier. Needless to say, this poem does not appear in Harley 682. The English speaker is understandably more careful to be oblique and to use metaphor as a cloak; this speaker's inner self tends to couch the political in the personal and to take refuge in the "hermitage of thoughtfull fantase," focusing on "the cofir of remembraunce," the "book of pleasant penser," and the "treasure of his thought." Charles's speaker reports, in other words, a very highly developed sense of "inwardness" that manifests itself in several ways.

As Maus explains, inwardness in the Renaissance context is a complicated theological and philosophical matter as well as a matter of sometimes pressing concern in trials of religious faith and political loyalties. Here, especially in the English sequence, the political problem is expressed fully as a personal problem. Captured by cousin and enemy; writing in two languages for hosts who were also jailers; political prisoner, not just prisoner of love; prince of royal blood but utterly subject to those around him; French but living half his life among the English—the dualisms inherent in Charles's situation divide his identity in any number of respects. Clever talking was definitely useful to one in Charles's position, as the above poems illustrate. One chronicler reports that Charles surreptitiously (although apparently not surreptitiously enough) squeezed the arm of one of his foreign visitors, Hugues de Lannoy, as if to convey that his words were to be taken as feigned and not truthful.[40] Charles's awareness of his dual position leads to a kind of arm squeezing in the poetry, too. He is a prisoner and tropes his speaker as prisoner of love; he is captive and calls his speaker "the most wofull caitiff of Fraunce." He is under close political scrutiny and writes of hiding from spying love-gossips. The old love-adversary Daunger necessarily means more than one thing to someone in Charles's position.

His delicate position thus somewhat resembles that of the Elizabethan courtier-poet, a bold supplicator who asserts himself cleverly in seeking favor from people who control his very life. The dual position may tend to foster the development of a lyric speaker whose polysemy, puns, double entendre, and speech-acts add up to a pleasing rhetorical play that creates a safe space of sorts. *Sprezzatura,* in other words, and the conditions that made it necessary and advantageous were in operation in England long before Castiglione theorized it or Hoby translated it (as, e.g., Patterson's study of Clanvowe, Scattergood's study of the court of Richard II, Stevens's *Music and Poetry,* and R. F. Green's *Poets and Princepleasers* demonstrate). The difficulties inherent in such dual social positions may have encouraged similar poetic responses in both periods. In fact, Seth Lerer, in *Courtly Letters in the Age of Henry VIII: Literary Culture and the Arts of Deceit,*[41] has recently explored the Tudor manifestations of the very sorts of politico-poetic dissimulations I have discussed here as foundational to Charles's English poetry. In the work of both Charles and the Elizabethan courtier-poets, the delicate social position seems to result in a verbal dexterity and an intense focus on inwardness.

Inwardness or interiority or interiorized subjectivity has been held by scholars from Jacob Burckhardt to Stephen Greenblatt to Francis Barker to Joel Fineman to be a particular feature of the change from medieval to Renaissance (or early modern) consciousness. Fineman, for example,

---

40. Recounted fully in Champion, *Vie,* 200–205: "Charles prit alors messire Hughes par la main, et, qui plus est, le pinça au bras très fort, par deux ou trois fois. On voyait bien qu'il n'osait pas dire toute sa pensée" (202–3). Michael K. Jones, in "'Gardez mon corps, sauvez ma terre': Immunity from War and the Lands of a Captive Knight: The Siege of Orléans Revisited" (in *Charles of Orleans in England, 1415–1440,* ed. Mary-Jo Arn [Woodbridge, Suffolk: Boydell and Brewer, forthcoming]), provides detailed historical information and debunks several myths about Charles's captivity and relations with his English host-captors.

41. Cambridge: Cambridge University Press, 1997.

claims that Shakespeare "invented" modern subjectivity; Greenblatt identifies self-fashioning as a way of being in the world that arises in the Tudor courts. But David Aers and Lee Patterson have argued persuasively against the kind of static Robertsonian view of the Middle Ages on which must depend such pronouncements about a Renaissance or early modern revolution in subjectivity. Aers points out that this view of the "Renaissance" of subjectivity makes for odd political bedfellows—on the one hand, conservative, exegetical-school medievalists who posit a stable Middle Ages and a collective rather than an individual subjectivity; and on the other hand, liberal early modern New Historicists who posit a sudden disruption of that stability into "self-fashioning," the "tremulous private body," and the uniquely "perjur'd eye." To read Charles (or Ovid, for that matter) is to be reminded that an unsettled, self-conscious, and astute sense of interiority is not nearly so late a development.[42]

Aers, moreover, thinks that Western poetic subjectivity begins not with Shakespeare but with Augustine;[43] this genealogy certainly explains a great deal about medieval autobiographical writing and about much poetry called Petrarchan, since Petrarch's engagements with Augustine are strong, as in turn are sixteenth-century poets' engagements with Petrarch. In fact, a literary historian hoping to write a linear narrative of Charles in literary history (but aware that in Charles's case there is no codicological support for direct influence) might seize upon Augustine (or, following him, Petrarch) as a common ancestor for the inwardness and writerly subjectivity of Charles and the sixteenth-century lyric writers. To explain Charles's anticipatory poetics, such a critic might want to argue that Charles had simply absorbed an Augustinian mode, or had adopted a Petrarchan poetics a century and a half ahead of the Tudor poets. But Charles's poetry does not fit in this line. It is not confessional in the same way that Augustine's is—the point is not to narrate the course of serious changes in a soul. (And despite considerable attention to writing and reading, there is no "tolle, lege" moment in Charles.) Hoccleve's kind of

---

42. Aers, "A Whisper in the Ear of Early Modernists; or, Reflections on Literary Critics Writing the 'History of the Subject,'" in *Culture and History, 1350–1600*, ed. David Aers (Detroit: Wayne State University Press, 1992), 178–80 and 186–89, 191, 195. Patterson makes related points in "Court Politics and the Invention of Literature: The Case of Sir John Clanvowe," in the same collection, 7–42, and in the introduction to *Negotiating the Past*. Interiority certainly exists in Old English poetry ("The Wanderer," "The Seafarer") as well. Lyric genres seem to be especially congenial to "inwardness."

43. "Whisper in the Ear," 182–85.

"inwardness" makes a nice contrast with Charles's in this respect: Hoccleve *is* concerned with that moment of self-awareness (looking in the mirror, in his case) and with the state of the changes in his own soul, what these changes imply for him spiritually and textually, and how those changes are to be perceived in the world. Charles's speaker, on the other hand, seems quite sure about the dreadfully fragmented state of his inner self, quite unconcerned to repent or explain himself in confessional mode, and quite certain that it all needs to be concealed (even as he playfully reveals it). I would further differentiate between an Augustinian mode of poetry-as-confessional, in which the explorations of the self are aimed at a higher religious or philosophical matter, and another mode—perhaps we could call it a contingent mode—in which the explorations of the self and the interiority or subjectivity revealed in the poetry come about as a result of some immediate political or social pressures. Wyatt, like perhaps the later Raleigh, would exemplify a hybrid of confessional and contingent modes: he connects the religious ideal with the immediate political pressures, and his agonized inwardness responds to both. Charles's English work is more in the Wyattesque-contingent than the purely Augustinian-confessional line and, if anything, is even more concerned to trope immediate worldly pressures.

Charles's poetry, furthermore, is surprisingly and fundamentally un-Petrarchan in several significant respects. First, there is no dreamy idealized scene setting—no white does in green grass in the sweet season. Petrarch's imagistic work is powerfully focused on a demi-reality that also describes, mirrors, or inverts the speaker's inner situation. Charles's non-imagistic English settings, nearly pragmatic by comparison with Petrarch's settings, in fact work to specify rather than to generalize the view of the inner speaker's experience, or to contrast the named day with the feeling of the speaker, as is the case in a few of the Valentine and May poems. "This ioyous tyme this fresshe cesoun of May" is when Charles finds himself singularly miserable: "O loue allas! Not se y lo this day / Oon wight but that he hath sum suffisaunce— / Saue y—in loue" (Ballade 17). Charles's speaker connects May day and his inner state, once in contrast (in Ballade 48 he chides his sorrowing heart for not joining the spirit of the season) and once in a sort of pathetic fallacy on a stormy day (in Ballade 53 his heart is "Fortrobelid als with thondir, wynde, and rayne"). One Valentine's day, traditionally, "An oost of fowlis semblid in a croft . . . and pletid ther latyne," but Charles, bereft of his lady, rails at them,

> Ye birdis ought
> To thank Nature (where as it sitteth me nought)
> That han yowre makis to yowre gret gladnes
> Where y sorow the deth of my maystres
> Vpon my bed so hard of noyous thought.
>
> (Ballade 72)

The conventional birds may be singing love, but Charles's speaker uses that setting to set off his own particular woefulness rather than to create an idealized image of love-talk or of the lady.

There is also a distinct lack of classicism here. While Charles's rhetorical displays are noteworthy, he does not indulge in one of the prime habits of poets following Petrarch, a deliberate invocation and renovation of classical poetry and poetics. There are only two dozen references to classical entities in the whole 6,531-line English sequence. Predictably, Cupid receives the most frequent mention, and Venus the next most frequent. Diana, Alcestis, Flora, Penelope, and Pygmalion show up, as do Dido, Cressida, and Helen. Such figures, traditionally associated with various sorts of love stories, are not surprising occasional visitors in a love-lyric sequence. Even the Parcae, Argus, Lucina, and Tisiphone are mentioned, as are Hippocrates, Galen, and King Scipio.[44] But the classical allusions are not only relatively few, they are placed in service of the speaker's expressions of personal woe rather than as part of a transformative or historically self-conscious (i.e., "Renaissance") poetics. The speaker alludes, for example, to "the gret kerver, the prince Pigmalioun" so as to complain that the current lady's heart is harder than any legendary stone (Ballade 90). The phoenix, likewise, is a simple image of the lady's uniqueness in Ballade 9: "She is the sovl fenyx of Araby." In Ballade 62 the phoenix appears in a simile for the lady's uniqueness and the dreadful impossibility of her death: "For when she lyuyd she fayrist lyuyd in ded / Right as the fenyx lyueth withouten ayre." There was only one such, says the speaker, and now she is dead; should he take a new lover? Unthinkable, in Ballade 62. (Soon, however, this image of singularity is undercut by his subsequent

---

44. Charles also mentions Saint Gabriel, Saint Ives, Saint Anthony, Saint Quentin, and Saint Giles, as well as Jesus and John. Medieval as opposed to strictly classical references include Macrobius, Lady Nature, and several personifications common since de Meun and de Lille. My sense is that his allusions may have been locally useful gestures to "the past," a generalized rather than a self-consciously historical past, and that in this poetry no strict distinction was observed or intended among biblical, classical, or historical references.

loving.) Allusions to classical entities serve local effects in the various lyrics and do provide metaphors and similes that add interest. They also imply that the poet assumed a certain kind of audience familiarity with a basic repertoire of classical characters. But although his extensive library would have encouraged it,[45] Charles, unlike Petrarch and his followers, evidences no larger excavatory or renovatory engagement with classical literature.

The nature of love and the lovers is also un-Petrarchan here. As we have seen, Charles makes considerable space for the erotic and for the mutual satisfactions as well as the mutual suspicions and disappointments of love. He praises but does not sanctify the lady; each mistress has many superior qualities but each treads on ground, kisses, and flirts with this speaker. In fact, Ballade 119 almost scornfully reminds the lady that she too is human: "Ne wotith not eche wight as wel as ye / That ye are made as men of flesshe & blood?" He has clearly not mistaken his ladies for Beatrice or Laura. Charles experiences both erotic success and at other times disillusionment, despair, a worldliness that is more Ovidian or pragmatic than Petrarchan. We have seen several examples of Charles's use of economic metaphors to figure the exchange-values of loving. And as we have also seen, in English the tone can be lofty or sensuous but is often rough, colloquial, concrete—anything but consistently laureate. The English poetry is playful and specific in impression, not lush and entrancing as is Petrarch's Italian poetry.

And although the first lady of the vernacular sequences dies, Charles definitely does not take advantage of this poetic or personal event to structure the rest of the sequence as an idealizing, transcendent *in morte* section. In fact, the speaker rather quickly asks himself, "Shal I me make a lady new?" and punningly figures love as a chess game. (The puns, as usual, are a big part of the game: a "lady" or "dame" is the chess piece corresponding to a queen; to "make" can be to checkmate or capture.) The speaker mourns, of course, and quite convincingly, but not for Petrarch's obsessive decades. Charles's speaker at first vows he'd rather die than live without the lady, but later makes new vows to a new lady. The speaker is released from Love's traditional service into a nontraditional state of renunciatory detachment (he calls this inner place "no care"), after which he offers to true lovers his "Iubilee" or banquet of small poems (love poems, more than

---

45. Champion, *Librairie*. As stated in note 3, Huizinga even sees Charles's poetry as part of a productive anticlassicism, part of a strain in late medieval poetry that is in some sense "modern" (*Autumn of Middle Ages,* 389). For line numbers to these classical references, see Arn, ed., *Fortunes Stabilnes,* 623–24, where proper names are listed.

a hundred roundels and chansons expressing similarly varied lover's experiences). But the food of love plays on; soon enough, Venus descends with her eroticized "kercher of plesaunce," and the speaker sees a new lady, who uncannily resembles the former one. The reader has to conclude that in this collection, one lady is pretty much like another. Charles's speaker can implicitly "love both fair and brown," though unlike Donne's speaker he still claims to value fidelity and makes new vows of eternal (or at least annual) service. In disillusioned moments he swears he will stay in "no care," a state of detachment from love, but he does later return to loving and continues to write refreshingly varied, sensual, and witty poems. Nothing in the beginning of the sequence asks for pity or pardon ("pietà, non che perdono," as Petrarch put it in his first sonnet), and nothing in the end of the sequence promises a higher spiritual connection. Charles does not form his vernacular collections on an Augustinian confessional pattern nor on a Petrarchan pattern of frustration, renunciation, and transcendence. This lyric book, in other words, may take the Petrarchan template of the single-author collection, but it does not represent romantic love as the idealizing, Christianizing, spiritually transcendent experience Petrarch established.

I would have expected, in fact, a much greater degree of Petrarchism, if we can even quantify such a thing, from the son of Louis d'Orléans and Valentina Visconti. Valentina Visconti, from the Milanese family of Petrarch's patrons, was herself a bibliophile and musician and often welcomed poets to their court. The records show, however, that Charles owned only Petrarch's *Epistole,* plus an unnamed book translated into French,[46] and no *Rime.* Yet he must surely, in such an environment, have encountered Petrarch's sonnets.[47] As we saw in chapter 5, Charles is at his most Italian-humanist or postcourtly in the Grenoble 873 manuscript, under the influence of Professor Astesano, but even under that influence, the sequence is never incarnated as an imitation of the *Rime.* Charles sounds more Boethian than Petrarchan, which is perhaps to say more like Christine de Pisan or Alain Chartier.[48] Fox notes that "the time was not right in Northern France for poets to adopt Italian humanism or to imitate

---

46. Arn, ed., *Fortunes Stabilnes,* 48; Champion, *Librairie.* Harrison, "Charles d'Orléans and the Renaissance," *Rocky Mountain Review of Language and Literature* 25 (1971), 92, claims that the *Trionfi* may have influenced Charles.

47. Cocco, "Italian Inspiration," points out many particular elements of the *dolce stil nuovo* in Charles's poems. In my opinion, the "Complainte de France" echoes Petrarch's "Italia mia," but otherwise I find the resemblances largely unremarkable.

48. In, for example, a ballade in Fairfax 16, "O thou Fortune which hast the gouvernaunce."

the poetry it produced."⁴⁹ In fact there is evidence that the opposite was true, and that at this time, it was the Italians who were busily imitating the Valois, Europe's major cultural arbiters.⁵⁰ Gordon Braden has remarked that Charles's poetry may be rooted in his native traditions of troubadour lyric instead of in Petrarchism, and this does seem especially true of the roundels and the *puys* poems of the post-1440 period.⁵¹ I also see a tempered Ovidian strain in these poems, as Astesano apparently saw, too: recall his preface, which places Charles in the line of Ovid (but does not mention Petrarch, which may corroborate Petrarch's fifteenth-century reputation as primarily a writer of prose, not poetry). Although we could imagine a literary line in which Charles and Petrarch (and Ovid, Du Bellay, and others) could be read together as "poets of exile," Charles's exile was for different reasons. Prince and patron himself, his relation to systems of patronage and to central powers was distinct from that of other exiled poets in such a line. And his variable use of translation distinguishes him from other prisoners and exiles: Charles's translations suppress the political in English (for a local context), and emphasize it in Latin (for a world context).⁵² Above all, given Charles's Visconti lineage, the lack of overt Petrarchism in this verse should give very serious pause to critics who wish to draw direct lines of Petrarchan influence through France to England, who would see the fifteenth century as transitional in that linear way, or who would wish to claim Petrarch as a common ancestor for Charles and the sixteenth-century English poets he resembles.

Tudor Connections and Other
Medieval-Renaissance Continuities

How, then, to explain an essentially non-Petrarchan and yet postmedieval poetics of this sort? Although Petrarch (or Augustine) does not turn out to be the common ancestor, there are other specific literary and historical con-

---

49. Fox, *Lyric Poetry,* 49. Arn further states that "the matter is one of no great import to his work, for whatever contact he had with Italian humanism and poetry must have taken place . . . after his captivity in 1440, when the English poems had already been written" (*Fortunes Stabilnes,* 49 n. 130). Still, I think that he likely did encounter Petrarchan poetry in his youth but that it simply had not taken hold in France by 1415 (nor in England 1415–40) and did not take hold of his young imagination nor of his English experiments.

50. Wallace, *Chaucerian Polity,* 45, 52–54.

51. Braden, personal communication. Simon Gaunt, *Troubadours and Irony* (Cambridge: Cambridge University Press, 1989), explores the ironic stance and variable voice of troubadour lyrics; Charles's dialogic proclivities may recall the *tenzone.*

52. Du Bellay's Latin and French poems written during his exile might make a nice contrast here.

nections between Charles and the courts of the French and English Renaissance (even beyond the continuing intermarriage of royal and noble families, a significant sustaining connection between the two cultures and periods). Charles's early life was spent among "medievals," Deschamps, Chartier, and de Pisan; his later life among "pre-Renaissance" poets like Villon. Patron of arts and letters, Charles was also uncle of Francis I, the exemplary Renaissance monarch, and of Marguerite de Navarre, exemplary Renaissance author. Charles's poetry was extensively copied, but it was also printed in large numbers by Antoine Vérard in the early sixteenth century in collections popular across Europe (including England). Charles's poems were read in England across a much wider readership over a much longer time than has previously been remarked, as chapter 4 explained.

Especially interesting is one of the particular contexts in which Charles's poetry was available to the Tudor kings. The huge Orléans ransom materially funded the Tudor dynasty over a period of 102 years, including its reinvasions of France (as historian Michael K. Jones has demonstrated),[53] and the Tudors continued to claim France as part of the kingdom. The early Tudors also absorbed, as Janet Backhouse has shown, a great deal of French literary material.[54] One important manuscript, BL Royal F 16.ii, is essentially a royal conduct book, a book of instruction to princes. It is heavy on instructions about love: 166 of Charles's poems (attributed) open the volume, followed by a prose discourse on love that purports to be letters between Heloise and Abelard. Next comes a set of traditional prose and verse love questions ("Ensuyuent les demandes en amours"). The final section is "le liure dit grace entiere sur le fait du gouvernement dun prince," which opens and closes in verse, with prose in the middle. The book is all in one hand and was supposedly prepared for Prince Arthur (and owned by Henry VII and later Henry VIII). Bernard André, tutor to the Tudor princes, poet laureate, *orator regis,* and court biographer to Henry VII, is generally thought to be responsible for this book.[55] André's foundational role as "the senior figure of England's

---

53. "Henry VII, Lady Margaret Beaufort, and the Orléans Ransom," in *Kings and Nobles in the Late Middle Ages,* ed. Ralph Griffiths and James Sherborne (New York: St. Martin's, 1986), 254–73.

54. Backhouse documents the Tudor preference for French manuscripts in "Illuminated Manuscripts Associated with Henry VII," in *The Reign of Henry VII: Proceedings of the 1993 Harlaxton Symposium,* ed. Benjamin Thompson (Stamford: Paul Watkins, 1995), 175–87.

55. The Royal manuscript is discussed in Warner and Gilson, *Catalogue of Western Manuscripts,* 2:203–4; Backhouse, "Founders of Royal Library," places this book among the earlier efforts. André, *Historia Regis Henrici Septimi,* ed. James Gairdner (London: Longman, Brown, Green, Longman, and Roberts, 1858).

humanist culture" in Tudor court contexts has been explored by David Carlson in several recent articles;[56] André's *Historia Regis Henrici Septimi* can be seen as an early construction of Tudor monarchy that would be extended by sixteenth-century historiographers like Holinshed. That a blind Frenchman was not only poet laureate but royal tutor and biographer, and that Charles's poetry makes up such a significant portion of his Tudor royal conduct book, may remind us again of how pervasive was the French literary presence in England even into the sixteenth century, including specifically the absent presence of Charles d'Orléans.

Another way to connect the two eras without recourse to influence models might be to consider the similarity of contextual pressures on the literature: the social or political pressures already mentioned, as well as the pressure of a language in considerable flux and the pressure of genre. Paula Blank has shown that during the Tudor period the language itself was not as fixed or "modern" as some editorial practices might have it. The language of Tottel's collection, like that of Turberville, Gascoigne, and other "Renaissance" poets, resembled fifteenth-century English, which continued to change from within and without during both centuries, not suddenly stabilizing after Caxton into "Modern English," as we might mistakenly think if we read only modernized versions of Wyatt or Surrey or Sidney.[57] The orthographic, metrical, and lexical continuity between "medieval" and "Renaissance" appears in modernized editions less than it probably really was, or at least less than it appears to the reader of unmodernized editions. (Another manifestation of the distortions of post hoc periodization.) Macaronic poetry in the two eras seems to be one common response to linguistic flux and multiple possibility, expressing flexibility and multilingual facility on the part of writer and audience and opening a polyvocality for the poetic persona that writers like Charles and Skelton exploit fully.[58] The language of Skelton or Hawes, of Copeland or Caxton,

---

56. "Reputation and Duplicity," 262; Carlson also notes his "high position and international acclaim" (262–64). See also Carlson's "King Arthur" and "Politicizing Tudor Court Literature."

57. Blank, *Broken English: Dialects and the Politics of Language in Renaissance Writings* (London: Routledge, 1996), 6, 12–15, 33–68. Her concern is for multiple dialects, but she does acknowledge the continuing interventions of French in England (12, 40–52, 101–2, 118–19, 165–76, 177 n. 4).

58. See John Fox, "Glanures/Charles d'Orléans: Three Macaronic Randeaux," in *Charles of Orleans in England, 1415–1440,* ed. Mary-Jo Arn (Woodbridge, Suffolk: Boydell and Brewer, forthcoming), on several of Charles's macaronic verses. Charles's experiments in English in dimeter and trimeter lines resemble Skelton's work, and they share a certain attitude of detachment. Skelton's *Dyvers Balettys,* though not a lyric sequence as Charles's is, might make a useful point of comparison in this regard.

of Roos or Suffolk, was as much like that of Charles as it was of Sidney, and any line drawn to divide this continuum will be arbitrary. Yet Charles was not a native speaker (though chroniclers say he left England speaking better English than French), and the language clearly exerts an odd sort of pressure in Charles's translations: working outside the "courtly" French vocabulary—an abstract, literary vocabulary—and needing to add metric cheville to every line, he perhaps seizes on the lexicon he knows best first, that of concrete daily experience. Many of his quirky expressions—those like "shertith," "kast him a kayle," and the exclamations like "A pak, madame! What do y say?"—are those he would have heard spoken around him every day. In bringing the living language he hears into the English poems, he steps still further away from the old French-courtly conventions.

The pressure of genre also creates continuity across the great, artificial, medieval-Renaissance chasm—or rather, the choice to create a lyric sequence or lyric book imposes certain constraints and elicits similar poetic solutions. It is perhaps unfashionably transhistorical to admit this, but any writer of a lyric sequence, on vellum, in print, or in cyberspace, faces the problem of creating a variable yet credibly consistent lyric persona. Even in ages that expect fixed-form poetry, writers of fixed-form sequences risk repetitive results unless they take pains to add interest to their several hundred uniform poems. One way to do this is to vary the speaking voice at line level; to imply dramatic encounters, to include the restless turning in apostrophe and interrogation that Charles (like Du Bellay, Spenser, or Sidney) finds useful. Writing a sequence of several hundred fixed-form poems actually demands a greater attention to line-level interest and to a consistent, credible, yet variable and interesting "voice" or speaker. Creating a speaker with *sprezzatura* gives both immediate effects and also advantages for a long uniform sequence, for it permits wide variability of expression without sacrificing the strong, unified, central position of the persona. And as we have seen, Charles's English lyric draws a fair amount of its special character from a rather flamboyant or at least playful and self-conscious use of words, another attribute that cannot finally be pinned to any historical condition. It also contains experiments in meter, rhyme scheme, and lineation in what had been fairly well fixed French forms, as Steele and Day, John Fox, Hans Meier, and Mary-Jo Arn have demonstrated.[59] Part of the unexpected interest of the bilingual

---

59. Fox, *Lyric Poetry,* 111ff.; Meier, "Middle English Styles"; Arn, ed., *Fortunes Stabilnes,* 85, 90, 92–94, 96, 391.

oeuvre is the extent to which Charles departs from the French courtly traditions in which he was so well versed. That Charles did not bring the well-codified traditions of French courtliness wholesale into an English incarnation may indicate his sense of the limits of his English audience's tastes for Frenchness, or for what was at that time in their language an utterly new thing, the one-author lyric book. Particular inflections will differ historically of course, but the demands of a lyric sequence help explain why this poetry seems out of its moment. The chosen literary mode seems to have a conditioning power all its own.

To summarize: Like the lyric speaker's voice and *sprezzatura,* other anticipatory features of this work—the move away from allegory and narrative toward experiential, concrete, colloquial lyric, the self-conscious textual performance, the erotic specificity and success, the puns, the departures from the dominant conventions of his moment, the intense expressions of "inwardness"—respond to the generic and historical contexts of the translation itself. The initial historical condition or problem to which Charles responded was his long imprisonment in a foreign land; the literary condition or problem was his choice to write a lyric book. The former is historically contingent and determines not only the fact of the translation but its analogous appearance in two languages, his own and that of his captors. The latter condition, that of any lyric poet, is nearly timeless or at least is less precisely historical and appears to have stimulated much of the experimental poetics of this lyric. The choice to write a long uniform book of lyric makes great demands on the poet and may actually foster modal shifts and other innovations. To translate such a sequence into a language as yet still forming its lyric conventions would encourage further innovation, demanding, as translation always does, that the poet decide when and how to include, alter, or reject features of another literary tradition. To translate such a sequence in foreign captivity would permit the poet to incorporate the living language into the new texts. And to translate from the dual sociopolitical position of guest-and-captive would indeed stimulate a dual subjectivity and a courtierlike, but distinctly non-Petrarchan, inwardness.

Literary Period Categories as Useful Tautologies; Translation as a Challenge to Literary Periodization

What further literary-historical and theoretical sense can we make of this strange, very large, blip on the graphs of early modern literary history?

Since Charles d'Orléans was born in 1394 and died in 1465, the title of this chapter implies challenges to literary periodization in general and to the period categories "medieval" and "Renaissance" (or "early modern") in particular.[60] But despite the implied challenges to period that I have posed throughout this book, I am not trying to recategorize Charles d'Orléans for the Renaissance, nor to advocate that we redraw period boundaries or definitions to accommodate him, nor to abolish a useful periodization. The grand periodization wars are already well joined by Besserman, Fredric Jameson, and others, and the medieval-Renaissance skirmishes by Patterson, Aers, Wallace, and others. This chapter has provisionally relied on period categories like "medieval" and "Renaissance" and their associated literary qualities—relying, in other words, on the constructed categories to be stable at least long enough to interrogate particular features of the poetry in terms of literary history. Beneath an undeniable, immediate utility, though, I assume that literary period categories are after-the-fact tautologies, inappropriately teleological, and historically unrepresentative; that period labels are insufficient synecdoches for the phenomena under study; that periodization is a mirror process, as much about us as about the objects of study, thus fostering a regressive critical narcissism; that even pedagogically, where they are most useful, period categories suppress continuity, overemphasize disjunctions between periods, and may keep students thinking in boxes. The curricular and professional consequences of strict periodization can be deadly, too. But this chapter only sought to do what had not been done before for this large and understudied oeuvre: to look across accepted period boundaries for particular similarities and to reconsider its multiply liminal position. As it turns out, Charles's poetry's deviations from the fifteenth-century English practice of poetry and its considerable reshapings of the English conception of the lyric book do call into question some accepted critical narratives, and some of the usual literary-historical models don't answer.

---

60. For recent discussions of the history and theory of periodization, see Lawrence Besserman, ed., *The Challenge of Periodization: Old Paradigms and New Perspectives* (New York: Garland, 1996), especially 3–27. For application of some of the problems of periodization to medieval literature (specifically, to Chaucer's *Canon's Yeoman's Tale*), see Lee Patterson, "The Place of the Modern in the Late Middle Ages," in Besserman, *The Challenge of Periodization,* especially 51–54. On the problem of the term *Renaissance* see Findlen and Gouwens introducing a special issue of the *American Historical Review* on the topic; "The Persistence of the Renaissance," *AHR* 103, no. 1 (1998): 51–54. For a review of the *early modern* versus *Renaissance* labeling controversy in literary studies, see Leah Marcus, "Renaissance/Early Modern Studies," in *Redrawing the Boundaries,* ed. Stephen Greenblatt and Giles Gunn (New York: Modern Language Association, 1992), 41–63.

For example, influence models, even cross-cultural ones, do not suffice. We have seen what a stretch it would be to place Charles in a major "line," whether Augustinan, Petrarchan, or Chaucerian. For although there is more evidence than we usually hear that Charles's poetry was read in Renaissance England (as we saw in chapter 4), that evidence does not prove direct borrowing or even general influence as it is usually construed. Nor is this a case like that of a "minor" literature, theorized by Gilles Deleuze and Félix Guattari as the colonized and collective "deterritorialization" of literary language; in such cases, the language question (like the literary consequences of it) is an impossible one of the survival and identity of a deracinated minority.[61] Nor is this a matter of cultural appropriation of the sort that translation theorists like Lawrence Venuti study. In fact, the usual models for dealing with translation—developmental, appropriative, source-and-target, or influence models—might predict that fifteenth-century French poetry, periodized as a highly developed, latest-medieval moment just before the *rhétoriqueurs* and the Renaissance, would have a lot to offer the fifteenth-century English literary system, a bare generation after Chaucer and over a century before the flourishing of Tudor lyric poetics. Such models might also predict that Charles's translations would bring an advanced French lyric poetics to England. In one major respect that prediction is accurate: the signal accomplishment of the first one-author English lyric book results from this bilingual effort. But it is much more true, poem by poem, to say that Charles's English work is not only more innovative than the English poetry of its era, but also is innovative in ways quite unlike his analogous French poetry: innovative not chiefly as an import, appropriation, colonization, or influence. On the contrary, the English poems go their own way (and this tendency increases over the course of the sequence); it is as if the English contexts—linguistic, historical, generic—stimulate Charles's poetic experiments. Remarkably, without any material evidence of influence, and without a shared Petrarchism, many of these innovations resemble the practices of English Renaissance lyric poets.

So the real challenge to periodization—the larger challenge that underpins this book's modest, practical adjustment to the facts and emphasis of

---

61. As with their example, the Jewish communities of Prague (Deleuze and Guattari, *Kafka,* chap. 3). Translator as preserver, as missionary, as proselytizer, as merchant, as money-changer, as imperious colonizer, as oppressed colonized, as thief, as gleaner, as busy bee in literary fields: these old and new metaphors will not fit the case, and the case is too significant to be ignored.

literary history—is posed by translation itself, which tends to leap unexpectedly across period categories too often imposed on literatures monoculturally (and after the fact). Any literary translation is a point of contact between two languages, two cultures, two literary systems, and two literary histories. More precisely, a translation connects two literatures (in Itamar Even-Zohar's terms, "systems" or "fields")[62] that necessarily exist in different stages or states. In the early modern period, at least, this "polysystems effect" of translation most often occurs because of historical distance, as exemplified by the "diachronic imitation" Greene analyzes.[63] Most discussions of Renaissance translations from the classics, for instance, rightly assume the navigation of historical distance to be a central issue. With or without historical distance, however, one of the usual actions of translation is to import practices from one literary tradition that may (or may not) then be taken up as innovations in the other literature.[64] If a translation brings new or new-old literary practices in this way from one tradition into another, that translation will not only have crossed national and language boundaries, but will have necessarily crossed critical or period boundaries as well. Again, no two literatures can ever be in the same state; so, regardless of actual historical distance between source and translation, a literary-historical distance—and thus a cross-cultural challenge to periodization—is inevitable.

But the challenge posed by translation's inherent polysystems effect is implicitly broader (and more practical). This theoretical point about translation and period bears not only on the case of Charles's trilingual corpus, but on much literature of the European fifteenth and sixteenth centuries, because (1) literary texts were much more often polyglot, including translation, plurilingualism, and appropriation, than we now tend to assume; and (2) the fifteenth and sixteenth centuries were a time of rapid linguistic and cultural change; and (3) those changes involved both historical distance between versions and, significantly, the inevitable atemporal

---

62. *Papers in Historical Poetics* (Tel Aviv: Porter Institute for Poetics and Semiotics, 1978).

63. *The Light in Troy*, chapter 1. See also studies by Pigman, "Versions of Imitation"; Carron, "Imitation and Intertextuality"; A. K. Hieatt, "The Genesis of Shakespeare's Sonnets: Spenser's *Ruines of Rome*," *PMLA* 98, no. 5 (1983): 800–814; Marc Bizer, *La Poésie au miroir: Imitation et conscience de so: dans la poésie latine de la Pléiade* (Paris: Champion, 1995); and others.

64. Or may transform its practice, as Copeland, *Rhetoric, Hermeneutics, and Translation*, demonstrates in the case of "rhetorical and hermeneutic" translations. For a new anatomy of translation practices, chiefly in the sixteenth century, see my "Thomas Watson," especially 4–9.

literary-historical distance I am emphasizing here. Karlheinz Stierle has gone so far as to say that the "co-presence of cultures" inherent in contemporaneous translations is a prime mark of the "Renaissance" (the "vertical" model of translation, one involving authoritative distances, being the mark of "medieval" literature).[65] From this view, fifteenth-century literary translations—especially ones like Charles's in which the "co-presence of cultures" is so powerful—can help us reconceptualize the move from "medieval" to "Renaissance" or "early modern" literature as one in which poems in various languages could simultaneously enjoy multiple significances. Charles's multiply liminal phenomenon is in some sense a unique contribution to English lyric history but is also more broadly representative of the rich pluriculturalism of the early modern period. The case has potential bearing on a wide range of other works, because so much earlier poetry was biculturally or multiculturally positioned. This is certainly true of England: William Ringler, for instance, proves that translations accounted for "slightly more than 34 percent" of English verse published between 1475 and 1500; between 1501 and 1558 the proportion is about 50 percent.[66] In other words, most early modern poetry can be fruitfully read for its polysystems effects, for its period and culture and literary-historical crossings, for its entries into and repositionings in other literary systems.[67]

As we have seen, the self-translations that connect this whole oeuvre both cross and connect the languages and literatures and nations that were in an immensely complex process of separation; yet in unexpected ways, these translations also cross, connect, and challenge the critical categories of "medieval" and "Renaissance" we have since created. Perhaps critical attention to works like Charles's—multilingual, out-of-period, and thus

---

65. Stierle, "*Translatio studii* and Renaissance," 64; general discussion is on 64–65.
66. *Bibliography and Index*, 6.
67. Two brief examples will suffice, where a thousand exist: Spenser's *Ruines of Rome* and *Visions* poems can be best studied not only in their English Renaissance field, among the *Complaints* and other sonnet sequences, but also in the fields into which their earlier versions were placed: among early Elizabethan emblem books and Dutch and French Protestant literature, among DuBellay's oeuvre and the midcentury sonnet sequences, among Marot's poems, among Petrarch's poems. Likewise, the early English printed verses "On the Beauty of Women" could best be considered not only comparatively against their French and Italian analogues, but from a polysystems view, comparing their positions in the English literary field with the positions of the analogues in Italian and French fields. It is important, as Anne Prescott reminded me, to try not to assume the stability of one version so as to compare another to it; polysystems theory offers a solution to that problem (conversation, Folger Shakespeare Library, early 1999).

undercanonized works—a literary-historical sibling of the "comparative historicism" David Wallace advocates in *Chaucerian Polity,* can take account of what we, in a largely monolingual age, tend to underestimate: the pluricultural nature of the poetry of this period, its inherent yet sometimes less-visible liminalities, its surprising appearances in multiple literary histories. One thing found in translation is this perspective, this willingness to ask different questions of older poetry. To treat poems as plurilingual—meaning, to read for their culture- and system-crossing attributes—will be to treat them not only as "medieval" or "Renaissance" texts but more fully, and more nearly, to read them as they were written.[68]

---

68. Final caveat: of course one can never read anything "as it was written," but efforts more nearly to approximate that ideal are worthwhile, as two decades of historicist scholarship have shown; this book merely seeks to extend that larger, contextualizing effort to include specifically plurilingual literary contexts. We might wish to reshape our sense of "context" to match that of the writers and readers we study; theirs was, I believe, a cosmopolitan and polyglot sense of literary context.

Appendix: Bibliographic Observations on Grenoble Ms. 873

Observations on Bibliothèque Municipale de Grenoble, Manuscrit 873 (Rés. U.1091)

Charles of Orleans, French Poems, with Latin translation and other materials by Antonio Astesano; c. 1461.

Vellum, c. 310 × 236 mm. Twenty quires. Collation: 1–13 (in eights), 14 (in seven), 15–19 (in eights), 20 (in seven). No quire signatures. Catchwords between quires 15–16, 16–17, 17–18, and 18–19.[1]

1. fols. 1r–7r. Ad illlustrissimum principem . . . / . . . / ex urbe Astensi xiij maio 1458.
    Prefatory and dedicatory material in Latin by Astesano, dated 1456, 1457, and 1458.
2. fol. 9r. Cum Gallis . . . / . . . / Aurelianensis talia verba movens.
    Astesano's Latin preface to the poetry.
3. fols 9v–111r. Au temps passe . . . / . . . / Et ta Rendu guienne et normandie.
    Selected French poems with Latin translations in facing-column format on the subjects of love and politics.
4. fols. 113r–158v. Si michitata . . . / . . . / Hunc deus omnipotens iussit ad astra vehi.
    Latin works by Antonio Astesano on various subjects addressed to numerous individuals; some dated as early as 1435.[2]

---

1. I wish to thank the curators and librarians of the *fonds ancien* of the Bibliothèque Municipale de Grenoble for their expertise and graciousness: Yves Jocteur-Montrozier, Marie-Françoise Bois-Delatte, Marie-Christine Hébré, Marie-Thérèse Imbert, Marguerite Pénicaut, and Monique Samé.

2. On folio 139v, "ex urbe Astensi anno Christi mccccxxxv"; on fol. 140v, "Ex pa[]ia anno Christi mccccxxxvj" (I use brackets here to indicate letters of which I am uncertain). These early dates are not noted in the catalog listing for this manuscript, which does contain additional information I omit here: see P. Fournier, E. Maignien, and A. Prudhomme, *Catalogue général des manuscrits des bibliothèques publiques de France: Départements,* vol. 7, *Grenoble* (Paris: Librairie Plon, 1889), entry 266, pp. 264–66, which also refers to Aimé Champollion-Figeac, *Louis et Charles d'Orléans* (Paris, 1844), 367; to Léopold Delisle, *Le Cabinet des*

General Description, Bindings, Provenance

This sumptuously decorated vellum manuscript, dated at approximately 1461, but containing dates as early as 1435, is made up of 159 folios measuring about 310 mm × 236 mm, ruled in two-column format. The book contains a selection of the French poetry of Charles, duke of Orleans, with translations into Latin by Antonio Astesano, the duke's secretary.[3] Also here are Astesano's Latin prefaces to the poetry, and in a substantial section of back matter, Astesano's own epistolary and narrative Latin works. Each page of the duke's poetry is arranged in columns, French poems on the left and Latin translations on the right.

This manuscript is currently in an early-nineteenth-century binding, but the Bibliothèque Municipale de Grenoble also owns a seventeenth-century leather binding of it. This earlier binding, faded ivory-beige leather, measures approximately 330 mm × 625 mm fully opened; closed it would contain a book of about 50-cm thickness, matching what would be the unbound size of the present manuscript quires. On its spine is marked "117" in dark brown or faded black ink. The binding has nine pairs of holes along the sides of the spine, four of which have bits of small skin thongs still attached. Measuring from the bottom up, the holes appear at 0.5 cm, 5.5 cm, 8.5 cm, 13 cm, 16.5 cm, 20 cm, 23.8 cm, 28 cm, 32 cm. Although there is some evidence of cropping on a few folios in Astesano's Latin back matter (folio 153r, for example, where words in the outer margin are cut off), the book has evidently existed in the same physical state at least since the early seventeenth century. I speculate that this may not always have been the case: in the Latin material, dates as early as 1435 lead me to think that Astesano had composed and perhaps assembled some quires of his Latin works well before the late 1440s and 1450s, when the poetic translations were probably done.[4]

---

manuscrits de la Bibliothèque Impériale (Paris: Imprimerie Impériale, 1868–81), 1:111 (full information is in 2:98–120); and to Berriat-Saint-Prix, in *le Magasin encyclopédique* (1802), among others.

3. For more information on Astesano, see Balzaretti, "Antonio Astesano traduttore"; *Dizionario biografico degli Italiani,* vol. 4, s.v. "Astesano"; Muratori, *Rerum Italicarum Scriptores,* vol. 14, s.v. "Antonio Astesano." Thanks to Mary-Jo Arn for providing the following references: Giacomo Gorrini, *Il Comune astigiano e la sua storiografia* (Firenze: C. Ademollo, 1884), 203–24; on Nicolas Astesano, brother of Antonio and said to be the scribe of this manuscript, see *Enciclopedia universal ilustrada europeo-americana,* vol. 6 (Barcelona: José Espasa é Hijos, 1912), s.v. "Astesano, Nicolas"; and *Nouvelle Biographie générale,* vol. 3 (Paris: Firmin Didot Frères, 1856), s.v. "Astesan, Nicolas."

4. Charles, after all, arrived at Asti in October of 1447; we know that Astesano was at Blois in 1450–51 and at Tours in 1452, but he returns to Asti some time in 1452 (*Dizionario biografico degli Italiani,* vol. 4). The prefatory quire is dated 1456, 1457, and 1458; we do not know how it was returned to Blois to be bound by 1463, nor when it was decorated (but plausibly was decorated all at once, given the uniformity and hierarchy of decoration), nor where it was decorated (my guess is in central France rather than in Italy, judging from the style of decoration).

On the top right margin of folio 1r are the words "ex libris claudio expillij 1607" (see fig. 5). Expilly (1561–1636) was a book collector, antiquarian, magistrat, and prominent citizen of Grenoble. The book was later held by Mgr. de Caulet (1693–1771) and the bishops of Grenoble, from whom the city acquired it. Before Expilly, however, provenance is more difficult to ascertain. The earliest mention of this manuscript, according to the *Catalogue général,* is that in 1463, twenty "sous tournois" were paid to the widow of Jean Fouqueré, a binder at Blois, for its binding. The *Catalogue* notes that this places the book as part of the Blois library. Marginalia on folios 18 and 34 indicate a slightly more tenuous connection with Charles's court at Blois: "Symon Cailleau" is marked, with flourish, on the top right of folio 18 and very faintly, about 50 mm wide, with capitals 5–6 mm and flourish 24 mm, on the bottom right of folio 34 (not folio 54, as the *Catalogue* states). Symon Cailleau may have been related to Jehan Cailleau, Charles's doctor and the person who handled his manuscripts at Blois; there is also an Anthoine Cailleau noted at Blois during Charles's stay there, according to the *Catalogue* entry.[5] As Arn and Champion note, headings to some of Charles's poems in BN f. fr. 25458 also signal Cailleau. A more tenuous connection of this manuscript to Blois, pointed out by Professor Arn in an unpublished essay on Charles's personal manuscript (BN f. fr. 25458), is Charles's purchase, in 1455, of "xiij peaulx de veslin" from Michau Boudet, a Blois merchant. Arn speculates that this would have been enough vellum to create around fourteen quires, depending upon the size of the skins.[6] It may or may not be coincidental that the duke's poetry, with a quire of prefaces, occupies fourteen quires in this manuscript.[7]

Page Numbering and Quire Construction

A paper binding leaf (pastedown) and endpaper are found at the front and at the back of the manuscript, probably dating from the early nineteenth-century rebind-

---

5. See also Ernest Wickersheimer, *Dictionnaire biographique des médécins en France au moyen âge* (Paris: Librairie Droz, 1936), s.v. "Jean Caillau"; thanks to Mary-Jo Arn for providing this reference.

6. "Order of Composition"; private correspondence. Arn's point is that Champion's assumption (that this household entry of vellum purchase proves additions to the duke's personal manuscript) may not be correct. The entry itself, by the way, seems to allow the possibility that Charles's poetry and Astesano's Latin works were originally conceived as two projects and then put together at Blois: "le livre des Balades de Monseigneur le duc d'Orleans, tant en françois comme en latin *et autres livres en icelluy*" (emphasis added), cited in d'Héricault, ed., "Notice Bibliographique," *Poésies complètes,* 287.

7. There is, as I have said, the possibility that at least parts of the six quires of Latin material by Astesano were copied much earlier than the poetry, beginning in 1435. On the other hand the vellum does not vary much throughout the manuscript. The unanswerable questions are, as Arn notes ("Order of Composition"), how large were the skins and how many quires were made from them?

ing of the book at Grenoble. Folios are numbered on the top right of each recto, in a seventeenth-century hand, numerals measuring about 1–1.5 mm high. The numbering of folio 158 ends in a grand flourish, but the lightly ruled blank folio 159 looks to have been numbered later, in a pencil or charcoal, in a different hand. There is a misnumbering in the manuscript: number 36 has been skipped; folio 37 follows folio 35, in other words. (The quire is intact; no page is missing here.) Folio 131 was evidently misnumbered as 130, and has been overwritten as "13I" [sic]. Otherwise the numbers are unremarkable.

The manuscript is made up of twenty quires, with standard construction throughout (hair-facing-hair, flesh-facing-flesh); binding threads (stitches approximately 3 cm long) are visible in most quires. All quires are in eight; quires 14 and 20, however, contain seven leaves. This is a significant feature of the construction of this manuscript, since quire 14 ends the poetry section and quire 20 ends Astesano's Latin section (and the book). In quire 14, folio 111r ends the poetry (the rest of that page is ruled and blank), and folios 112r and 112v are ruled and blank. There is a stub between folios 111 and 112 (or rather, between leaves 6 and 8 of this quire), and the flesh-hair pattern of the rest of the quire indicates that the stub results from the removal of the leaf that is conjugate with folio 107, the quire's second leaf. In other words, the page removed would have been the quire's seventh leaf, which in the copying turned out to be an unneeded blank page left at the end of the quire: common enough at the end of a work to take out an extra blank folio. Likewise in quire 20, the text ends on the left column of folio 158v, and folios 159r and 159v are ruled and blank. In this case, the stub is after folio 159 (after the seventh leaf of the quire; the stub would have been the eighth leaf). Considered with the consistent flesh-hair pattern of the rest of the quire, this indicates that a blank folio that formed the rest of the bottom sheet of the quire (conjugate with folio 153, in other words) was removed. This removal of blank extras at the end of the copied texts makes for "end quires" with seven leaves where Charles's poetry ends and also where Astesano's Latin works end, which could conceivably indicate that the fourteen quires of poetry and the six quires of Astesano's Latin may have been executed separately or thought of at some point as potentially distinct books; then at some point (surely well before 1463) the two projects became one book.

Catchwords are found only in the Latin back matter, and only between quires 15–16, 16–17, 17–18, and 18–19. Some are lightly decorated catchwords, outlined in pen flourishing; an example is visible in figure 6, folio 120v. This could further indicate that Astesano had assembled quires 15–20, or at least 16–19, containing his earlier Latin material, before the assembly of the whole work. That would imply that the ruling in columns, the page size, and page format, had been preconceived by Astesano and pursued as a single project over nearly three decades. We should not underestimate the Italian humanist desire for permanent fame, of course, which could well have led Astesano to piggyback his own carefully saved and copied works onto Charles's more flamboyant and elegantly literary Selected and Translated Works. In this view, the long-held idea of this book would have been Astesano's, and Charles's poetry, while surely central and prestigious, was necessary but in some sense instrumental, almost a vehicle for Astesano's own fame. But another explanation, from this same evidence of quires and catchwords, would be that the earlier Latin work of Astesano was simply copied into these last six quires some time in the 1450s (previous dates copied in as well?), and that the catchwords imply a binder (perhaps in the house of Fouqueré) who read French but not Latin. In this view the book would have been more wholly Charles's conception and project, and Astesano's Latin work in the back matter (some of which does deal with Charles's captivity, his family, and so on) was necessary but ultimately instrumental. In support of this latter view is the extremely consistent format of the whole book, its ruling, spacing, and decoration (which would have been done later in any case but which is alike throughout, and distinctly French) and especially the consistent quality and look of the vellum itself.[8] The physical evidence of the book, in other words, presents intriguing and important interpretive issues.

Leaves, Lines, and Decoration

The 159 folios are uniformly ruled and lined in columns throughout. Folios 5v, 7v, 8r, 8v, 111v, 112r, 112v, 134v, 159r, and 159v are ruled but blank. These blank pages appear at the ends of conceptual sections: after each part of the prefatory material, after the poetry, and after sections of Latin material. The copying, in other words, like the decoration plan, is based on literary rather than material considerations. The page ruling and writing space measurements vary only slightly throughout. As a general rule, the columns of writing space each measure 8.5–9 cm × 22 cm high, the space between columns 1–1.5 cm, the margins roughly 1.6–2 cm at the top and 3.5–4 cm at the bottom, 1 cm at inner edges and 2 cm at outer edges.

Columns have anywhere from thirty to thirty-four lines, generally more in the Latin (around thirty-two to thirty-three lines) than in the visually less cluttered French-Latin poetry (around thirty lines). Spacing between lines, stanzas, and poems is much more generous in the poetry than in the front and back matter, perhaps as a function of lyric forms found in the French. There are very few blank or skipped lines in the Latin back matter, and one would not see much need for spacing between copied lines in epistolary verse or hexameters, except at breaks in content. Rondeaux and ballades, on the other hand, have intrinsic

---

8. Handwriting is inconclusive: although the back-matter writing seems more cramped than that of the poetry, it looks to be the same hand. Likewise, although the ink in the back matter looks like plain black ink, somewhat faded, and the ink in the poetry tends to be golden brown ranging to faded blackish, the difference is not great enough to be conclusive. Eyes more expert than mine could probably determine more definitive results. (Incipits, excipits, and some marginalia are in red.)

formal breaks at refrains, stanzas, and envois, that make spacious layout more pleasing and natural. A typical page of poetry will have either one ballade or two rondeaux or chansons, often centered top-to-bottom in the column of writing space. In the short poems this makes for very generous spacing and means that sometimes several lines are left blank above and below the poems in addition to lines left blank between parts of the poem. Sometimes envois to longer ballades spill over onto a subsequent page, and of course complaintes and stanzaic portions simply fill the columnar writing space, with appropriate spacing left between stanzas and envoi. The Latin spacing, furthermore, differs from the French when it is appropriate. For example, a rondeau will have spacing at the natural break around the refrain lines, but if the corresponding Latin distich breaks differently, the spacing is around the distich. Or, as in figure 7, a reduced image of folio 43r, the ballade has a space left before the envoi, while the spacing in the Latin translation emphasizes the distich that introduces the refrain. Whoever handled the spacing had a feel for the poetry in both languages. The overall effect of spacing is not only of a literary sensibility but gives the impression of a well-planned, generous layout that displays the poems to best aesthetic advantage.

On decorated pages, as figures 2, 3, 4, and 5 show, the margins are partially or fully filled with extraordinarily detailed rinceaux in black ink with heavy, gessoed gilding inside leaves, at vine-stem junctures, and in other parts of berries, flowers, and leaves; on many pages the amount of gold in tiny globules all over the border is truly stunning. Some of the most heavily decorated pages actually seem to glow, and to make it look as if gold is also in the ink used for writing. Acanthus leaves often include gold or gold-brushed portions sometimes arranged symmetrically with blue portions. Leaves, flowers, fruits, berries, and nuts are in yellow, gold-brush, blue, rose, mauve, red, and green, including fine black outlines and inside detail strokes. The elaborate rinceaux and border elements resemble those of the Master of the White Inscriptions in shape and color but are even less broadly foliated and more reticulated; nor do large elements like acanthus leaves or larger flowers intrude so frequently in the tracery of vines and small leaves, giving overall a finer and more even look than many fifteenth-century manuscript borders.[9] The borders resemble those of the Coëtivy master working in the Loire Valley circa 1460–70,[10] or some of the work associated with

---

9. A more delicate look, for instance, than the borders in J. Paul Getty Museum ms. Ludwig XIII 7 (83.MP.150), fol. 274v, a Master of the White Inscriptions manuscript of Froissart's *Chroniques* dated circa 1480–83; the large decorated initials are similar, however. This page is reproduced in Michelle P. Brown, *Understanding Illuminated Manuscripts* (Malibu, Calif.: J. Paul Getty Museum in association with the British Museum Press, 1994), 40.

10. As in J. Paul Getty Museum ms. 42 (91.MS.11), Boethius, *La Consolation de Philosophie.* See Brown, *Understanding Illuminated Manuscripts,* 10, for a reproduction of leaf 1.

the Boucicaut master.[11] The border style is very much like the work of the decorator of some of the fifteenth-century French books of hours now found in the Musée de Cluny.[12]

On the lightly zoomorphic bas-de-page decoration of folio 9r (fig. 8) are two pheasants, or, perhaps, a two-headed pheasant, at the right side. At the left bas-de-page is a peacock in splendid gold and blue.[13] Two smaller, more common birds are hiding in the right-hand border, one redheaded, white with brownish wings, and the other in flight, with black tips on brown and white wings. In the very large personated heraldic initial that begins the work is an angel holding the Visconti-Valois arms, showing the serpent in silver and black and three fleur-de-lis in blue and white, in appropriate fields. The upper front portions of this angel's white wings, however, are shaded lightly with red. The arms, but not the angel, appear again in the manuscript on folio 113r (fig. 2), in the center bas-de-page, roughly 30 mm × 34 mm, in much clearer colors, the silver metal less tarnished.

Page decorations as well as letter decorations occur in a clear, coherent, and consistent hierarchy throughout. By that I mean that one finds full page decoration—top, inner, outer, bottom, and intercolumn borders fully decorated—on folios that begin a major section of the work. This is true of folio 9r and 9v, where the poetry begins, and folio 113r, where the Latin back matter begins (see figs. 2 and 8). The next level of hierarchy is more frequent, occurring between sections of poetry, at folios 22v, 38r, 53r, 68r, 83r, and 97v (see figs. 3 and 4). At this level one finds the top, bottom, and intercolumn center spaces decorated, but not the outside

---

11. As in the Balfour Hours, circa 1415–20 (J. Paul Getty Museum ms. 22 [86.ML.571]). See fol. 48, reproduced in Brown, *Understanding Illuminated Manuscripts,* 107. A Boucicaut connection would not be surprising, since Charles's father Louis d'Orléans and Boucicaut had long been friends. Sometime before 1406 Louis (Gian Galeazzo Visconti's son-in-law, you will recall) had appointed Boucicaut governor of Genoa. In the Marshal's late years he and Charles were close as well; Charles is praised in Boucicaut's will. See Millard Meiss, *French Painting in the Time of Jean de Berry: The Boucicaut Master* (London: Phaidon, 1968), 10 and nn. 35, 36, 39. The large decorated letters are almost exactly like the Boucicaut workshop letters shown in this book, in size, color, shape, and penwork detail. On the other hand, in 1448 a "Jean Haincelin enlumineur" received payment from Charles for unknown work; Meiss speculates that the Bedford Master was Paris illuminator Jehan Haincelin (62 and n. 25).

12. Very close indeed is a book of hours I saw in December 1998 in couloir 15 of the Musée de Cluny, listed as "Cl. 1252, Livre d'heures, Paris, vers 1410–20, Fonds du Somerard." This book's decoration has gold leaf and vine patterns very close to those of the Grenoble manuscript, with slightly more bright red. See also Alain Erlande-Brandenburg, *Musée national du Moyen Âge* (Paris: Réunion des musées nationaux, 1993), which shows a more broadly foliated example, Cl. 22715.

13. Just beneath the peacock, in pale ink, is a small, illegible word: *Velit? Iller? Vecie?* Note that room seems to have been left for an incipit at the top of this preface. I speculate that the dedications in folios 1r–6r may have obviated the necessity for an additional "Ad illustrissimum . . ." here.

margins. A third level of organization is evident in the prefaces, on folios 1r and 6r, where the border decorations cover only half of the page (see fig. 5).

Furthermore, letters of five sorts are distributed in the whole manuscript according to a coherent plan that marks different literary sections and levels of organization of the work—including Astesano's Latin back matter. (This indicates, given the above information, that even though the copying and certainly the composition of the Latin back matter may have begun years before the translation and copying of the French-Latin poems, the decoration at least was conceived and executed for the volume as a whole.) Nearly all the letters include, in the margin beside them, a very small, faint guide letter.

1. Very large letters: four to as many as eight lines high (as on folio 1r), measuring generally 30–35 mm high × 35–40 mm wide, but can, like the personated letter on folio 9r, measure up to 40 mm high × 50 mm wide. These are made of a thick gold background, after which the letters themselves inside the gold ground have been colored in blues, reds, pinks, gold, and white, often with elaborate inner penwork in white within. These letters begin major sections of the poetry, and occur on pages with full-border decoration and partial-border decoration.

2. Large decorated letters: generally two lines high, these measure 10–12 mm high × 18–20 mm wide, and begin new poems within sections. In these, the letters themselves are gold, and the background to the letters are red or blue, including penwork in black or white, and including foliate and other flourishing.

3. Medium colored capitals: These red or blue letters, one full line high, mark stanzas within poems (or sections within Latin work). These measure 6–8 mm high × 10–12 mm wide. They can include exterior pen flourishing at the corners of the letter.

4. Capitals and second letters begin lines or important words, and measure generally a line high, or 6–7 mm high, 5 mm wide.

5. Small letters in the text are generally 3–4 mm high, but the writing seems more cramped, and the ink at once blacker and more variable in fading, in the quires that contain the Latin works of Astesano.

Letters in the French poems and Latin translations, furthermore, are decorated in a manner that emphasizes their relation to one another. The decorated letters alternate not only down a page—red, blue, red, blue—but across as well, in a "shoelace" pattern. For example, if the background to a large, poem-beginning letter is red in the French, the corresponding Latin letter will be blue; the following medium, stanza-beginning letters will reverse this pattern (French in blue, Latin in red); medium letters beginning the subsequent stanzas in the poem will continue the alternation. (This pattern is not perfectly invariable but predominates: compare the colors in figure 3, folio 53r, with the less typical color pattern of figure 4, folio 97v.) This color pattern has interpretive significance, for it stresses the interrelated and mirroring nature of the French and Latin versions and gives visual form to the venerable theoretical idea of translation's dance between sameness and difference. Most of all, it encourages a particular way of reading, subtly and pleasurably guiding the eye back and forth across the page in a comparative process.

There are relatively few irregularities of decoration in the manuscript. Some represent consistent differences between Astesano's Latin material and the poetry. For example, red and blue paraphs appear in some of the Latin sections, instead of fully decorated letters (fols. 6r, 6v, 7r, for example, and more frequently in the back matter). Also in the back matter are red marginalia and tiny (10–11 mm) penwork margin hands with ruffled cuffs pointing to key passages, one or two of which seem appropriately sententious (131v, 235v, 125r). The incipits and explicits are in red ink, and a few explicits are accompanied by a larger, penwork "LAUS DEO," sometimes with various quincunx line-designs. One of these appears on the last folio of quire 19, the only quire in Astesano's Latin sections not to be joined to its follower by a catchword; perhaps this represents some prior terminus in Astesano's idea of the work, or perhaps not. When I described these differences to Gilbert Ouy, he pointed out that some are typical features of humanist manuscripts.[14] I would also say that humanist tendencies are evident in the classical allusions and claims to permanent fame Astesano makes in the preface to Charles's poetry, and Astesano's biography would also be consonant with such tendencies. We might not be exaggerating to call this volume a marriage of the humanist and the courtly or courtierlike, a conjunction also frequently found in English Tudor poetics.

Other slight irregularities in the manuscript are perhaps less consistently revealing. For example, an error in the decoration of a gilded letter on folio 85v tells us only that the illuminator was probably not a reader of Latin. Instead of "Supplicat. . . ," the logical Latin translation here, a large initial "D" beautifully decorated in gold according to the usual plan renders the Latin version a nonsensical "Dupplicat," an unwittingly ironic bilingual pun of the sort Charles d'Orléans might well have appreciated.

Rich Possibilities for Future Research

Some of the most interesting aspects of this manuscript, aspects unfortunately outside the scope of this study, are its many historical and political connections. Any student of fifteenth-century French and Italian history, social history, or politics can find fascinating "inside stories" in virtually every quire of Astesano's Latin back matter. Not only are important topical events bewailed or rhapsodized (e.g., the earthquake in Naples in 1456 and an apparition of Christ in 1457), but successes and failures in warfare are recorded and interpreted. Charles's imprisonment and family histories appear, of course, as well as King Charles's capture of Genoa, and an unusual early mention of Joan of Arc ("de Iohanna gallica virgine bellica," fol. 136r), and most important, letters, poems, and epigrams to and

---

14. Conversation, Centre National des Recherches Scientifiques, Villejuif, France, December 1998. I am grateful for Professor Ouy's encouragement and assistance.

about, and epitaphs about, an amazingly long list of the era's major and minor figures. A partial list would include not only King Charles, Charles d'Orléans, Joan of Arc, Jean d'Angoulême, the comte de Dunois, Gian Giacomo marchese di Montferrato, Theodore and Boniface of Montferrato, the marchese di Saluzzo, and the doge of Genoa, but include a host of lesser addressees as well: "ad Thomam Francum Grecum, phisicum regium"; "ad humanissimum patrem . . . Bernardum Carretum Sancti Quintini abbatem"; "ad baptisam spinulam virum clarum"; "ad magistrum antonium marengum genuensem"; "ad jacobum bracellum eloquentissimum Genue cancellarium"; "ad clarissimum jureconsultum gulielmum iuvenalem cancellarium regium"; and too many more to record here. Many epitaphs of Great Ones and their contacts appear on folios 155r and following, including a truly remarkable range of people from Carmelite friars to cardinals to political appointees to Isabelle, Charles's royal first wife. There is also an "exclamatio contra Anglicos" (fol. 154r), and a noteworthy passage comparing deeds of war and acts of poetry. Two nineteenth-century editions of this manuscript, each respectable but neither comprehensive, are difficult to obtain.[15] A modern edition is needed, but until then, this work is available on microfilm and should prove extremely useful to researchers in several fields.

---

15. Champollion-Figeac, ed., *Poésies du duc Charles d'Orléans;* Chalvet, ed., *Poésies de Charles d'Orléans.*

References

Adams, Robert. "Langland's *Ordinatio:* The *Viso* and the *Vita* Once More." *Yearbook of Langland Studies* 8 (1995): 51–84.

Aers, David. "A Whisper in the Ear of Early Modernists; or, Reflections on Literary Critics Writing the 'History of the Subject.'" In *Culture and History, 1350–1600,* ed. David Aers, 177–202. Detroit: Wayne State University Press, 1992.

Alfred. *King Alfred's West-Saxon version of Gregory's Pastoral Care.* 2 vols. Early English Text Society, o.s. 45 and 50. London, 1871; rpt. Millwood, N.Y.: Kraus Reprints, 1988.

Allmand, Christopher. *Henry V.* Berkeley and Los Angeles: University of California Press, 1992.

André, Bernard. *Historia Regis Henrici Septimi.* Ed. James Gairdner. London: Longman, Brown, Green, Longman, and Roberts, 1858.

Aristippus, Henricus. *Plato latinus.* Ed. R. Klibansky, V. Kordeuter, and C. Labrowsky. London, 1940.

Aristotle. *Rhetoric.* Trans. John Henry Freese. Cambridge: Harvard University Press, 1975.

Armstrong, E. "English Purchase of Books from the Continent, 1465–1526." *English Historical Review* 94 (1979): 268–90.

Arn, Mary-Jo. "Charles d'Orléans: Translator?" In *The Medieval Translator 4,* ed. Roger Ellis and Ruth Evans, 125–35. Exeter: Exeter University Press, 1994.

———. "Charles of Orleans and the Poems of BL MS Harley 682." *English Studies* 74 (June 1993): 222–35.

———. "*Fortunes Stabilnes:* The English Poems of Charles of Orleans in Their English Context." *Fifteenth-Century Studies* 7 (1983): 1–18.

———. "The Order of Composition in Charles d'Orléans's Personal Manuscript (BN f. fr. 25458)." Manuscript.

———. "Poetic Form as a Mirror of Meaning in the English Poems of Charles of Orleans." *Philological Quarterly* 69, no. 1 (1990): 13–29.

———, ed. *Charles d'Orléans in England, 1415–1440.* Woodbridge, Suffolk: Boydell and Brewer, forthcoming.

———, ed. *Fortunes Stabilnes: Charles of Orleans's English Book of Love.* Binghamton, N.Y.: Medieval and Renaissance Text Society, 1994.

Aubailly, Jean-Claude. *Le Monologue, le dialogue, et la sottie.* Paris: Champion, 1976.

Backhouse, Janet. "Founders of the Royal Library: Edward IV and Henry VII as Collectors of Illuminated Manuscripts." In *England in the Fifteenth Century: Proceedings of the 1986 Harlaxton Symposium,* ed. Daniel Williams, 23–42. Woodbridge, Suffolk: Boydell Press, 1987.

———. "Illuminated Manuscripts Associated with Henry VII." In *The Reign of Henry VII: Proceedings of the 1993 Harlaxton Symposium,* ed. B. Thompson, 175–87. Woodbridge, Suffolk: Boydell Press, 1995.

Bacon, Roger. *Part of the Opus Tertium.* Ed. A. G. Little. University Press of Aberdeen, 1912; rpt. Farnborough, England: Gregg, 1966.

Balzaretti, Marco. "Antonio Astesano traduttore di Charles d'Orléans." *Studi Francesi* 29 (1985): 58–62.

Barban, Judith L. "Twentieth-Century (Re)Soundings of Charles d'Orléans: Song Settings by Debussy, Poulenc, and Francaix." *Medieval Perspectives* 9 (1994): 15–23.

Barber, M. J. "The Books and Patronage of Learning of a Fifteenth-Century Prince." *Book Collector* 12 (1963): 308–15.

Barnstone, Willis. *The Poetics of Translation: History, Theory, Practice.* New Haven: Yale University Press, 1993.

Barolini, Teodolinda. "The Making of a Lyric Sequence: Time and Narrative in Petrarch's Rerum Vulgarium Fragmenta." *Modern Language Notes* 104, no. 1 (1989): 1–38.

Barzun, Jacques. *An Essay on French Verse.* New York: New Directions, 1990.

Bates, Catherine. *Rhetoric of Courtship.* Cambridge: Cambridge University Press, 1992.

Beaufils, Constant. *Étude sur la vie et les poésies de Charles d'Orléans.* Paris, 1861.

Bennett, H. S. "The Production and Dissemination of Vernacular Manuscripts in the Fifteenth Century." *Library,* 5th ser., 1 (1946–47): 167–78.

Besserman, Lawrence, ed. *The Challenge of Periodization: Old Paradigms and New Perspectives.* New York: Garland, 1996.

Bizer, Marc. *La Poésie au miroir: Imitation et conscience de soi dans la poésie latine de la Pléiade.* Paris: Champion, 1995.

Blank, Paula. *Broken English: Dialects and the Politics of Language in Renaissance Writings.* London: Routledge, 1996.

Blayney, Margaret S., ed. *Fifteenth-Century English Translations of Alain Chartier's "Le Traité de l'Esperance."* 2 vols. London: Oxford University Press, 1974–80.

Bloom, Harold. *The Anxiety of Influence.* 2d ed. New York: Oxford University Press, 1997.

Boethius. *De Institutione arithmetica (Ms Bern 633); Boethian Number Theory.* Ed. and trans. Michael Masi. Amsterdam: Rodopi, 1983.

———. *In Isagogen Porphyrii commenta.* Ed. Samuel Brandt. Vindobonae: Tempsky, 1906.

Boffey, Julia. "Charles d'Orléans Reading Chaucer's Dream Vision." In *Mediaevalitas: Reading the Middle Ages,* ed. Piero Boitani and Anna Torti, 43–62. Cambridge: D. S. Brewer, 1996.

———. *Manuscripts of English Courtly Love Lyrics in the Later Middle Ages.* Bury St. Edmunds, Suffolk: D. S. Brewer, 1985.

Bonnassie, Pierre. *From Slavery to Feudalism in South-western Europe.* Trans. Jean Birrell. Cambridge: Cambridge University Press, 1991.

Bossy, Michel-André, ed. and trans. *Medieval Debate Poetry: Vernacular Works.* New York: Garland, 1987.

Bourdieu, Pierre. *Les Règles de l'art.* Paris: Seuil, 1992.

Braden, Gordon. *Petrarchan Love and the Continental Renaissance.* New Haven: Yale University Press, 1999.

British Museum. *A Catalogue of the Lansdowne Manuscripts in the British Museum.* London: R. and A. Taylor, 1819.

British Museum, Department of Manuscripts. *Illuminated Manuscripts in the British Museum.* Notes by George F. Warner. London, 1899.

Brown, Michelle P. *Understanding Illuminated Manuscripts.* Malibu, Calif.: J. Paul Getty Museum in association with the British Museum Press, 1994.

Brownlee, Kevin. *Poetic Identity in Guillaume de Machaut.* Madison: University of Wisconsin Press, 1984.

Bullrich, Georg. *Über Charles d'Orléans und die ihm zugeschreibene englische Übersetzung seiner Gedichte.* Berlin, 1893.

Burgundio of Pisa. Prologue to the translation of St. John Chrysostom's commentary on the Gospel of John. See Peter Classen, *Burgundio von Pisa: Richter-Gesandeter-Übersetzer,* 50–61. Heidelberg: Carl Winter, 1974.

Burke, John. *A Genealogical History of the Commoners of Great Britain and Ireland.* Vols. 1–4. London: R. Bentley, 1834–38; rpt. Baltimore: Genealogical Publishing, 1977.

Burrow, J. A. *English Verse, 1300–1500.* London: Longman, 1977.

———. "Hoccleve and the Middle French Poets." In *The Long Fifteenth Century: Essays for Douglas Gray,* ed. H. Cooper and S. Mapstone, 35–49. Oxford: Clarendon, 1997.

———. *Thomas Hoccleve.* Newcastle-upon-Tyne: Athenaeum Press, 1994.

Calin, William. "The Density of the Text: Charles d'Orléans." In *Mélanges de langue et de littératures offerts à Alice Planche.* 2 vols. Paris: Les Belles Lettres, 1984.

———. *The French Tradition and the Literature of Medieval England.* Toronto: University of Toronto Press, 1994.

———. "Will the Real Charles of Orleans Stand! or Who Wrote the English Poems in Harley 682?" In *Conjunctures: Medieval Studies in Honor of Douglas Kelly,* ed. Keith Busby and Norris J. Lacy, 69–86. Amsterdam: Rodopi, 1994.

Camargo, Martin. *Middle English Verse Love Epistle.* Tübingen: Niemeyer, 1991.

Cappelli, Adriano. *Elements of Abbreviation in Medieval Latin Paleography.* Ed. and trans. David Heimann and Richard Kay. Lawrence: University of Kansas Libraries, 1982.

Carlson, David R. "King Arthur and Court Poems for the Birth of Arthur Tudor in 1486." *Humanistica Lovaniensa* 36 (1987): 147–83.

———. "Politicizing Tudor Court Literature: Gaguin's Embassy and Henry VII's Humanists' Response." *Studies in Philology* 85, no. 3 (1988): 279–304.

———. "Reputation and Duplicity: The Texts and Context of Thomas More's Epigram on Bernard André." *ELH* 58, no. 2 (1991): 261–80.

Carron, Jean-Claude. "Imitation and Intertextuality in the Renaissance." *New Literary History* 19, no. 3 (1988): 565–79.

Cerquiglini, Jacqueline. *"Un Engin si soutil": Guillaume de Machaut et l'écriture au XIVème siècle.* Geneva: Slatkine, 1985.

Chambers, E. K., and Frank Sidgwick. *Early English Lyrics....* London: Sidgwick and Jackson, 1911; rpt. 1937.

Champion, Pierre. "Du Succès de l'oeuvre de Charles d'Orléans et de ses imitateurs jusqu'au XVIè siècle." In *Mélanges offerts à M. Emile Picot.* 2 vols. Geneva: Slatkine, 1969.

———. *Un Inventaire des papiers de Charles d'Orléans (1444).* Paris: Librairie Ancienne Honoré Champion, 1912.

———. *Librairie de Charles d'Orléans.* Paris, 1910; rpt. Geneva: Slatkine, 1975.

———. *Le Manuscrit autographe des poésies de Charles d'Orléans.* Paris, 1907; rpt. Geneva: Slatkine, 1975.

———. *Vie de Charles d'Orléans.* 2d ed. Paris: Honoré Champion, 1969.

Champollion-Figeac, Aimé. *Louis et Charles d'Orléans.* Paris, 1844.

Charles d'Orléans. *Ballades et Rondeaux.* Ed. Jean-Claude Mühlethaler. Paris: Livre de Poche, 1992.

———. "Complainte de France." Paris: Sézille, 1944; La Haye: Stols, 1944.

———. *The English Poems of Charles of Orleans.* Ed. Robert Steele and Mabel Day. 2 vols. London: Oxford University Press, 1941 and 1946; rpt. (2 vols. in 1), 1970.

———. *Fortunes Stabilnes: Charles of Orleans's English Book of Love.* Ed. Mary-Jo Arn. Binghamton, N.Y.: Medieval and Renaissance Text Society, 1994.

———. *Poems Written in English by Charles, Duke of Orleans during his captivity in England after the battle of Azincourt.* Ed. George Watson Taylor. London: Nicol, for the Roxburghe Club, 1827.

———. *Poésies.* Ed. Pierre Champion. 2 vols. Paris: Librairie Ancienne Honoré Champion, 1923–24.

―――. *Poésies complètes de Charles d'Orléans* . . . . Ed. Charles d'Héricault. 2 vols. Paris, 1874; rpt. Paris: Gosselin, 1896.

―――. *Poésies de Charles d'Orléans* . . . . Ed. J.-Marie Guichard. Paris: Gosselin, 1842.

―――. *Poésies de Charles d'Orléans, père de Louis XII et oncle de François Ier, rois de France.* Ed. Vincent Chalvet. Grenoble: Giroud, 1803.

―――. *Poésies du duc Charles d'Orléans* . . . . Ed. Aimé Champollion-Figeac. Paris: J. Belin-Leprieur, 1842.

Chartier, Alain. *Les Oeuvres.* Ed. André Duchesne. Paris, 1617; rpt. Geneva: Slatkine, 1975.

―――. *The Poetical Works of Alain Chartier.* Ed. J. C. Laidlaw. London: Cambridge University Press, 1974.

―――. *La Chasse et le départ d'amours.* Paris: Vérard, 1509.

Chaucer, Geoffrey. *The Riverside Chaucer.* 3d ed. Ed. Larry D. Benson. Boston: Houghton Mifflin, 1987.

Cholakian, Rouben. *Deflection/Reflection in the Lyric Poetry of Charles d'Orléans: A Psychosemiotic Reading.* Potomac, Md.: Maryland Press, 1984.

Cicero. *De optimo genere oratorum.* Trans. Henry Hubbell. Cambridge: Harvard University Press, 1949.

Cigada, Sergio. "Christine de Pisan e la traduzione delle poesie di Charles d'Orléans." *Aevum* 32 (1958): 509–16.

Clanvowe, John. *The Works of Sir John Clanvowe.* Ed. V. J. Scattergood. Cambridge: D. S. Brewer, and Totowa, N.J.: Rowman and Littlefield, 1975.

Clark, Cecily. "Charles d'Orléans: Some English Perspectives." *Medium Aevum* 40 (1971): 254–61.

Classen, Albrecht. *Die Autobiographische Lyrik des Europäischen Spätmittelalters.* Amsterdam: Rodopi, 1991.

Cocco, Mia. "The Italian Inspiration in the Poetry of Charles d'Orléans." *Mid-Hudson Language Studies* 2 (1979): 46–60.

Coldiron, A. E. B. "Charles d'Orléans and Thomas Park's Copy of the *Specimens of the Early English Poets.*" *Notes and Queries,* n.s. 44 (December 1997): 465–69.

―――. "Thomas Watson and Renaissance Lyric Translation." *Translation and Literature* 5, no. 1 (1996): 3–25.

―――. "*Translatio,* Translation, and Charles d'Orlèans's *Parole*d Poetics." *Exemplaria* 8, no. 1 (1996): 169–92.

―――. "Translation, Canons, and Cultural Capital." In *Charles d'Orlèans in England, 1415–1440,* ed. Mary-Jo Arn. Woodbridge, Suffolk: Boydell and Brewer, forthcoming.

Cooper, Helen, and Sally Mapstone, eds. *The Long Fifteenth Century: Essays for Douglas Gray.* Oxford: Clarendon, 1997.

Copeland, Rita. *Rhetoric, Hermeneutics, and Translation in the Middle Ages.* Cambridge: Cambridge University Press, 1991.
Courthope, W. J. *History of English Poetry.* 3 vols. T. Tegg, 1840; 6 vols., London: Macmillan, 1895–1910.
Croft, Thomas. *The Retrospective Review, and Historical and Antiquarian Magazine* (London), 2d ser., 1 (1827): 147–56.
Crow, M. M. "John of Angoulême and His Chaucer Manuscript." *Speculum* 17 (1942): 86–99.
Damrosch, David, ed. *New Longman Anthology of British Literature.* New York: Addison Wesley Longman, 1999.
Daniel, Samuel. *Complete Works in Verse and Prose.* Ed. A. B. Grosart. London: Hazell, Watson, and Viney, 1885–96; rpt. New York: Russell and Russell, 1962.
———. *Poems and a Defense of Rhyme.* Ed. A. C. Sprague. Cambridge: Harvard University Press, 1930.
Davies, R. T. *Medieval English Lyrics.* Evanston, Ill.: Northwestern University Press, 1964.
Defaux, Gerard. "Charles d'Orléans ou le poétique du secret: À propos du rondeau XXXIII de l'édition Champion." *Romania* 93 (1972): 194–243.
de la Rue, l'Abbé. *Essais historiques sur les bardes, les jongleurs, et les trouvères normands et anglo-normands.* Paris, 1834.
Deleuze, Gilles, and Félix Guattari. *Kafka: Pour une littérature mineure.* Paris: Éditions de Minuit, 1975.
Delisle, Léopold. *Le Cabinet des manuscrits de la Bibliothèque Impériale.* 3 vols. Paris: Imprimerie Impériale, 1868–81.
DeNeef, A. Leigh. "Epideictic Rhetoric and the Renaissance Lyric." *Journal of Medieval and Renaissance Studies* 3 (1973): 203–31.
Derrida, Jacques, et al. "Table Ronde sur la traduction." In *L'Oreille de l'autre: Otobiographies, transferts, traductions.* Montreal: VLB, 1982.
Deschamps, E. *Oeuvres complètes d'Eustache Deschamps,* ed. Gaston Raynaud. 11 vols. Paris: Librairie de Firmin Didot et cie., 1891.
Deschères, Théodore. "Charles d'Orléans." In *Le Plutarque français.* Paris: Crapelet, 1838.
Dictionnaire de biographie française. Paris: Librairie Letouzey et Ané, 1975.
Dizionario biografico degli italiani. Ed. A. M. Ghisalberti. 50 vols. Rome: Istituto della Enciclopedia italiana, 1960–73.
Donne, John. *Poems with Elegies on the Author's Death.* London: Marriot, 1633; rpt. New York: Da Capo, 1970.
d'Orléans, Charles. See Charles d'Orléans.
Drayton, Michael. *Poems.* Ed. John Buxton. London: Routledge and Paul, 1953.
———. *Works.* Ed. K. M. Tillotson, J. W. Hebel, and B. H. Newdigate. 5 vols. Oxford: Blackwell, 1931–41.

Dryden, John. "Preface to the Translation of Ovid's Epistles." In *Essays of John Dryden*. Ed. W. P. Ker. New York: Russell and Russell, 1961.

DuPlessis, Robert. *Transitions to Capitalism in Early Modern Europe*. Cambridge: Cambridge University Press, 1997.

duPont-Ferrier, Gustave. *Jean d'Orléans, Comte d'Angoulême d'après sa bibliothèque (1467)*. Paris: Félix Alcan, 1897.

Edwards, John R. *Multilingualism*. London: Routledge, 1994.

Ellis, George. *Specimens of the Early English Poets*. London: Edwards, Pall Mall, 1790. 2d ed., London: G. and W. Nicol, 1801. 3d ed., 1803.

Enciclopedia universal ilustrada europeo-americana. Barcelona: José Espasa é Hijos, 1912.

Erlande-Brandenburg, Alain. *Musée national du Moyen Âge*. Paris: Réunion des musées nationaux, 1993.

Evans, Ruth. "Translating Past Cultures?" In *The Medieval Translator 4*, ed. Roger Ellis and Ruth Evans, 20–45. Binghamton, N.Y.: Medieval and Renaissance Text Society, 1994.

Even-Zohar, Itamar. *Papers in Historical Poetics*. Tel Aviv: Porter Institute for Poetics and Semiotics, 1978.

Fehrenbach, R. J., and E. Leedham-Green, eds. *Private Libraries in Renaissance England*. 5 vols. to date. Binghamton, N.Y.: Medieval and Renaissance Text Society, 1992–.

Fenoaltea, Doranne, and David Rubin, eds. *The Ladder of High Designs: Structure and Interpretation of the French Lyric Sequence*. Charlottesville: University Press of Virginia, 1991.

Findlen, Paula, and Kenneth Gouwens. "AHR Forum: Introduction: The Persistence of the Renaissance." *American Historical Review* 103, no. 1 (1998): 51–54.

Fineman, Joel. *Shakespeare's Perjured Eye*. Berkeley and Los Angeles: University of California Press, 1986.

———. *The Subjectivity Effect in Western Literary Tradition: Essays toward the Release of Shakespeare's Will*. Cambridge: MIT Press, 1991.

Fisher, John H. "Caxton and Chancery English." In *Fifteenth-Century Studies: Recent Essays*, ed. R. F. Yeager, 161–85. Hamden, Conn.: Archon, 1984.

Fisher, John H., Malcolm Richardson, and Jane L. Fisher. *An Anthology of Chancery English (1384–1462)*. Knoxville: University of Tennessee Press, 1984; digital text, University of Virginia Electronic Text Center.

Forster, Leonard. *The Poet's Tongues: Multilingualism in Literature*. Cambridge: Cambridge University Press, 1970.

Fournier, P., E. Maignien, and A. Prudhomme. *Catalogue général des manuscrits des bibliothèques publiques de France: Départements*. Vol. 7, *Grenoble*. Paris: Librairie Plon, 1889.

Fox, Alistair. *Politics and Literature in the Reigns of Henry VII and VIII*. Oxford: Basil Blackwell, 1989.

Fox, John. "Glanures/Charles d'Orléans: Three Macaronic Rondeaux." In *Charles of Orleans in England, 1415–1440*, ed. Mary-Jo Arn. Woodbridge, Suffolk: Boydell and Brewer. Forthcoming.

———. *The Lyric Poetry of Charles d'Orléans*. Oxford: Clarendon, 1969.

Freeman, Michelle A. *Poetics of "Translatio studii" and "Conjointure."* French Forum Monographs, 12. Lexington, Ky., 1979.

Fryde, E. B. *Peasants and Landlords in Later Medieval England*. New York: St. Martin's, 1996.

Furnish, Shearle. "*Ordinatio* of Huntington Library MS HM 149: An East Anglian Manuscript of Nicholas Love's *Mirrour*." *Manuscripta* 34, no. 1 (1990): 50–65.

Gaunt, Simon. *Troubadours and Irony*. Cambridge: Cambridge University Press, 1989.

Gellrich, Jesse. *Idea of the Book in the Middle Ages*. Ithaca: Cornell University Press, 1985.

Gilson, Étienne. *Les Idées et les lettres*. Paris: J. Vrin, 1932.

Goez, Werner. *Translatio imperii: Ein Beitrag zur Geschichte des Geschichtsdenkens und der politischen Theorie im Mittelalter und in der frühen Neuzeit*. Tübingen: Mohr, 1958.

Goodrich, Norma. *Charles, Duke of Orleans: A Literary Biography*. New York: Macmillan, 1963.

Gorrini, Giacomo. *Il Comune astigiano e la sua storiografia*. Firenze: C. Ademollo, 1884.

Goujet, l'Abbé. *Bibliothèque françoise ou histoire de la littérature françoise*. Vol. 9. 1745.

Gower, John. *Complete Works of John Gower*. Ed. G. C. Macaulay. 4 vols. Oxford: Clarendon, 1899; rpt. Grosse Pointe, Mich.: Scholarly Press, 1992.

Green, R. F. "Hearts, Minds, and Some English Poems of Charles d'Orléans." *English Studies in Canada* 9 (1983): 136–50.

———. *Poets and Princepleasers*. Toronto: University of Toronto Press, 1980.

Greenblatt, Stephen. *Renaissance Self-Fashioning*. Chicago: University of Chicago Press, 1980.

Greene, Roland. *Post-Petrarchism: Origins and Innovations of the Western Lyric Sequence*. Princeton: Princeton University Press, 1991.

Greene, Thomas. *The Light in Troy*. New Haven: Yale University Press, 1982.

Griffiths, Jeremy, and Derek Pearsall. *Book Production and Publishing in Britain, 1375–1475*. Cambridge: Cambridge University Press, 1989.

Guillory, John. *Cultural Capital: The Problem of Literary Canon Formation*. Chicago: University of Chicago Press, 1993.

Hadfield, Andrew. *Literature, Politics, and National Identity: Reformation to Renaissance*. Cambridge: Cambridge University Press, 1994.

Hammond, Eleanor Prescott. "Charles d'Orléans and Anne Molyneux." *Modern Philology* 22 (1924–25): 215–16.

———. *English Verse between Chaucer and Surrey.* Durham, N.C.: Duke University Press, 1927; rpt. New York: Octagon Books, 1965.
Hanford, James Holly. "The Debate of Heart and Eye." *Modern Language Notes* 26 (1911): 161–67.
Hardison, O. B. *The Enduring Monument.* Chapel Hill: University of North Carolina Press, 1962; rpt. Westport, Conn.: Greenwood, 1973.
Harrison, Ann Tukey. "Charles d'Orléans: The Reluctant Traveler." *Fifteenth Century Studies* 10 (1984): 79–90.
———. *Charles d'Orléans and the Allegorical Mode.* Chapel Hill: University of North Carolina Department of Romance Languages, 1975.
———. "Charles d'Orléans and the Renaissance." *Rocky Mountain Review of Language and Literature* 25 (1971): 86–92.
———. "Orleans and Burgundy: The Literary Relationship." *Stanford French Review* 4 (1980): 475–84.
Herman, Peter, ed. *Rethinking the Henrician Era.* Urbana: University of Illinois Press, 1994.
Hieatt, A. K. "The Genesis of Shakespeare's Sonnets: Spenser's *Ruines of Rome.*" *PMLA* 98, no. 5 (1983): 800–814.
Hill, W. Speed, ed. *New Ways of Looking at Old Texts.* Binghamton, N.Y.: Medieval and Renaissance Text Society/Renaissance English Text Society, 1993.
Hitching, F. K., and S. Hitching. *References to English Surnames, 1601.* Walton-on-Thames: Bernau, 1910.
Hoccleve, Thomas. *Hoccleve's Works.* Ed. F. J. Furnivall. 3 vols. Early English Text Society, nos. 61, 72, 73. London, 1892–1925.
Hopkins, John. "Coupling Theory and the Translation of Poetry: A Haiku Example." *Pacific Quarterly Moana* 5, no. 1 (1980): 47–51.
Horace. *Odes and Epodes.* Trans. C. E. Bennett. Cambridge: Harvard University Press, 1978.
———. *Satires, Epistles, and Ars Poetica.* Trans. H. R. Fairclough. Cambridge: Harvard University Press, 1966.
Huizinga, J. *Autumn of the Middle Ages.* Trans. Rodney J. Payton and Ulrich Mammitzsch. Chicago: University of Chicago Press, 1996.
Huot, Sylvie. *From Song to Book.* Ithaca: Cornell University Press, 1987.
Imbert, Barthélémy. *Annales Poétiques ou Almanach des Muses.* Paris, 1778.
Ingberg, A. C. "The Enigma of the Translator: A Poststructuralist Reading of Theories of Translation." Ph.D. diss., Purdue University, 1986.
Ivy, G. S. "The Bibliography of the Manuscript Book." In *The English Library before 1700,* ed. Francis Wormald and C. E. Wright, 32–65. London: Athlone Press, 1958.
Jansen, J. P. M. "Charles d'Orléans and the Fairfax Poems." *English Studies* 70 (June 1989): 206–24.

———. "The French Manuscripts of the English Poems of Charles of Orleans." *Notes and Queries,* n.s. 35 (December 1988): 439–40.

———, ed. *The "Suffolk" Poems: An Edition of the Love Lyrics in Fairfax 16 Attributed to William de la Pole.* Groningen: Universiteitsdrukkerij, 1989.

Le Jardin de Plaisance. Paris: Vérard, 1501.

Jauss, Hans. *Toward an Aesthetic of Reception.* Trans. Timothy Bahti. Minneapolis: University of Minnesota Press, 1982.

Jerome. *Select Letters of St. Jerome.* Trans. F. A. Wright. Cambridge, Mass.: Harvard University Press, 1954.

Jones, Michael K. "'Gardez mon corps, sauvez ma terre'—Immunity from War and the Lands of a Captive Knight: The Siege of Orléans Revisited." In *Charles d'Orléans in England, 1415–1440,* ed. Mary-Jo Arn. Woodbridge, Suffolk: Boydell and Brewer, forthcoming.

———. "Henry VII, Lady Margaret Beaufort, and the Orléans Ransom." In *Kings and Nobles in the Later Middles Ages,* ed. Ralph Griffiths and James Sherborne, 254–73. New York: St. Martin's, 1986.

Keiser, George. "*Ordinatio* in the Manuscripts of John Lydgate's *Lyf of Our Lady:* Its Value for the Reader, Its Challenge for the Modern Editor." In *Medieval Literature: Texts and Interpretation.* Binghamton, N.Y.: Medieval and Renaissance Text Society, 1991.

Kelly, Douglas. *Medieval Imagination: Rhetoric and the Poetry of Courtly Love.* Madison: University of Wisconsin Press, 1978.

Kennedy, William. *Authorizing Petrarch.* Ithaca, N.Y.: Cornell University Press, 1994.

Ker, Neil. *Medieval Libraries of Great Britain: A List of Surviving Books.* London: The Royal Historical Society, 1941; rpt. 1964.

Keralio, Mlle de. *Collection des meilleurs ouvrages françois . . . .* Vol. 3. Paris: Lagrange, 1787.

Kermode, Frank. *The Sense of an Ending.* New York: Oxford University Press, 1967.

Knapp, Ethan. "Bureaucratic Identity and the Construction of the Self in Hoccleve's *Formulary* and *La male regle.*" *Speculum* 74 (1999): 357–76.

Kosta-Théfaine, Jean-François. "Charles d'Orleans: Bibliographie récente." *Le Moyen Français* 38 (1996): 144–50.

Kuhn, Sherman M., gen. ed. *Middle English Dictionary.* Ann Arbor: University of Michigan Press, 1954–.

LeBlanc, Yvonne. *Va Letter Va: The French Verse Epistle, 1400–1500.* Birmingham, Ala.: Summa Press, 1995.

Lefevere, André. *Translating Literature.* New York: Modern Language Association, 1992.

———, with Susan Bassnett, ed. *Translation, History, Culture.* London: Pinter, 1990.

Le Fèvre, Jean, Seigneur de Saint-Rémy. *Chronique.* 2 vols. Paris: Librairie Renouard, 1876–81.

Leicester, H. Marshall, Jr. *The Disenchanted Self: Representing the Subject in "The Canterbury Tales."* Berkeley and Los Angeles: University of California Press, 1990.

Lemaire de Belges, Jean. *Le Triomphe de l'amant vert.* Paris, 1531.

Lerer, Seth. *Chaucer and His Readers: Imagining the Author in Late Medieval England.* Princeton, N.J.: Princeton University Press, 1993.

———. *Courtly Letters in the Age of Henry VIII: Literary Culture and the Arts of Deceit.* Cambridge: Cambridge University Press, 1997.

Lorris, Guillaume de, and Jean de Meun. *Roman de la Rose.* Ed. Daniel Poirion. Paris: Garnier Flammarion, 1974.

Lyotard, J.-F. "The Different, the Referent, and the Proper Name." *Diacritics* 14 (1984): 4–14.

MacCracken, Henry. "An English Friend of Charles of Orleans." *PMLA* 26 (1911): 142–80.

Machaut, Guillaume de. *Poésies lyriques.* Ed. V. F. Shishmarev. Paris, 1909; rpt. Geneva: Slatkine, 1973.

Marks, Diane. "Poems from Prison: James I of Scotland and Charles of Orleans." *Fifteenth Century Studies* 15 (1989): 245–58.

Marot, Clément. *Les Traductions.* Vol. 6 of *Oeuvres complètes.* Ed. C. A. Mayer. Geneva: Slatkine, 1980.

Marotti, Arthur. "Malleable and Fixed Texts." In *New Ways of Looking at Old Texts,* ed. W. Speed Hill, 159–74. Binghamton, N.Y.: Medieval and Renaissance Text Society/Renaissance English Text Society, 1993.

———. "Manuscript, Print, and the English Renaissance Lyric." In *New Ways of Looking at Old Texts,* ed. W. Speed Hill, 209–22. Binghamton, N.Y.: Medieval and Renaissance Text Society/Renaissance English Text Society, 1993.

———. *Manuscript, Print, and the English Renaissance Lyric.* Ithaca: Cornell University Press, 1995.

Martin, Christopher. *Policy in Love: Lyric and Public in Ovid, Petrarch, and Shakespeare.* Pittsburgh: Duquesne University Press, 1994.

Matisse, Henri. *Poèmes de Charles d'Orléans, manuscrits et illustrés par Henri Matisse.* Paris: Tériade, 1950.

Maus, Katharine Eisaman. *Inwardness and Theatre in the English Renaissance.* Chicago: University of Chicago Press, 1995.

May, Steven W. "Manuscript Circulation at the Elizabethan Court." In *New Ways of Looking at Old Texts,* ed. W. Speed Hill, 273–80. Binghamton, N.Y.: Medieval and Renaissance Text Society/Renaissance English Text Society, 1993.

McLeod, Enid. *Charles of Orleans: Prince and Poet.* London: Chatto and Windus, 1969.

Meale, Carol. "Patrons, Buyers, and Owners: Book Production and Social Status." In *Book Production and Publishing in Britain, 1375–1475,* ed. Jeremy Griffiths and Derek Pearsall, 201–38. Cambridge: Cambridge University Press, 1989.

Meier, Hans. "Middle English Styles in Translation: The Case of Chaucer and Charles." In *So Meny People, Longages, and Tonges: Philological Essays in Scots and Mediaeval English Presented to Angus McIntosh,* ed. Michael Benskin and M. L. Samuels. Edinburgh: Authors Press, 1981.

Meiss, Millard. *French Painting in the Time of Jean de Berry: The Boucicaut Master.* London: Phaidon, 1968.

Michel, Francisque. *Rapports à M. le Ministre de l'instruction publique sur les anciens monuments de l'histoire et de la littérature de la France qui se trouvent dans les bibliothèques de l'Angleterre et de l'Ecosse.* Paris: Comité Historique des Arts et Monuments, 1838.

Milton, John. *Paradise Lost.* Ed. Alastair Fowler. 2d ed. New York: Longman, 1998.

Minnis, A. J. *Medieval Theory of Authorship.* 2d ed. Philadelphia: University of Pennsylvania Press, 1988.

Moore, Samuel. "Patrons of Letters in Norfolk and Suffolk, c. 1450." *PMLA* 27 (1912): 188–207 and 28 (1913): 79–105.

Muratori, Ludovico Antonio. *Rerum Italicarum Scriptores.* Vol. 14. Mediolani: Typographia societatis palatinae, 1738–42; rpt. Bologna: A. Forni, 1965.

Muscatine, Charles. *Chaucer and the French Tradition.* Berkeley and Los Angeles: University of California Press, 1957.

Nathan, Leonard. "Tradition and New Fangledness in Wyatt's 'They Fle Frim Me'." *Journal of English Literary History* 32 (1965):1–16.

Nelson, Deborah. *Charles d'Orléans: An Analytical Bibliography.* London: Grant and Cutler, 1990.

Norton-Smith, John, ed. *Bodleian Library MS Fairfax 16.* Facsimile edition. London: Scolar Press, 1979.

Nouvelle Biographie générale. Vol. 3. Paris: Firmin Didot Frères, 1856.

Oldmixon, John. *Amores Britannici.* London: John Nutt, 1703.

Ormont, H. "Les Manuscrits des rois d'Angleterre au château de Richmond." In *Études Romanes dédiées à Gaston Paris par ses élèves français.* Paris: Émile Bouillon, 1891.

Parkes, Malcolm. "The Influence of the Concepts of *Ordinatio* and *Compilatio* on the Development of the Book." In *Medieval Learning and Literature,* ed. J. J. G. Alexander and M. T. Gibson, 115–41. Oxford: Clarendon, 1976.

———. "Literacy of the Laity." In *The Medieval World,* ed. David Daiches and Anthony Thorlby, 555–78. London: Aldus, 1973.

Paston Letters and Papers of the Fifteenth Century. 3 parts (2 parts to date). Oxford: Clarendon, 1971–.

Patterson, Lee. *Literary Practice and Social Change in Britain, 1380–1530*. Berkeley and Los Angeles: University of California Press, 1990.

———. "The Place of the Modern in the Later Middle Ages." In *The Challenge of Periodization,* ed. Lawrence Besserman, 51–66. New York: Garland, 1996.

Payne, Paula H. "The Poet Orator's Praise: Epideictic Discourse in Sidney's *Astrophel and Stella.*" *Sidney Newsletter* 9, no. 1 (1988): 11–21.

Pearsall, Derek. "Hoccleve's *Regement of Princes:* The Poetics of Royal Self-Representation." *Speculum* 69 (1994): 386–410.

———. *John Lydgate.* London: Routledge and Kegan Paul, 1970.

Petrarch, Francis. *Petrarch's Lyric Poems.* Ed. and trans. Robert M. Durling. Cambridge: Harvard University Press, 1976.

Phelps, Ruth. *The Earlier and Later Forms of Petrarch's Canzoniere.* Chicago: University of Chicago Press, 1925.

Phillips, Helen. "Frames and Narrators in Chaucerian Poetry." In *The Long Fifteenth Century: Essays for Douglas Gray,* ed. H. Cooper and S. Mapstone, 71–98. Oxford: Clarendon, 1997.

Piaget, Arthur. "Une Édition gothique de Charles d'Orléans." *Romania* 21 (1892): 581–96.

Pigman, G. W., III. "Versions of Imitation in the Renaissance." *Renaissance Quarterly* 33 (1980): 1–32.

Pisan, Christine de. *Oeuvres poétiques.* Éd. M. Roy. 3 vols. Paris: Firmin et cie, 1886–96.

Planche, Alice. *Charles d'Orléans ou la recherche d'un langage.* Paris: Editions Honoré Champion, 1975.

Platts, Graham. *Land and People in Medieval Lincolnshire*. Lincoln: History of Lincolnshire Committee, 1985.

Plomer, H. R. "The Importation of Low Country and French Books in England, 1480 and 1502–3." *Library,* 4th ser., 9 (1929): 164–68.

Poirion, Daniel. "La Nef d'Espérance." In *Mélanges de langue et de littérature du Moyen Âge et de la Renaissance offerts à Jean Frappier.* (2 vols), 2:913–28. Geneva: Droz, 1970.

———. *Le Poète et le prince.* Paris: Presses Universitaires de France, 1965.

Porter, Roy. *Rewriting the Self.* London: Routledge, 1997.

Postan, M. M., ed. *Cambridge Economic History of Europe.* 2d ed. 8 vols. Cambridge University Press, 1966–87.

Quixley, Robert, trans. *Quixley's Ballades Royal (?1402).* Leeds, 1908; rpt. *Yorkshire Archaeological Journal* 20 (1909): 33–50.

Reed, Thomas L. *Middle English Debate Poetry and the Aesthetics of Irresolution.* Columbia: University of Missouri Press, 1990.

Ringbom, Sixten. "Some Pictorial Conventions for the Recounting of Thought and Experiences in Late Medieval Art." In *Medieval Iconography and Narra-*

tive, ed. Flemming Andersen, Esther Nyholm, Marianne Powell, and Flemming Stubkjaer, 38–69. Odense: Odense University Press, 1980.

Ringler, William. *Bibliography and Index of English Verse in Manuscript, 1501–1558.* Prepared and completed by Michael Rudick and Susan J. Ringler. London: Mansell, 1992.

———. *Bibliography and Index of English Verse Printed, 1476–1558.* London: Mansell, 1988.

Ritson, Joseph, ed. *Ancient Songs and Ballads from the Time of King Henry the Third to the Revolution.* London, 1790, 1792, 1829. Ed. W. Carew Hazlitt (London: Reeves and Turner, 1877).

———, ed. *English Anthology.* London: C. Clarke, 1793.

Robbins, R. H. "Some Charles d'Orléans Fragments." *Modern Language Notes* 66 (1951): 501–5.

———, ed. *Historical Poems of the 14th and 15th Centuries.* New York: Columbia University Press, 1959.

———, ed. *Secular Lyrics of the XIVth and XVth Centuries.* Oxford: Clarendon, 1952.

Robinson, Douglas. *The Translator's Turn.* Baltimore: Johns Hopkins University Press, 1991.

Russell, J. Stephen. *The English Dream Vision.* Columbus: Ohio State University Press, 1988.

Rymer, Thomas. *Foedera. Acta Regis. . . .* London: J. and J. Knapton, 1731.

———. *Syllabus in English of the Documents. . . .* 3 vols. London: Public Record Office; rpt. New York: AMS Press, 1973.

Sallier, l'Abbé de. *Mémoires de l'Académie Royale des inscriptions et belles lettres.* Vol. 13. 1740.

Sallust. *Works.* Trans. J. C. Rolfe. Cambridge: Harvard University Press, 1931; rpt. 1995.

Salter, Elizabeth, and Derek Pearsall. "The Role of the Frontispiece." In *Medieval Iconography and Narrative,* ed. Flemming Andersen, Esther Nyholm, Marianne Powell, and Flemming Stubkjaer, 100–123. Odense: Odense University Press, 1980.

Santé, Luc. "Living in Tongues." In *Best American Essays,* ed. Ian Frazier, 123–31. Boston: Houghton-Mifflin, 1997.

Sauerstein, Paul. *Charles d'Orléans und die englische Übersetzung seiner Dichtungen.* Halle, 1899.

Scattergood, V. J. *Politics and Poetry in the Fifteenth Century.* London: Blandford Press, 1971.

———. *Reading the Past: Essays on Medieval and Renaissance Literature.* Portland, Oreg.: Four Courts Press, 1996.

Seneca. *Ad Lucilium epistulae morales.* Ed. and trans. Richard Grummere. London: W. Heinemann, 1925.

Sénemaud, Edmond. *La Bibliothèque de Charles d'Orléans, Comte d'Angoulême, au château de Cognac en 1496.* Paris: A. Claudin, 1861.
Sidney, Sir Philip. *Sir Philip Sidney.* Ed. Katherine Duncan-Jones. Oxford: Oxford University Press, 1989; rpt. 1990.
Simmons, Autumn. "A Contribution to the Middle English Dictionary: Citations from the English Poems of Charles, Duc D'Orléans." *Journal of English Linguistics* 2 (1968): 43–56.
Sims, R. *Index to the Pedigrees and Arms Contained in the Heralds' Visitations, and other genealogical manuscripts in the British Museum.* London: John Russell Smith, 1849.
Smith, Barbara Herrnstein. *Contingencies of Value.* Cambridge: Harvard University Press, 1988.
———. *Poetic Closure.* Chicago: University of Chicago Press, 1968.
Smith, G. G., ed. *Elizabethan Critical Essays.* 2 vols. London, 1904; rpt. 1937.
Spearing, A. C. *Medieval Dream-Poetry.* Cambridge: Cambridge University Press, 1976.
———. *Medieval to Renaissance in English Poetry.* Cambridge University Press, 1985.
———. "Poetic Identity." In *A Companion to the "Gawain"-Poet,* 35–51. Woodbridge, Sulfolk: D. S. Brewer, 1997.
———. "The Poetic Subject from Chaucer to Spenser." *Subjects on the World's Stage: Essays on British Literature of the Middle Ages and the Renaissance,* 13–37. Newark: University of Delaware Press and London: Associated University Presses, 1995.
———. "Prison, Writing, Absence: Representing the Subject in the English Poems of Charles d'Orléans." *Modern Language Quarterly* 53 (1992): 83–99.
Spence, Sarah, ed. and trans. *Chansons.* New York: Garland, 1986.
Spiller, Michael. *The Development of the English Sonnet.* London: Routledge, 1992.
Spivak, Gayatri. "Imperialism and Sexual Difference." *Oxford Literary Review* 8 (1986): 225–40.
Stemmler, Theo. "Zur Verfasserfrage der Charles d'Orléans zugeschriebenen englischen Gedichte." *Anglia* 82 (1964): 458–73.
Stevens, J. E. *Music and Poetry in the Early Tudor Court.* London: Methuen, 1961.
Stevenson, Joseph. *Letters and Papers Illustrative of the wars of the English in France during the reign of King Henry the Sixth, King of England.* London: Longman et al., 1861–64.
Stevenson, Robert L. *Familiar Studies of Men and Books.* New York: Dodd and Mead, 1887.
Stevick, Robert, ed. *One Hundred Middle English Lyrics.* Indianapolis: Bobbs-Merrill, 1964.
Stierle, Karlheinz. "*Translatio studii* and Renaissance." In *The Translatability of*

Cultures, ed. Wolfgang Iser and Sanford Budick, 55–66. Stanford, Calif.: Stanford University Press, 1996.

Stillwell, Margaret Bingham. *Incunabula and Americana, 1450–1800.* New York: Columbia University Press, 1931.

Strohm, Paul. "A Note on Gower's Persona." In *Acts of Interpretation: The Text in Its Contexts, 700–1600,* ed. M. J. Carruthers and Elizabeth D. Kirk, 203–98. Norman, Okla.: Pilgrim, 1982.

Taylor, Henry. *St. Clement's Eve.* In *Works.* 5 vols. London: Kegan Paul, 1877–78.

Tchemerzine, Avenir. *Bibliographie d'éditions originales et rares d'auteurs français des XVe, XVIe, XVIIe, et XVIIIe siècles. . . .* 10 vols. Paris: M. Plée, 1927.

Thibault, Pascale. *La Bibliothèque de Charles d'Orléans et de Louis XII au château de Blois.* Blois: Les Amis de la bibliothèque de Blois, 1989.

Thomas, Max W. "Reading and Writing the Renaissance Commonplace Book: A Question of Authorship?" In *The Construction of Authorship,* ed. M. Woodmansee and P. Jaszi, 401–15. Durham, N.C.: Duke University Press, 1994.

University of London, Institute of Historical Research. *Victoria History of the Counties of England: Lincoln.* Ed. William Page. 2 vols. London: Archibald Constable, 1900–1906.

Urwin, Kenneth. "The 59th English Ballad of Charles d'Orléans." *Modern Language Review* 38 (1943): 129–32.

Vance, Eugene. "Chaucer, Spenser, and the Ideology of Translation." *Canadian Review of Comparative Literature* 8, no. 2 (1981): 217–38.

Venuti, Lawrence. "Genealogies of Translation Theory: Schleiermacher." *Traduction Terminologie Redaction* 4, no. 2 (1991): 125–50.

———. "The Translator's Invisibility." *Criticism* 28 (1986): 179–212.

Vernet, André. "Les Traductions latines d'oeuvres en langues vernaculaires au Moyen Âge." In *Traduction et Traducteurs au Moyen Âge,* ed. G. Contamine, 225–41. Paris: Éditions du CNRS, 1989.

Vinsauf, Geoffroi de. *Poetria Nova.* Ed. and trans. Margaret F. Nims. Toronto: Pontifical Institute of Medieval Studies, 1967.

Visceglia, M. A. "Rente féodale et agriculture dans les Pouilles à l'époque moderne, XVIè–XVIIIè siecles." In *Prestations paysannes, dîmes, rente foncière, et mouvement de la production agricole à l'époque pré-industrielle,* ed. Joseph Goy and E. L. R. Ladurie, 2 vols., 1:237–58. Paris: Mouton Editeur, 1982.

Vitruvius. *De Architectura.* Ed. and trans. Frank Granger. 2 vols. Cambridge, Mass.: Harvard University Press, 1995.

Wallace, David. *Chaucerian Polity.* Stanford, Calif.: Stanford University Press, 1997.

Walpole, Horace. *Catalogue of Royal and Noble Authors.* 2d ed. London: R. and J. Dodsley and J. Graham, 1759. Reprint. Edinburgh, 1796.

———. *The Works of Horatio Walpole, Earl of Orford.* 5 vols. London: G. G. and

J. Robinson and J. Edwards, 1798. Rev. ed. Thomas Park, London: John Scott, 1803, 1806.

Warner, George F., and Julius P. Gilson. *Catalogue of Western Manuscripts in the Old Royal and King's Collections in the British Museum.* 4 vols. London: Trustees, 1921.

Warton, Thomas. *History of English Poetry from the Twelfth to the close of the Sixteenth Century.* Ed. W. Carew Hazlitt. 4 vols. London, 1871; rpt. Hildesheim: Georg Olms Verlagsbuchhandlung, 1968.

Weinreich, Uriel. *Languages in Contact.* The Hague: Mouton, 1974.

Weissbort, Daniel, ed. *Translating Poetry: The Double Labyrinth.* London: Macmillan, 1989.

Wickersheimer, Ernest. *Dictionnaire biographique des médécins en France au Moyen Âge.* Paris: Librairie Droz, 1936.

Wilde, Oscar. *The Picture of Dorian Gray.* New York: Signet, 1962.

Wilkins, Nigel. "Music and Poetry at Court: England and France in the Late Middle Ages." In *English Court Culture in the Later Middle Ages,* ed. V. J. Scattergood and J. W. Sherborne, 183–204. London: Duckworth, 1983.

Wright, C. E. *Fontes Harleiani.* London: Trustees of the British Museum, 1972.

Wyatt, Thomas. *The Complete Poems.* Ed. R. A. Rebholz. London: Penguin, 1978; rpt. 1988.

Yeager, R. F. *Fifteenth-Century Studies: Recent Essays.* Hamden, Conn.: Archon, 1984.

———. *John Gower's Poetic.* Cambridge: D. S. Brewer, 1990.

———. "'Oure Englishe' and Everyone's Latin." *South Atlantic Review* 46 (1981): 41–53.

Yenal, Edith. *Charles d'Orléans: A Bibliography of Primary and Secondary Sources.* New York: AMS Press, 1984.

Yorkshire Archaeological Society. *Subsidy Rolls.* Records series 16, 21, 74 (1894–1929).

Zink, Michel. "Plurilingualism, Hermeticism, and Love in Medieval Poetics." *Comparative Literature Studies* 32 (1995): 112–30.

Zumthor, Paul. "Charles d'Orleans et le langage de l'allégorie." In *Mélanges offerts à Rita Lejeune,* ed. J. Ducoulot-Gembloux, 2 vols., 2:1481–1502. N.p., 1969.

———. *Essai de poétique médiévale.* Paris: Éditions du Seuil, 1972.

General Subject Index

Absence/presence, 33–36, 71–76
Address, shifting, 47ff., 152
Agincourt, battle of, 1, 25–26
"Albe y fer forget me nevyr," 71–75, 76
Alfred the Great, 17–18
Allegorical modes and traditions, 34, 53–54, 61–62, 71, 153–59
Amores Britannici, 89
Anadiplosis, 170
Anaphora, 51
André, Bernard, 79–80, 182–83
d'Angoulême, Jean, 25
Antipophora, 170
Apostrophe. *See* Address, shifting
Aristotle, 48
Arrangement. *See* Ordinatio
Astesano, Antonio, 15–16, 56, 112–44, 191–200
Augustine, Saint, 175–77
Authorship question, 14–16, 106

Bilingualism/trilingualism, 1–13, 98–99, 184, 188–89
Book, idea of. *See* Lyrics, lyric book
Bourgogne, duc de (Jean Sans Peur), 89
Bourgogne, duc de (Phillippe le Bon), 136–42

Caesar, Sir Julius, 83
Cailleau, Symon, 193
Catalexis, 75
Canon, 9–10, 76–111. *See also* Reception, of Charles's poetry
Champion, Pierre, 92–94

Chansons, reordered, 126–71. *See also* Ordinatio
Charles d'Orleans. *See* d'Orleans, Charles
Chartier, Alain, 5, 12, 87, 90–91
Chaucer, ed. of 1561. *See* Stowe, John
Chaucerian aspects of Charles's poetry, 86, 148–53. *See also* Petrarch; Sidney, Philip; Wyatt, Thomas
Cheville, 32, 53, 68, 139
Chiasmus, 37, 167
  phonetic chiasmus, 53
Clanvowe, *Boke of Cupid,* 70, 148
Closure, 47, 71–75, 127–29
Comparative historicism, 6–8, 11–12, 189–90
Complaintes, reordered, 125–26
Concreteness, greater in English poetry, 33–34, 59
Correctio, 171
Critical tradition. *See* Reception, of Charles's poetry
Croft, Thomas, 106
Cultural capital, 76–77

Daniel, Samuel, 56
Décasyllabes, 32
Decoration. *See* Hierarchy of decoration
Deschamps, Eustache, 90–91
Dialogues, 56–61, 66–67, 162–66
Donne, John, 11, 32n. 52, 161, 164
Double entendre. *See* Wordplay

219

Doubling. *See* Reduplicatio
Dryden, John, 19–20

Elizabeth I, 83
Ellis, George, 10, 95, 97–99, 102, 169
English and French literature, relative states of. *See* Polysystems
English language, 21–24. *See also* Polysystems; Vernaculars
Envois, 46–56, 74–75, 167
Epideixis, 39–41, 47–49
Epimone, 171
Epistolary modes, 46–47, 136–42
Erotic emphasis, 136–42, 157–60, 162–66
Exegi monumentum, 75, 115–16

Fairfax, Charles, 82

Garencières, Jean de, 91
Gelle, Elizabeth, 80
Genre and translation. *See* Lyrics; Polysystems; Translation, discontinuities or nonequivalences in; Translation, and literary history; Translation, and periodization
Gloucester, Humphrey, 86
"Go little bille" topos. *See* Envois
Goujet, l'Abbé, 91–92
Gower, John, 86, 150–51
Grenoble 873. *See* Manuscripts, Grenoble 873

"Hearne fragment." *See* Manuscripts, "Hearne fragment"
Heart poems, 61–71, 158–59
and heart's duplicities, 36–37
Halesby, John, 80
Henry V, 25–26, 85–86, 90
Henry VI, 86
Henry VII, 80, 182–84. *See also* Tudors
Henry VIII, 12, 80. *See also* Tudors
Hierarchy of decoration, 121–44, 191–200. *See also* Manuscripts, Grenoble 873

Hoccleve, Thomas, 148–49, 151, 176–77
Holland, Joseph (fl. 1580), 82
Holt, Rycardus, 80

Illumination. *See* Hierarchy of decoration; Manuscripts
Imbert, Barthélémy, 91–92
Imitatio, 37–38, 43. *See also* Renaissance literature, Charles's connections and continuities with; Translatio; Translation, vertical and horizontal
"Inwardness," 172–81, 185
Isabella, widow of Richard II and first wife of Charles, 89, 200

James I of Scotland, 11, 45, 151
Jekyll, Joseph, 83

Keralio, Mlle de, 91–92, 99

Lannoy, Hugues de, 45
Latin manuscript. *See* Manuscripts, Grenoble 873
Louis d'Orléans. *See* d'Orléans, Louis
Lydgate, John, 149–50
Lyrics
lyric books, 116–21, 123–25, 142–47, 187–90
and lyric "I," 39–75
and lyric speaker, intensity and prominence of in English versions, 58–60
and lyric speaker, speechless, 59–60
See also Poetic subject; Subjectivity; Writerly identity; Writerly position

Manuscript presence, in England. *See* Reception, of Charles's poetry
Manuscripts
BL Harley 682, 1; general contents of, 3–5; 14–15, 39, 80–81
BL Harley 6916, 82–83
BL Harley 7333, 82–84

BL Royal F 16.ii, 8, 44–45, 79–85, 182–85
Bodleian Rawlinson K 38/42, 84
Cambridge UL Addit. 2585, 84
Fairfax 16, 81–82
Grenoble 873, 10–11, 112–44, 180–81, 191–200
"Hearne fragment," 84
Lansdowne 380, 82–83
Matisse, Henri, 93
Medieval period, and the "Renaissance," 11–13, 145–90. *See also* Periodization
Medieval conventions, Charles's relation to, 34, 53–54, 59–62, 69–71, 145–47, 147–59, 171, 176–78, 183, 185–90. *See also* Periodization
Medieval translation, 17–20, 26–29, 87–88
Merismus, 171
Metanoia, 171
Milton, John, 32n. 2

Occupare amplexu, 162–66
Octosyllabes, 32, 139
Oldmixon, John, 89
Openings of poems, 159–61
Orality/textuality, 33, 49–56. *See also* Writing and speech
Ordinatio, 10–11, 112–44, 191–200
Original vs. originel, 37–38, 39, 42
d'Orléans, Charles
  captivity of, 20–24
  diplomatic activities of, 28
  English poems of: Ballade 3, 47; Ballade 6, 63–66, 70; Ballade 7, 70; Ballade 9, 47–48, 160, 178; Ballade 10, 30–38; Ballade 12, 37; Ballade 16, 159; Ballade 17, 177; Ballade 19, 51–52; Ballade 20, 166–67; Ballade 21, 36, 49; Ballade 22, 47; Ballade 24, 47, 173; Ballade 25, 172–73; Ballade 26, 70; Ballade 28, 48; Ballade 31, 51–53; Ballade 32, 159; Ballade 33, 62–63, 66–67; Ballade 36, 159; Ballade 37, 62, 68; Ballade 38, 52, 155; Ballade 39, 52; Ballade 42, 70, 173; Ballade 43, 52, 63, 68, 69, 70; Ballade 45, 167; Ballade 48, 177; Ballade 51, 69, 162; Ballade 52, 153; Ballade 53, 167, 177; Ballade 55, 48, 69; Ballade 56, 69; Ballade 57, 48; Ballade 60, 37, 161, 167–68; Ballade 62, 178–79; Ballade 64, 48; Ballade 70, 57–58, 159; Ballade 72, 58–59, 177–78; Ballade 74, 69; Ballade 76, 159; Ballade 79, 59–60; Ballade 90, 178; Ballade 91, 50–51; Ballade 97, 167; Ballade 99, 168–69; Ballade 100, 169–71; Ballade 102, 159; Ballade 108, 154; Ballade 110, 160; Ballade 111, 138–42; Ballade 112, 68–69; Ballade 113, 138–42; Ballade 114, 160; Ballade 115, 161; Ballade 116, 162–66; Ballade 118, 159; Ballade 119, 179; Ballade 120, 51, 53, 173; Ballade 121, 71–76; "Go forth myn hert," 98; "Lende me your praty mouth madame," 96; "My hertly loue," 98; "Ne ware my trewe and innocent hert," 98; Roundel 9, 161; Roundel 43, 159; Roundel 69, 155, 162; "Ye schal be payd," 154–55
  French poems of: Ballade VI, 63–66; Ballade XXXIII, 62–68; Ballade XXXVII, 62, 68; Ballade LXIII, 58; Ballade LXXXVIII, 136–42; Ballade LXXXVIIIa, 137–42; Ballade XCIV, 173–74; "Bien defendu bien assailly" and "Bien assailly bien defendu," 127; Chanson XXIII, 154; Chanson XLI, 158–59; "Comment voys-je ces anglais esbahis," 26–28, 131, 133–34; "Complainte de France," 25–26, 129–32, fig. 4; complaintes, 126–27; "Des nouvelles d'Albion," 8, 142, fig. 1; "En regar

d'Orléans, Charles, French poems of (*continued*)
  dant vers le pays de France," 45; "Me fauldrez vous a mon besoing," 128; "Priez pour paix," 132; "Que faut-il plus a un cueur amoureux?" 127–28; "Que voulez-vous que plus vous die?" 128; Rondeau XII, 154; Rondeau CCLXVIII, 154; verse letters to Burgundy, 136–42
  library of, 20–21
  poetry of: calendrical/seasonal poems, 127; closure in, 47, 71–75, 127–29; départie poems, 127; English versions of as more colloquial, 35, 60, 66–67, 164–65; English versions of as more concrete, 33–34, 59; English versions of as more extreme, 5, 33–34, 58–60; erotic emphasis in, 136–42, 157–60, 162–66; eye poems, 126–27; kiss poems, 126, 158, 161–66; openings in, 55, 153, 159, 161; Chaucerian and un-Chaucerian aspects of, 86, 148–53; Petrarchan and un-Petrarchan aspects of (*see* Petrarch); (*see also* Dialogues; Heart poems; Lyrics; Medieval conventions, Charles's relation to; Poetic subject; Translation; Wordplay; Writing and speech)
  readership and, 77–111
  writerly position of, 8, 28–29, 34–37, 39–45, 47, 173–76, 184–85 (*see also* Lyrics; Manuscripts; Reception, of Charles's poetry; Poetic subject; Subjectivity; Writerly identity; Writing and speech)
d'Orleans, Louis, 1, 11–12
Oxymoron, 167–68

Paradox, of translated subjectivity. *See* Self-translation
Park, Thomas, 10, 89, 95, 100–105, 169–71
Pentameter, 32, 139
Periodization, 9, 11–12, 143–44, 180–85
  and canon formation, 107–8
  translation as challenge to, 185–90
  See also Donne, John; Gower, John; Hoccleve, Thomas; Lydgate, John; Medieval conventions, Charles's relation to; Petrarch; Renaissance literature, Charles's continuities and connections with; Shakespeare, William; Sidney, Philip; Spenser, Edmund; Stowe, John; Wyatt, Thomas
Persona. *See* Lyrics, and lyric "I"; Lyrics, and lyric speaker; Poetic subject; Subjectivity; Writing and speech
Personifications, 152–57
Petrarch, 4–5, 20, 88, 123–24, 131, 142–44, 145, 161, 168, 172–81, 188
Phonetic technique, 34–37, 53
Pisan, Christine de, 5, 12, 91
Poetic subject, 39ff., 42, 57–66, 150–52
  not autobiographical, 39–45, 46, 68–70, 71–75
  See also Lyrics, and lyric "I"; Subjectivity; Writing and speech
Political poems, 119ff., 129–34
Politics, of selection and translation, 134–44
Polysystems, 10–12, 20–24, 76–78, 87–88, 146–47, 187–90. *See also* Lyrics; Translation, discontinuities or nonequivalences in
Prosopopoeia, 5
Pryor, Thomas, 80
Puns. *See* Wordplay
Puttenham, George, 169–71
Puys, 91, 146

Readership, literary, 22
Reception, of Charles's poetry, 9–10
  during eighteenth century, 94–105

during nineteenth and twentieth centuries, 105–11
with Charles as historical figure in England, 85–87
in English literary canons, 94–111
in French literary canons, 90–94
in manuscripts in England, 78–85
in print in England, 87–90, 94–111
Reduplicatio, 32, 59
Renaissance literature, Charles's continuities and connections with, 9–12, 20, 32, 44–45, 49–50, 54–56, 71, 74, 145–47, 150–52, 153, 160, 167–71, 172–90. *See also* Medieval conventions, Charles's relation to; Periodization
Reordering of manuscript books, 123–24. *See also* Hierarchy of decoration; Lyrics, lyric book; Ordinatio; Politics, of selection and translation
Ritson, Joseph, 10, 95–97, 102
Rohan, Cardinal de, 83
Romanticism, 37–38

St. Clement's Eve, 89
Sallier, l'Abbé, 91–92, 94
Sallust, 25–26
"Selected works," 10, 114–21, 142–44. *See also* Manuscripts, Grenoble 873
Selection, 112–44
Self-fashioning, 9
Self-translation, 5–6, 8–9, 39–45, 66. *See also* Translation
Shakespeare, William, 54, 56, 89
 Henry V, 89
 1 Henry VI, 89
 2 Henry VI, 89
Shirley, John, 83
Sidney, Philip, 11, 32n. 52, 50–51, 56, 71, 73, 153, 154, 157, 161, 166, 174, 183–84
Sonnets, Renaissance, 54–56, 166–67
Speaker. *See* Lyrics, and lyric "I"; Lyrics, and lyric speaker; Poetic subject; Subjectivity; Writing and speech
Speech, vs. writing. *See* Writing and speech
Spenser, Edmund, 32n. 52, 49–51, 56, 167–68
Stanley, John (MP Surrey), 81
Stevenson, Robert Louis, 107
Stillingfleet, Edward, Bishop of Winchester, 81
Stowe, John, 82
Subjectivity, 4, 6–7, 8, 28–29, 39–45, 58–60, 68–70, 145, 175–77, 184–85
Suffolk, Duke and Duchess of (William and Alice de la Pole), 7, 12, 85–86
Symploche, 170
Syntactic mimesis/anti-mimesis, 32–33

Taylor, Henry, 89
Text-consciousness, and self-consciousness, 39ff.
Text-referentiality, and self-referentiality, 46ff.
Text, as mediator, 52–54. *See also* Envois
Translated authorship, 14–16
Translatio, 8, 14–29, 75
 translatio imperii, 17–19, 24–29, 129–31
 translatio poesis, 20–23
 translatio studii, 17, 20–24, 29, 56, 117–19
 translatio sui or suater, 29, 44
Translation
 discontinuities or nonequivalences in, 5–6, 29–38, 53–54, 70–71, 71–75, 136–42
 English versions as more concrete, 33–34, 59
 English versions as more colloquial, 35, 60, 66–67, 164–65
 English versions as more extreme, 5, 33–34, 58–60
 equivalence, fidelity, or replicativity in, 17–18, 29–30, 37

Translation (*continued*)
  from French in early modern period, 87–88
  and influence, 2–3, 5–6
  and literary history, 2–3, 8–9
  and periodization, 2–3, 8–10, 185–90
  politics of, 134–44
  self-translation, 5–6, 8–9, 39–45, 66
  vertical and horizontal, 17, 20, 189
  visibility in, 39
Tredecrofft, Yohanne, 80
Tudors, 8–9, 79–85, 87–88, 182ff.

Valedictory poem, 71–76, 128–29
Vérard, Antoine, 91
Vernaculars, 1–13, 21–24, 114–17. *See also* Polysystems
Villon, François, 91, 146
Visconti, Valentina, 5, 11–12, 180

Vitruvius, *De Architectura,* 115
Walpole, Horace, 10, 95–99, 103, 105
Warham, Archbishop, 83
Waterton, Robert, 85
Watson Taylor, George, 103–6
Wilde, Oscar, 89–90
Wordplay, 34–37, 52–53, 74–75, 157–59, 162–66
Writerly identity, 3, 6–9, 66
Writerly position, 8–9, 28–29, 34–37, 39–45, 47, 173–76, 184–85. *See also* Lyrics; Poetic subject; Subjectivity
Writing and speech, 49–57, 59–60, 71–76, 128, 160–62. *See also* Text-consciousness, and self-consciousness; Text-referentiality, and self-referentiality
Wyatt, Thomas, 4, 11, 68–69, 88, 152–55, 166, 183
Wyssedune, Tomas, 80

Fig. 1. BL ms. Royal F 16.ii, folio 73. (Used with the permission of the British Library.)

Fig. 2. Grenoble ms. 873, folio 113r, depicting full border illumination opening a major section of the book. (Used with the permission of the Bibliothèque Municipale de Grenoble.)

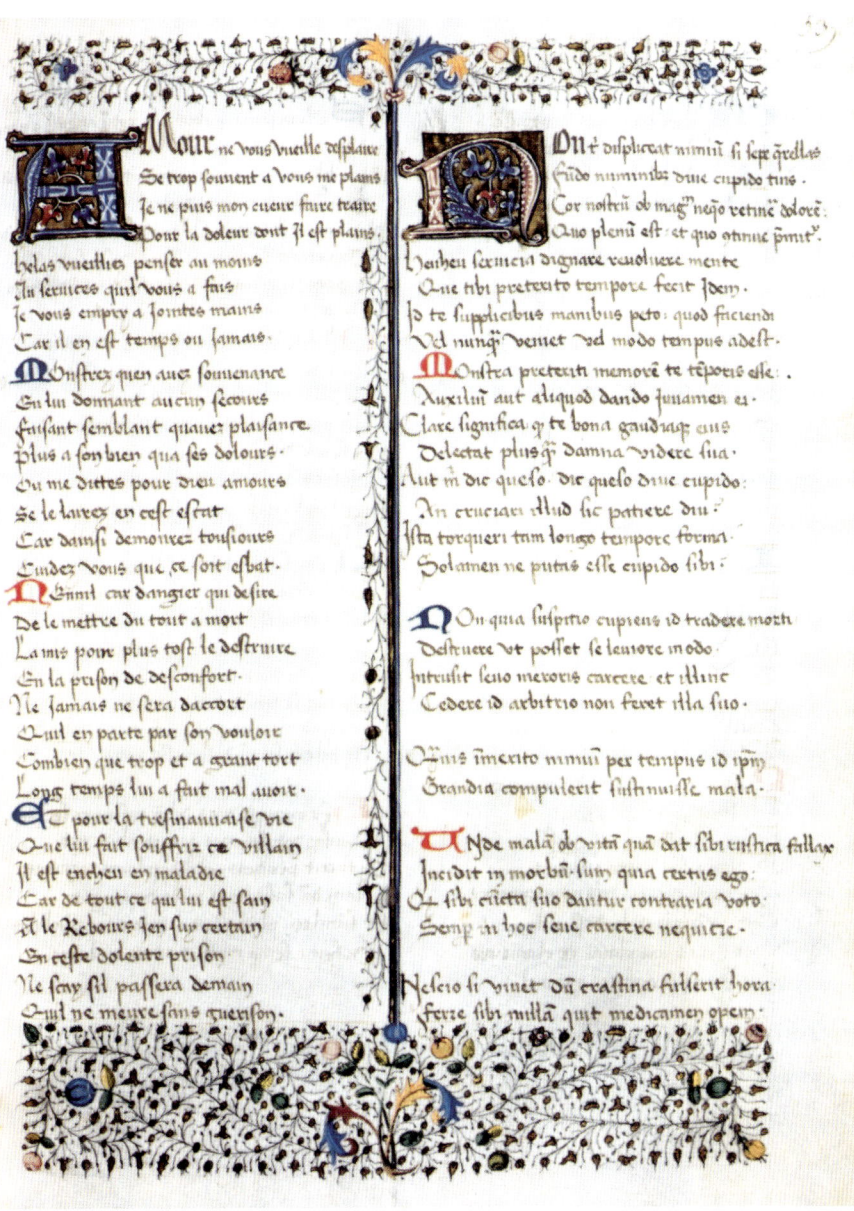

Fig. 3. Grenoble ms. 873, folio 53r, depicting partial border illumination opening a section of poetry. (Used with the permission of the Bibliothèque Municipale de Grenoble.)

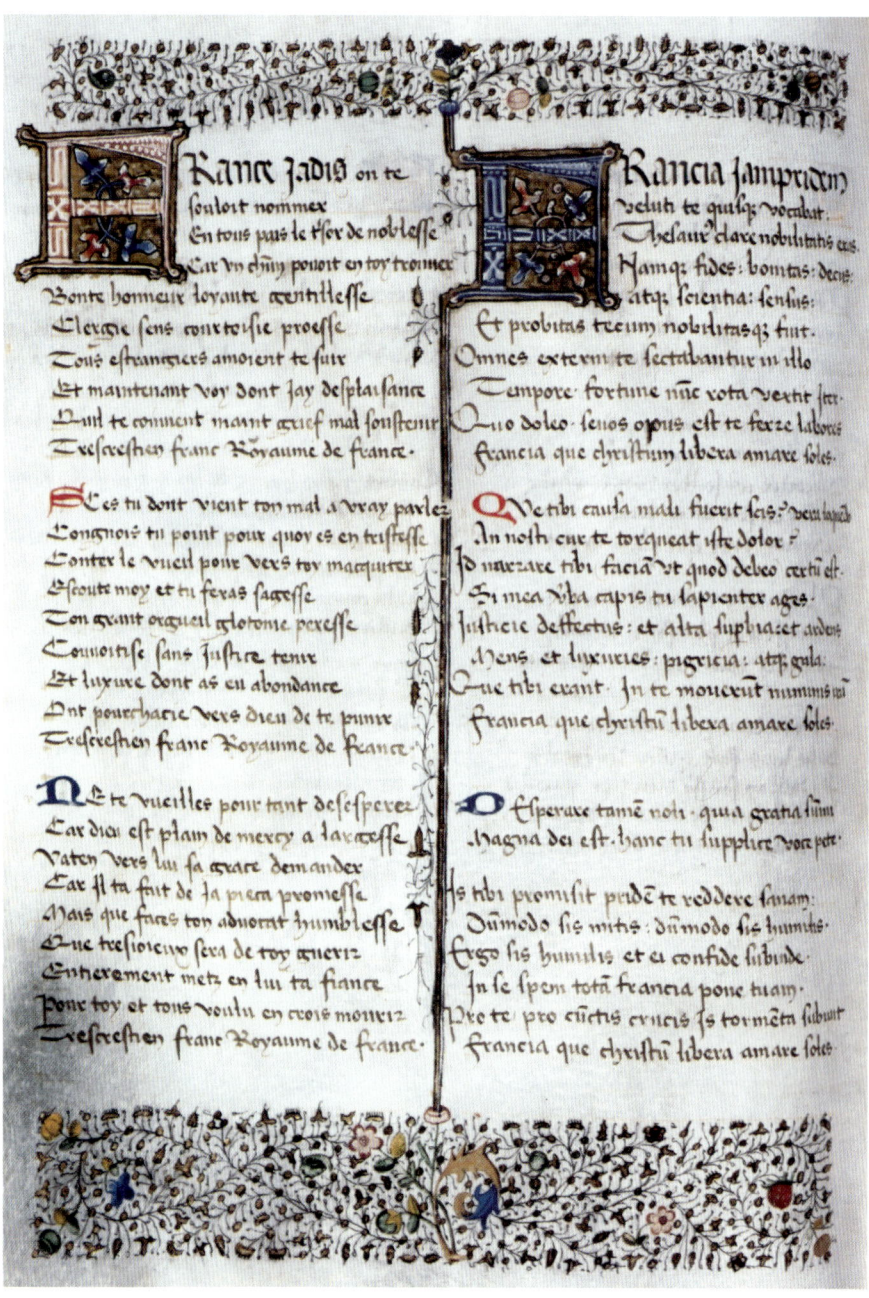

Fig. 4. Grenoble ms. 873, folio 97v, the "Complainte de France." (Used with the permission of the Bibliothèque Municipale de Grenoble.)

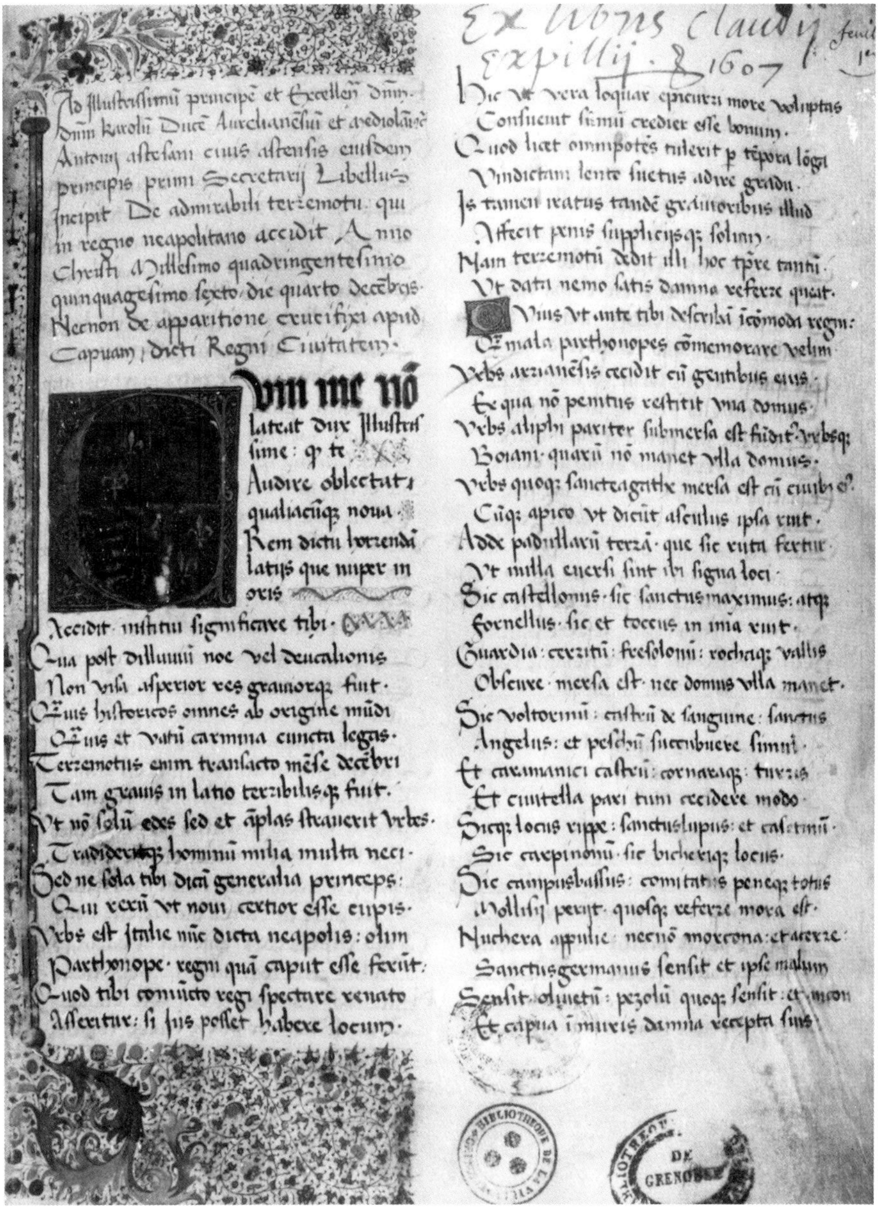

Ex libris Claudij
expillij. 1607

Ad Illustrissimum principem et Excellen dnm
dnm karoli Duce Aurelianensi et Mediolani
Antonij astesani eius astensis euisdem
principis primi Secretarij Libellus
incipit De admirabili terremotu qui
in regno neapolitano accidit Anno
Christi Millesimo quadringentesimo
quinquagesimo sexto die quarto decebris
Necnon de apparitione crucifixi apud
Capuam, dicti Regni Civitatem.

vm me no
lateat dux Illustris
sime: quod te
Audire oblectat,
qualiacuq noua
Rem dictu horrendi
latijs que nuper in
oris

Accidit mihi tu significare tibi
Qua post dilluuium noe vel deucalionis
Non visa asperior res grauiorq fuit.
Quius historicos omnes ab origine mundi
Quius et vatii carmina cuncta legas.
Terremotus enim transacto mese decebri
Tam grauis in latio terribilisq fuit.
Ut no solu edes sed et aplas strauerit vrbes.
Tradiderit q hominum milia multa neci.
Sed ne sola tibi dici generalia princeps:
Qui rexii ut noui certior esse cupis.
Vrbs est italie nuc dicta neapolis: olim
Parthenope regni qui caput esse ferut.
Quod tibi coniucto regi spectare renato
Asseritur: si sus posset habere locum.

Hic ut vera loquar epicurii more voluptas
Consueuit simul credier esse bonum.
Quod licet omnipotes tulerit p tempora longa
Vindictam lente suetus adire gradu.
Is tamen reatus tande grauioribus illud
Afficit penis suppliciisq solum.
Nam terremotu dedit illi hoc tempore tanti.
Ut data nemo satis damna referre queat.
Vius ut ante tibi describi icomoda regni
Et mala parthonopes comemorare velim.
Vrbs auianesis cecidit cu gentibus eius.
Et qua no penitus restitit una domus.
Vrbs alipbi pariter submersa est hidnit rebusq
Boiani quaru no manet villa domus.
Vrbs quoq sancte agathe mersa est cu ciuibus eis
Cuiq apico ut dicit asculus ipsa ruit.
Adde padullaru terra que sic euita fertur
Ut nulla euersi sint ibi signa loci.
Sic castellonis sic sanctus maximus: atq
Foenellus sic et tocens in ima ruit.
Guardia cerexitu fresoloni rochaq vallis
Obscure mersa est nec domus villa manet.
Sic voltornii castrii de sanguine sanctus
Angelus: et pelosii succubuere simul.
Et cremanici castru cornaraq turris
Et ciuitella pari tum cecidere modo.
Sicq locus ripe sanctus lupus et caletru
Sic crepinonu sic bicheriq locus.
Sic campus ballus comitatus peneq totus
Vollisij perijt quosq referre mora est.
Nuchera appulie necno morcona et acerre
Sanctus germanus sensit et ipse malum
Sensit olivetu pezoli quoq sensit et mon
Et capua i mureis damna recepta suis.

Fig. 5. Grenoble ms. 873, folio 1r, depicting half-border decoration and marks of ownership. (Used with the permission of the Bibliothèque Municipale de Grenoble.)

Presertim quoniam informis gracilisque maxime
Non poterat venere sat satiare suam.
Miles ut instituit cornutus vadit at ille
Cum tenera in thalamo coniuge claudit eum
Sic clausus miles huic oscula figit et inquit
Gaude nympha tui simplicitate viri.
Sed mea ne tenera tibi nympha teneretur corpus
Arma premat armis me spoliabo prius.
Nec mora depositis nicolosa corripit arma.
Atque optata simul gaudia utergue cepit.
Cum vero miles satis est satiatus abunde.
Destinat amplexus deseruisse suos.
Dein thalamo egressus cornuto dicit ut uxor
Concubitu pregnas sit sua facta novo.
Ut puerum armatum paritura sed esse necesse
Per biduum coniux mingat ut ipsi nichil.
Nam si fors coniux urinam emiserit una
Emittet pueri semina facta sui.
Cornutus simplex vera ee cogitat esse.
Et statuit custos coniugis esse sue.
Ne biduo coniux urinam emittere possit.
Huic soceiro sui deserit ipse latus.
Advenit interea cuius sibi fuimus amicus:
Qui secum merces communicare solet.
Hunc rogat ut subito veniat ja ea pici
Imminet ingentis in cito tendat iter.
Cornutus quis fructus linqueret ipsam
Uxorem statuit mox celerare gradum.
Ut videat que sit tam magni causa pericli.
Cur ad se solus venerit ille citus.
Uxore tamen ante monet ne migat et inde
Ad socium tendit mox rediturus iter.
Cornuto egresso coniux retinere nequibat
Amplius urina plena puella suam.

forte fuit thalamo urinam proximus ortis.
Introit ergo ortum mox nicolosa suum.
Atque illic medias urinam emittit in herbas.
Uno limacu prius casu erat ortu loco.
Cornutus rediens reperit quod minxerat uxor
Quesivit et urine posse videre locum.
Uno cum visu sibi cum totum et cornibus esset
Limacu armatus equiparandus viris.
Hanc credit puerum de semine militis esse:
Que de ventre uxor minxerit ipsa suo.
Flere igitur cepit tam parum funera nati.
Que fortuna sibi traxerat ante diem.
Et gravia uxori dicit convicia que sic
Minxerit infante perdideritque suum.
Ne tamen ipse puer merito puet honore.
Infante in medio collocat ipse thoro.
Atque sacerdotes ad funus convocat omnes.
Qui tumulet natum non sine honore suum.
Ecce sacerdotes venunt qui funera credunt
Esse viri ut celebrent funus honore pio.
Cum mox cornutum se versos esse putantes
Afficiunt pena supplicioque gravi.
Ad humanissimum patrem dominum Bernardum
Caretunum Sancti Quintini abbatem

Cire cupis veneranda pater cur prospera quosdam
fortuna ad superos evehat usque polos.
At quosdam ferme stygias detrudet ad umbras.
Tantum adversatur sena aliquando viris.
Difficile est nostris tibi respondere tabellis.
Et quesitu satis solvere posse tua.
Nam nec ego studui rerum cognoscere causas.
Nec tantum ingenio dij tribuere meo.
Que fabella tamen vetus est vulgataque dici.
Quam puto quesitu solvere posse tuum.

Temporibus ipsis

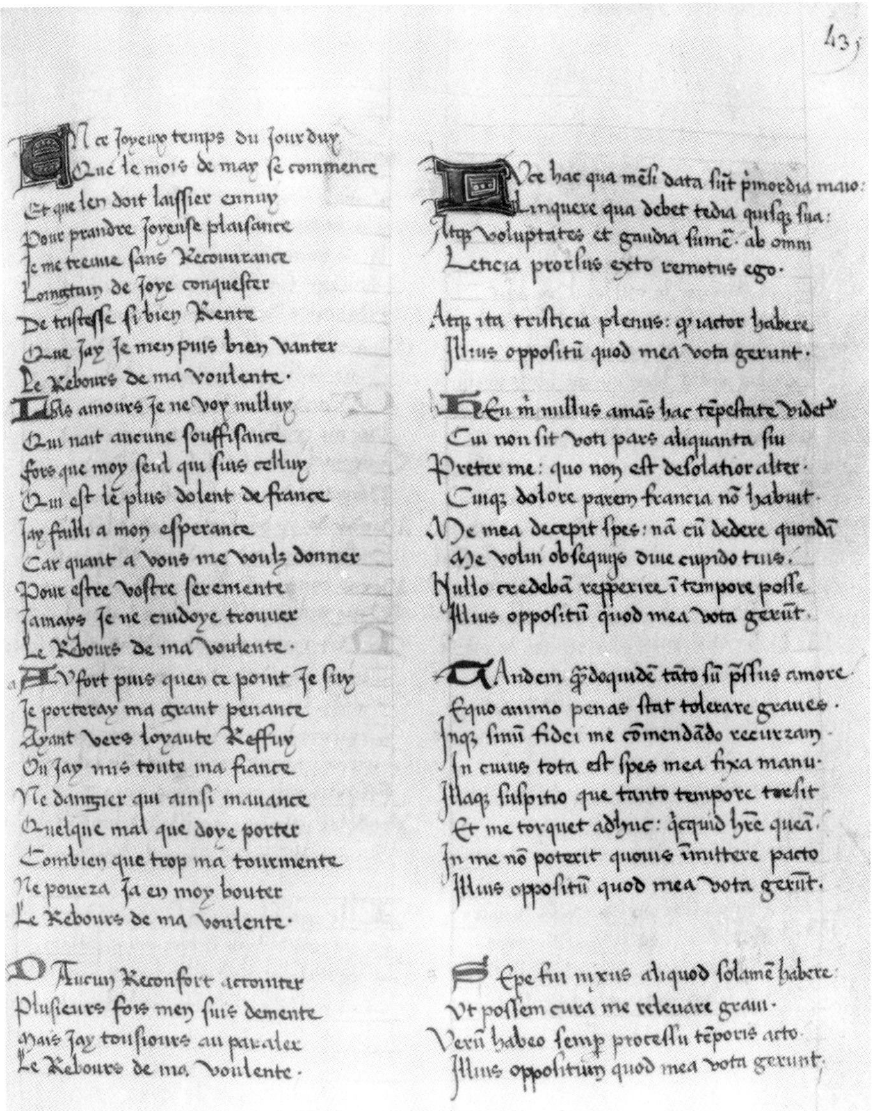

Ce joyeulx temps du jour duy
Que le mois de may se commence
Et que len doit laissier ennuy
Pour prandre joyeuse plaisance
Je me treuue sans Recourrance
Loingtain de joye conquester
De tristesse si bien Rente
Que jay je men puis bien vanter
Le Rebours de ma voulente.

Es amours je ne voy nulluy
Qui nait aucune souffisance
Fors que moy seul qui suis celluy
Qui est le plus dolent de france
Jay failli a mon esperance
Car quant a vous me vouls donner
Pour estre vostre seremente
Jamays je ne cuidoye trouuer
Le Rebours de ma voulente.

Vfort puis quen ce point je suy
Je porteray ma grant penance
Ayant vers loyaute Reffuy
On jay mis toute ma fiance
Ne danngier qui ainsi mauance
Quelque mal que doye porter
Combien que trop ma tourmente
Ne pourra ja en moy bouter
Le Rebours de ma voulente.

Aucun Reconfort acointer
Plusieurs fois mey suis demente
Mais jay tousiours au paraler
Le Rebours de ma voulente.

Ce hac qua mēsi data sit pmordia maio:
Linquere qua debet tedia quisq; sua:
Atq; voluptates et gaudia sume ab omni
Leticia prorsus exto remotus ego.

Atq; ita tristicia plenus: q; iactor habere.
Illius oppositū quod mea vota gerunt.

Eu in nullus amās hac tēpestate videt'
Cui non sit voti pars aliquanta sui
Preter me: quo non est desolatior alter.
Cuiq; dolore parem francia nō habuit.
Je mea decepit spes: nā cū dedere quondā
Me volui obsequiis diue cupido tuis.
Nullo creedebā repperire ī tempore posse
Illius oppositū quod mea vota gerunt.

Andem q;doquidē tāto sū pssus amore
Equo animo penas stat tolerare graues.
Inq; sinū fidei me comendādo recurzam
In cuius tota est spes mea fixa manu.
Illaq; suspirio que tanto tempore tresit
Et me torquet adhuc: q;cquid hēc queā.
In me nō poterit quouis imittere pacto
Illius oppositū quod mea vota gerunt.

Epe sui nixus aliquod solamē habere:
Vt possem cura me releuare graui.
Verū habeo semp procellu tēporis acto
Illius oppositum quod mea vota gerunt.

Fig. 7. Grenoble ms. 873, folio 43r, comparing French and Latin spacing.
(Used with the permission of the Bibliothèque Municipale de Grenoble.)

Fig. 8. Grenoble ms. 873, folio 9r, Astesano's preface, showing red-winged angel with Valois-Visconti arms, zoomorphic border decoration, and spacing for incipit. (Used with the permission of the Bibliothéque Municipale de Grenoble.)